This Side *of* Heaven

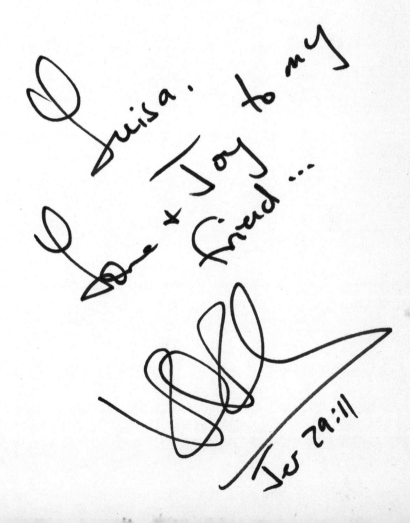

Luisa,
Joy to my
Love + Joy to my
+ Fried...

Jer 29:11

KAREN KINGSBURY

This Side *of* Heaven

CENTER
STREET®

New York Boston Nashville

Scriptures are taken from the HOLY BIBLE: NEW INTERNATIONAL VERSION®. Copyright © 1973, 1978, 1984 by International Bible Society. Used by permission of Zondervan Publishing House. All rights reserved.

Center Street
Hachette Book Group
237 Park Avenue
New York, NY 10017

Visit our Web site at www.centerstreet.com.

Center Street is a division of Hachette Book Group, Inc.
The Center Street name and logo are trademarks of Hachette Book Group, Inc.

Printed in the United States of America

First Edition: January 2009
10 9 8 7 6 5 4 3 2

Library of Congress Cataloging-in-Publication Data
Kingsbury, Karen
  This side of heaven / Karen Kingsbury.—1st ed.
     p. cm.
  Summary: "A story of family secrets, broken relationships, and a love strong enough to span a nation"—Provided by publisher.
  ISBN: 978-1-59995-678-7
  1. Fathers and daughters—Fiction. 2. Family secrets—Fiction. I. Title.
PS3561.I4873T47 2009
813'.54—dc22

                                                    2008038468

Book design by Charles Sutherland

To Donald, my Prince Charming

How I rejoice to see you coaching again, sharing your gift of teaching and your uncanny ability with basketball with another generation of kids. And best yet, now our boys are part of the mix. Isn't this what we always dreamed of, my love? I love sitting back this time and letting you and God figure it out. I'll always be here—cheering for you and the team from the bleachers. But God's taught me a thing or two about being a coach's wife. He's so good that way. It's fitting that you would find varsity coaching again now—after twenty years of marriage. Hard to believe that as you read this, our twentieth anniversary has come and gone. I look at you and I still see the blond, blue-eyed guy who would ride his bike to my house and read the Bible with me before a movie date. You stuck with me back then and you stand by me now, when I need you more than ever. I love you, my husband, my best friend, my Prince Charming. Stay with me, by my side, and let's watch our children take wing, savoring every memory and each day gone by. Always and always . . . The ride is breathtakingly beautiful, my love. I pray it lasts far into our twilight years. Until then, I'll enjoy not always knowing where I end and you begin. I love you always and forever.

To Kelsey, my precious daughter

You are nineteen now, a young woman, and my heart soars with joy when I see all that you are, all you've become. This year is a precious one for us, because you're still home, attending junior college and spending nearly every day in the dance studio. When you're not dancing, you're helping out with the business and ministry of Life-Changing Fiction™, so we have many precious hours together. I know this time is short and won't last, but I'm enjoying it so much—you, no longer the high school girl, a young woman and in every way my daughter, my friend. That part will always stay, but you, my sweet girl, will go where your dreams lead, soaring through the future doors God opens. Honey, you grow more beautiful—inside and out—every day. And always I treasure the way you talk to me, telling me your hopes and dreams and everything in between. I can almost sense the plans God has for you, the very good plans. I pray you keep holding on to His hand as He walks you toward them. I love you, sweetheart.

To Tyler, my lasting song

I can hardly wait to see what this school year will bring for you, my precious son. Last year you were one of Joseph's brothers, and you were Troy Bolton, and Captain Hook—becoming a stronger singer and stage actor with every role. This year you'll be at a new high school, where I believe God will continue to shape you as the leader He wants you to be. Your straight A's last year were a sign of things to come, and I couldn't be prouder, Ty. I know it was hard watching Kelsey graduate, knowing that your time with your best friend is running short. But you'll be fine, and no matter where God leads you in the future, the deep and lasting relationships you've begun here in your childhood will remain. Thank you for the hours of music and song. As you seize hold of your sophomore year, I am mindful that the time is rushing past, and I make a point to stop and listen a little longer when I hear you singing. I'm proud of you, Ty, of the young man you're becoming. I'm proud of your talent and your compassion for people and your place in our family. However your dreams unfold, I'll be in the front row to watch it happen. Hold on to Jesus, Ty. I love you.

To Sean, *my happy sunshine*

Today you came home from school, eyes sparkling, and showed me your science notebook—all your meticulous, neat sentences and careful drawings of red and white blood cells and various bones and bacteria. I was marveling over every page, remarking at the time you'd taken and the quality of your work, and together we laughed over the fact that neither of us really cares too much for science— but that it still matters that we do our best. You smiled that easy smile of yours and said, "Wait till you see Josh's—his blows mine away." You didn't know it at the time, but I was very touched by the tone in your voice. You weren't envious or defeated by the fact that Josh, in your same grade, might have managed to draw even-more-detailed pictures in his science journal. You were merely happy that you'd done your best, earned your A, and could move on from seventh-grade science proud of your effort. I love that about you, Sean. You could easily sulk in the shadow of your brother, a kid who excels in so many areas that the two of you share. But you also excel, my dear son. And one of the best ways you shine is in your happy heart, your great love for life and for people, and your constant joy. Sean, you have a way of bringing smiles into our family, even in the most mundane moment, and lately we are smiling very big about your grades. I pray that God will use your positive spirit to always make a difference in the lives around you. You're a precious gift, son. Keep smiling and keep seeking God's best for your life. I love you, honey.

To Josh, my tenderhearted perfectionist

So, you finally did it! You can beat me at Ping-Pong now, not that I'm surprised. God has given you great talents, Josh, and the ability to work at them with the sort of diligent determination that is rare in young teens. Whether in football or soccer, track or room inspections, you take the time to seek perfection. Along with that, there are bound to be struggles. Times when you need to understand again that the gifts and talents you bear are God's, not yours, and times when you must learn that perfection isn't possible for us, only for God. Even so, my heart almost bursts with pride over the young man you're becoming. After one of your recent soccer tournaments one of the parents said something I'll always remember. "Josh is such a leader," she told me. "Even when he doesn't know other parents are looking, he's always setting an example for his teammates." The best one, of course, is when you remind your teammates to pray before a game. What a legacy you and your brothers are creating here in Washington State! You have an unlimited future ahead of you, Josh. I'll be cheering on the sidelines always. Keep God first in your life. I love you always.

To EJ, *my chosen one*

Here you are in the early months of seventh grade, and I can barely recognize the student athlete you've become. Those two years of homeschooling with Dad continue to reap a harvest a hundred times what was sown, and we couldn't be more proud of you. But even beyond your grades, we are blessed to have you in our family for so many reasons. You are wonderful with our pets—always the first to feed them and pet them and look out for them—and you are a willing worker when it comes to chores. Besides all that you make us laugh, oftentimes right out loud. I've always believed that getting through life's little difficulties and challenges requires a lot of laughter—and I thank you for bringing that to our home. You're a wonderful boy, son, a child with such potential. Clearly that's what you showed the other day when you came out of nowhere in your soccer qualifiers and scored three goals. I'm amazed because you're so talented in so many ways, but all of it pales in comparison to your desire truly to live for the Lord. I'm so excited about the future, EJ, because God has great plans for you, and we want to be the first to congratulate you as you work to discover those. Thanks for your giving heart, EJ. I love you so.

To Austin, my miracle boy

I smile when I picture you hitting not one home run but three last baseball season—all of them for Papa—and I feel my heart swell with joy as I think of what happened after your second home run, when you had rounded the bases one at a time and accepted congratulations at home plate from your entire team. You headed into the dugout and a couple of your teammates tugged on your arm. "Tell us, Austin, how do you do it? How do you hit a home run like that?" That's when you smiled and shrugged your shoulders. "Easy. I asked God for the strength to hit the ball better than I could without Him." Papa must be loving every minute of this, Aus. I'm sure of it. What I'm not sure of is that missing him will ever go away. I can only tell you that our quiet times together are what I love most, too. That and our times of playing give-and-go out on the basketball court. You're my youngest, my last, Austin. I'm holding on to every moment, for sure. Thanks for giving me so many wonderful reasons to treasure today. I thank God for you, for the miracle of your life. I love you, Austin.

And to God Almighty, the Author of life,
who has—for now—blessed me with these.

ACKNOWLEDGMENTS

One night when I was putting the finishing touches on this book, Austin crawled up into bed next to me and stared at my laptop computer screen. "You know, Mom," he said, "I've been meaning to ask you about writing books. I have a couple questions." I smiled at him and asked him what he wanted to know. "Well," he said, "you know those beautiful covers on your books? They're so nice, with just the right colors and pictures, so do you do those? Do you make the covers?"

I shook my head. "No, buddy. I don't have anything to do with the covers, really. The publisher has these wonderful designers. They take care of coming up with a cover." He seemed a little disappointed for a few seconds. Then his eyes lit up. "I know, how about the design inside the book, the way the letters line up just so, and those little swirly things that make the first page of every chapter so nice." He scrunched up his face, slightly baffled. "Do you do that part?"

Again I shook my head. "No, honey. Actually there are designers at the publisher's offices who make sure the book looks nice on the inside." My smile turned a little sheepish. "They're the ones who do that."

His shoulders sank, and after a slight pause his brow rose, hopeful. "I know, how about the bookstores! Are you the one who gets all those books to the bookstores, so they can be there on the shelves for the people?"

Feeling the clear sense that I was disappointing him, I shook my head and managed a weak smile. "No, Aus, I don't do that, either. The publisher has a sales staff that handles getting the books to the bookstores. After that, other people at the bookstores open the boxes of books and put them on the shelves. I don't have anything to do with that."

"Wow." He climbed back down, but before he ran off he shrugged his shoulders. "You don't really do that much, do you?"

Austin has a point. No book comes together without a great and talented team of people making it happen. For that reason, a special thanks to my friends at FaithWords and Center Street who combined efforts to make *This Side of Heaven* all it could be. A special thanks to my dedicated editor, Anne Horch, who encouraged me often to stay with this story, however hard it was to write.

Also thanks to my amazing agent, Rick Christian, president of Alive Communications. Rick, you've always believed only the best for me. When we talk about the highest possible goals, you see them as doable, reachable. You are a brilliant manager of my career, and I thank God for you. But even with all you do for my ministry of writing, I am doubly grateful for your prayers. The fact that you and Debbie are praying for me and my family keeps me confident every morning that God will continue to breathe into life the stories in my heart. Thank you for being so much more than a brilliant agent.

A special thank-you to my husband, who puts up with me on deadline and doesn't mind driving through Taco

Bell after a basketball game if I've been editing all day. This wild ride wouldn't be possible without you, Donald. Your love keeps me writing; your prayers keep me believing that God has a plan in this ministry of fiction. And thanks for the hours you put in working with the guest-book entries on my Web site. I look forward to that time every day when you read through them, sharing them with me and releasing them to the public, praying for the prayer requests. Thank you, honey, and thanks to all my kids, who pull together, bringing me iced green tea and understanding about my sometimes crazy schedule. I love that you know you're still first, before any deadline.

Thank you also to my mom, Anne Kingsbury, and to my sisters, Tricia, Sue, and Lynne. Mom, you are amazing as my assistant—working day and night sorting through the mail from my reader friends. I appreciate you more than you'll ever know. Tricia, you are the best executive assistant I could ever hope to have. I treasure your loyalty and honesty, the way you include me in every decision and exciting Web site change. My site has been a different place since you stepped in, and the hits have grown tenfold. Along the way the readers have so much more to help them in their faith, so much more than a story with this Life-Changing Fiction™. Please know that I pray for God's blessings on you always, for your dedication to helping me in this season of writing, and for your wonderful son, Andrew. And aren't we having such a good time, too? God works all things to the good!

Sue, I believe you should've been a counselor! From your home far from mine, you get batches of reader letters every day, and you diligently answer them using God's wisdom and His Word. When readers get a response from "Karen's sister Susan," I hope they know how carefully you've prayed for them and for the response you give. Thank you for truly loving what you do, Sue. You're gifted with people, and I'm blessed to have you aboard.

A special thanks also to Will Montgomery, my road manager. I was terrified to venture into the business of selling my books at events for a couple of reasons. First, I never wanted to profit from selling my books at speaking events, and second, because I would never have the time to handle such details. Monty, you came in and helped me on both accounts. With a mission statement, "To love and serve the readers," you have helped me supply books and free gifts to tens of thousands of readers at events across the country. More than that, you've become my friend, a very valuable part of the ministry of Life-Changing Fiction™. You are loyal and kind and fiercely protective of me, my family, and the work God has me doing. Thank you for everything you're doing, and will continue to do.

Thanks, too, to Olga Kalachik, my office assistant, who helps prepare our home for the marketing events and research gatherings that take place there on a regular basis. I appreciate all you're doing to make sure I have time to write. You're wonderful, Olga, and I pray God continues to bless you and your precious family.

I also want to thank my friends with Extraordinary Women—Roy Morgan, Julie and Tim Clinton, Beth Cleveland, and the girls on the tour, along with so many others. How wonderful to be a part of what God is doing through all of you! Thank you for making me part of your family.

Thanks also to my forever friends and family, the ones

who rush to our side whenever we need you. Your love has been a tangible source of comfort, pulling us through the various seasons of life and making us know how very blessed we are to have you in our lives.

And the greatest thanks to God. The gift is Yours. I pray I might use it for years to come in a way that will bring You honor and glory.

FOREVER IN FICTION™

A special thanks to Gayle Flynn, who won Forever in Fiction at the Florida Solve Maternity Homes Auction. Gayle chose to honor her husband, Thomas Flynn, age fifty-seven, by naming him Forever in Fiction. Thomas is a personal injury attorney, a pillar in his community, a man with many friends and much integrity and faith. He and Gayle have been married thirty-four years and they have three grown children, with whom they love to vacation at their cabin in Kalkaska, Michigan.

Thomas likes collecting Native American artifacts, playing Ping-Pong, hunting, and fishing. He also likes reading fiction and particularly enjoys reading my books. Thomas is involved in a number of charities but he is particularly fond of Solve Maternity Homes, where he has served on the board of directors. Thomas's faith is key to him and his family, and he longs for a time when he and his wife can spend much of their time traveling to places like the West Indies or Australia.

He spent his younger years employed in social work but then became involved in the Home Repair Services business—a business devoted to helping the less fortunate in various Michigan neighborhoods. He loves woodworking and bird-watching, and when he travels to the Upper Peninsula of Michigan with his family, he tries to do a little of both. He enjoys slot machines, gambling for fun, and believing in miracles—not necessarily in that order.

Thomas's character in *This Side of Heaven* is that of a godly personal injury attorney, the one who demonstrates through fiction the importance of having godly men to represent those who are wrongly injured. As always with my Forever in Fiction characters, Thomas Flynn in this fictional setting is a created person with only some resemblance to the real Thomas Flynn.

That said, I pray that Gayle sees her husband, Thomas, as deeply honored by her gift and by his placement in *This Side of Heaven* and that she will always see a bit of Thomas when she reads his name in the pages of this novel, where he will be Forever in Fiction.

For those of you who are not familiar with Forever in Fiction, it is my way of involving you, the readers, in my stories, while raising money for charities. To date, Forever in Fiction has raised more than $100,000 at charity auctions across the country. If you are interested in having a Forever in Fiction package donated to your auction, contact my assistant, Tricia Kingsbury, at Kingsburydesk@aol.com. Please write *Forever in Fiction* in the subject line. Please note that I am only able to donate a limited number of these each year. For that reason I have set a fairly high minimum bid on this package so that the maximum funds are raised for charities.

Please understand that we receive hundreds of requests for this auction item, and not all requests can be met. Even so, I look forward to learning about the people in your life, people you would like to place Forever in Fiction.

. . . For Alyssa

"For I know the plans I have for you," declares the LORD, *"plans to prosper you and not to harm you, plans to give you hope and a future."*

—JEREMIAH 29:11

This Side *of* Heaven

The pain was a living, breathing demon, pressing its claws deep into his flesh and promising never to let go, not until death had the final word. But even with every vertebra and tendon in his back aching and burning, even with how he felt prisoner to his own body, and despite the eternal relief that was bound to come with his last breath, Josh Warren was certain of one thing that cool autumn night.

He didn't want to die.

Josh braced himself against the kitchen counter in his cramped apartment and stared at the clock. Just after midnight, early by his recent standards. His eyes blurred and battled for a moment of clarity. The problem was the meds, and whether he'd taken a double dose at ten o'clock, or at six. He leaned over his hands and tried to work up a complete breath. He drew three quick gasps, but only a fraction of his lungs offered any assistance. He was twenty-eight, but his body made him feel twice that.

"God"—he clenched his teeth and the whispered word filled his small kitchen—"I can't take this. I can't."

Three years. That's how long it had been. A hero, they

labeled him. Saved the lives of two teenage girls. But where were the news crews and reporters and cameramen now? Now, when every hour was a struggle to survive.

He tightened his grip on the countertop, his arms trembling, his lungs holding steady, refusing to inhale in a futile effort to keep the demon at bay. Another quick gasp and he hung his head. For a long moment he stayed that way, willing the pain to subside. But before he felt any relief, a drop of tepid water hit his hand. A grimace tugged at his eyebrows, and for a heartbeat he wondered if a pipe had broken upstairs the way it had last month, when the fog of pain and OxyContin was so strong he didn't notice the problem until a small stream started oozing from the plaster ceiling.

Another drop. He brushed at it as a third drop hit him, and at the same time he figured it out. He lifted his fingers to his forehead and touched a layer of wetness. No surprise there. He was sweating, his body giving way to the pain, handling the fire the only way it knew how. He wiped the back of his hand across his head and looked around.

Never mind when he'd taken the last dose. He needed more. Needed it now. He tried to straighten, but the demon weighed heavy on his shoulders, slumping him over as he shuffled toward the cupboard. He grabbed the bottle and fumbled with the lid before sliding one single pill into his palm. One pill wouldn't be too much. He downed it with a swig of water straight from the faucet.

Sleep would come, the way it always did eventually.

But first he needed to find Cara Truman. Josh made his way to the computer, set up on a desk against the dining room wall. He pulled his chair into place and fell into it.

Even then there was no relief. Sitting only intensified the pain in his lower back. He narrowed his eyes, logged in to his Facebook, and opened the instant message window—the one where Cara lived. Josh would never meet her in person. He was almost certain of that.

If he ever found his way free of the pain, he would call Becky Wheaton first, Becky who he had loved since he was fifteen. He'd heard from some of their old high school friends that her engagement had fallen through and she was single again. He thought about her constantly, but he couldn't call her. Not until he was healthy and whole and successful—the sort of guy she deserved.

Becky would have to wait, but when no amount of meds or sleep could take the edge off his constant pain, when concerned calls from his parents and his sister didn't bring relief, there was always Cara.

She knew him better than anyone, because she knew his story. The whole story. Even the part about his little girl on the other side of the country, the one no one else really thought was his. On late nights like this, across the invisible lines of cyberspace, he could share with Cara every crazy detail of the others, the stories that made up his life. And along the way Cara gave him a rare and priceless gift, one that kept him pushing through, battling the demon.

Cara believed him.

He studied the list of friends online, and she was there. He positioned his hands and tried to steady them as he tapped out the words. *Hey, it's me . . . you there?*

Half a minute passed and he saw that his neighbor Carl Joseph Gunner had tagged him in a few new photos. He clicked the album and for the first time that night he smiled.

Carl Joseph and his girlfriend, Daisy, both had Down syndrome. They lived with roommates in separate apartments in the adjacent building and both were very independent, with jobs and the ability to use the bus lines for errands.

The photos were taken by Carl Joseph last time he and Daisy stopped by the apartment. Carl Joseph had learned how to use the timer on his camera, so the pictures showed Carl Joseph, Daisy, and Josh standing in front of his TV, his refrigerator, and his patio slider—each one with the same cheeky smiles. Josh jotted a quick thank-you to Carl Joseph, and at the same time a response came from Cara.

I stepped away for a minute but I'm back.

Josh shifted positions, trying to find a more comfortable angle. *Can't sleep. I was hoping you were up.* Cara lived in Phoenix and she worked the swing shift at a data processing center. She usually didn't turn in until two in the morning.

Her next message appeared in the lower window on his computer screen. *I was thinking the other day about how we almost didn't meet. What would I have done without you?*

Josh smiled and moved his fingers over the keyboard. *Glad we'll never have to answer that. Just goes to show online poker's worth something. Even when you lose.*

The conversation came faster. *Lotta creeps play OP. You were like getting a royal flush, you know?*

Josh felt the compliment in the drafty corners of his heart. He leaned back against the vinyl chair and felt his body relax a little. *Thanks, sweetie. I'm just glad we found our way out of online poker and into this.*

Whatever this is.

Right. Josh chuckled. *Whatever it is. Hey, I talked to Keith yesterday. He's back with his wife . . . things are good.*

Really??? I'm so happy for him!! See, J . . . Where would he be without you?

Josh felt the warmth of her words deep to the center of his soul. Keith had been his best friend since grade school, but ten years ago he'd moved to Ohio. They still stayed in touch, and Keith sometimes joined him for online poker. That's how Cara knew him.

There was a pause in the conversation and then her next message appeared in the window.

How's your back?

Hurts like crazy . . . let's talk about something else. I go to court again next week.

To testify?

Yes. My lawyer says it should be the last time.

Yay! That means the settlement's coming! And then you can go after your daughter!

Josh read the line three times before his hands began moving across the keyboard. *That's why I wanted to talk to you tonight.*

Why?

Because you make her seem like a real person. My little girl.

She is real. Josh could hear Cara's indignant tone through the words of her message. *You're going to get custody of her one of these days, I just know it.*

The thrill of possibility sent tingles down Josh's arms. *Partial custody. But anything would be better than this.*

She's a lucky girl, J . . . I wish my kids had a daddy like you.

Josh stared at that part. Every time they had a conversation like this one, Josh wondered the same thing. Maybe he was wrong about never meeting her in person. Becky had probably moved on, anyway. If he and Cara got along so well, why not move their relationship from cyberspace to Phoenix? Or to Colorado Springs? Cara was a single mom of two kids—a boy and a girl. Her first husband had been abusive, and three years ago he'd moved out and found someone new. Cara found solace in online poker, and people who couldn't hit her, people who could pretend to be anyone they wanted to be.

Two years ago Josh was caught up in an online game with Cara—aka Miss Independent—when she said something that stayed with him still. In the comment section of the game, she wrote, *I play OP because my real life is on hold.*

That was exactly how Josh felt. Since the accident he'd been caught up in a web of depositions and hearings, meetings with lawyers, and waiting for workmen's comp checks in the mail. Since then, all of life had become a waiting game.

Waiting for the pain in his back to be healed.

Waiting for a decision in the trial against the drunk driver's insurance company.

Waiting for a chance at success so he could call Becky Wheaton and tell her he still loved her.

Waiting for his settlement money so he could pay back his parents and buy a house and take a paternity test so he could prove to all the world what he already knew: that Savannah was his daughter.

Another message appeared. *You're quiet. What are you thinking?*

Josh felt a tug on his heart. *How come you're there and I'm here?*

Yeah . . . I wonder that too sometimes.

Usually when they flirted with the possibility of taking their relationship to another level, one of them would change the subject before the conversation became too serious. But sitting in his stuffy apartment alone at one in the morning with the trial and the settlement becoming more of a reality each day, Josh suddenly couldn't stop himself. His fingers flew across the keyboard. *Okay, seriously, Miss Independent. Why don't we stop all this typing and find a way to hang out in person?*

There was a hesitation, and Josh's heartbeat sped up. Maybe he shouldn't have said anything. Maybe this was all she'd ever be capable of, and if that was the case, then so be it. Besides, he would always love Becky, and he owed it to both of them to see if she might feel the same way about him—once he was successful. If not, if she'd moved on, then maybe Cara was someone he could love. *Come on, Cara. . . .* He closed his eyes and remembered the words of the song he'd heard recently. *"I can only imagine . . . what it will be like. . . ."* God, please . . . *speak to her heart. If she's someone who could be in my life, then please . . .*

He opened his eyes just as the next message came across. *You're too good for me, J. You know that.*

Who are you kidding? . . . I'm lucky just to be your friend.

Another pause, shorter this time. *Tell me again about God, about you and Him.*

Disappointment stabbed at him because he really wanted to talk about the two of them. He swallowed hard. If she was going to change the subject, at least she wanted to talk about his newfound faith. He was still in pain, still sitting alone in a cheap apartment, but in the last six weeks his life had changed. He loved that Cara wanted to talk about it.

He breathed in and began typing. *I don't know, it's weird. My family's been talking to me about God forever, but I guess I had to figure it out on my own.*

What did it feel like . . . you know, when you heard that song and could tell God was talking to you?

Josh smiled again. He'd answered this question half a dozen times in the last six weeks, but Cara seemed to really need to understand.

He moved his hands across the keyboard faster this time. *I don't know, I mean . . . it was like God was talking straight to my heart. Telling me that I wasn't waiting for a settlement or a chance to see Savannah or for the next stage of my life. What I was really waiting for was Him. It was like He was calling me, and if I wanted to really live I needed to finally answer. You know? Stop running from Him and tell Him yes.*

I love that. She hesitated. *Can I tell you a secret?*

Always. He longed to hug her, put his hands on her shoulders, and look deep into her blue eyes. In lieu of that he clicked on her name in the instant message window and was instantly on her Facebook page. She had short brown hair and a narrow face. Not too tall or athletic or strikingly beautiful. A few extra pounds that drove her crazy, but the part Josh loved most was her smile. Cara's smile had a way of staying with him.

Her message flashed into view. *I've been talking with God.*

Online? He grinned at his own joke.

No, silly. In my heart. When I'm looking out the window at the summer sky or when a monsoon sweeps over Phoenix and lightning dances across the street outside my apartment complex.

He read her message slowly. *You should be a writer.*

I'm serious, J. You've changed me, your story about God. I think He's calling me, too. I'm taking the kids to church this Sunday.

Josh raised his eyebrows. *Seriously?* In the time he'd known her, Cara had been opposed to faith and God and anything dealing with Scripture. She never quite came out and said why, but on her Facebook page she described herself as agnostic. *Not interested in faith,* she'd written. That had changed in the last few weeks, and the reason had to be Josh's story about Wynonna and hearing God and realizing he'd been running away all this time.

Very seriously. So maybe I'll go to church this Sunday and all the answers will suddenly fall into place . . . and you'll get your settlement and buy a house in Scottsdale and we'll become best friends . . . and then . . . well, and then who knows? Right, J . . . maybe all that.

His heart did a somersault. *Right.* He wasn't sure if he should push the issue, but he couldn't stop himself. *Maybe all that and more.*

So . . . are you feeling better? ☺

He dropped his hands to his thighs and stared at the screen. He hadn't realized it until she asked, but he actually was feeling better. *You know what?* He typed the words quickly. *My back doesn't hurt like it did before.*

See, I knew it.

Knew what?

I'm good for you.

You are. Very good.

And you know what else, J?

He almost felt like she was sitting across from him. *What?*

You're very good for me, too. And that's enough for now.

Everything she'd said a moment ago suddenly felt like nothing more than wild-eyed dreams and make-believe. He wanted a cigarette so bad he would've walked three miles for one. *Yes,* he typed. *That's enough for now.*

They signed off, and Josh checked a few more profiles of his online friends before closing down the computer. He stood and the effort hurt, but it didn't slice through him the way it would've an hour ago. He wandered across the living room to the narrow wooden mantel above the electric fireplace. On it he had the photos that mattered. One of him and his family—back when he was in high school and all of life stretched out before him like a river of unlimited possibilities. Next to it was a picture of the two girls—the one that ran in the paper after the accident. And last was a photo of Savannah, taken three years ago when she was four. Maria sent it to him when she thought he was going to come through with thousands of dollars a month in child support.

But Josh didn't have that kind of money, not yet, and a few months after sending the photo she moved on—refusing his phone calls and never sending another photo.

Josh stared at the picture. *Please, God . . . keep her safe. I want so badly to be her dad.*

He heard no loud voice in response, no quiet whisper in the newly reclaimed territory of his soul. But a Bible verse played across his mind, one that the pastor had talked about last Sunday. He was going to church with Carl Joseph and Daisy, the same church where Carl Joseph's brother, Cody, and Cody's wife, Elle, attended. The sermon had been about holding on—even when there seemed to be no hope at all. The verse was from Psalm 119:50.

My comfort in my suffering is this: Your promise preserves my life.

Josh touched the frame surrounding Savannah's picture. *Thank You, God. . . . I feel Your comfort.* In the last few weeks, no words could have spoken more clearly to Josh than the ones from that single Bible verse. He kept a journal for Savannah and in his last entry he'd written to her about the Scripture. Never mind his relentless back pain, or the fact that the doctors weren't sure surgery would ever heal him. Forget about the depositions in the coming weeks, where the attorneys for the insurance company would certainly try to rip his testimony to shreds.

God's Word was reviving him.

Josh took a final look at the pictures on the mantel, then turned and walked slowly down the short hallway to his bedroom. He could walk a little straighter than before. Amazing, the power of having a true friend. No amount of pain medication could fully relieve the spasms in his back or the burning along his spine. But an hour of conversation with Cara and he felt like life was possible again. Like he could tackle another day.

In the beginning, their talks left them both drained because when they were honest with each other it was obvious things hadn't been easy for either of them. But now—now she was full of hope and life and encouragement, and Josh realized there could be only one reason for that: His new hope was spilling over into her life. And that was something that made him feel useful, like he had a purpose.

As he finished brushing his teeth, Josh smiled at the memory of their talk. Tonight they had tiptoed out of the safe confines of an instant message and stood for a brief moment on the balcony where the view was far grander. As Josh lay down and tried to find that elusive comfortable spot, as he begged God to keep the demon of deep, excruciating pain at bay, and as sleep finally found him, he thought about Cara and realized something else. Along the way God's Word wasn't only reviving him.

It was reviving both of them.

TWO

Annie Warren pulled the chilled raspberry cheesecake from her built-in Sub-Zero refrigerator, set it on her granite countertop, and sliced it onto a dozen china plates. The cheesecake was the same kind she served at the last function two weeks ago, and it was a huge hit. This time, she had a backup in the fridge just in case. It took no time to line the plates on a tray and steady it in her hands.

"Need help?" Her husband, Nate, rounded the corner, two coffee cups in his hands. He dropped them off near the sink. "They're hungry out there."

"No, thanks." She could feel the weariness in her smile as she walked past him toward the dining room. She tossed a quick glance back over her shoulder. "Maybe check the coffee. This crowd keeps every Starbucks in Colorado Springs in business."

Nate's laugh was low and discrete, muffled by the sounds as he worked the coffeemaker, fiddling with the springform top, the metal against metal. Annie eased her shoulder through a pair of double doors and found her practiced smile, the one she used whenever they entertained—and with Nate a member of the Colorado State

Board of Education, the Warrens entertained this way at least once a month.

Tonight it was the public librarians. Nate was up for reelection in a year and whatever he did he wanted the public librarians on his side. The board made decisions at every monthly meeting that directly affected them, and Nate wanted to make himself very clear: He was a friend of the public libraries. Hence the cheesecake.

Annie set the tray down near two nearly empty silver carafes of hot coffee.

"I told you." Babette, a librarian from the north side of the Springs, led her coworker closer to the dessert table. She smiled at Annie. "This is the cheesecake from Marigolds, right?"

"It is." Annie took a step back from the table. Good thing she bought two. "It was Nate's idea. 'Only the best for the librarians.'" Even as she said the words she could hear herself saying them last week about the teachers union. "*Only the best . . .*"

Babette was rail thin, but Annie had never known her to attend a party and eat less than three desserts. She helped herself to the first piece. "Best cheesecake in town, that's what I say." The other librarians made their way to the table as Babette took a few steps closer to Annie. "So . . ." She turned her back to the others. "I was thinking the other day about Josh, and he's what, now, in his late twenties? Because I was doing the math and it seems like this past June it was ten years since he and Blake graduated."

"Right." Annie's stomach tightened. She stood a little straighter. "Ten years, same as Blake."

Babette took three quick bites and seemed to swallow them whole. "Blake's an intern this fall, did I mention that? He ran into Becky Wheaton at the hospital the other day. She's a therapist now—beautiful girl. She was Josh's girlfriend way back when, wasn't she?"

"She was." Annie worked to keep her smile in place. "They haven't talked in a while."

"Blake says he might take her out for coffee. Just to re-connect." She waved her hand in the air, as if she'd forgotten her main point. "Anyway, Blake's the top intern in the program. I told you where he's at, right?"

"St. Anthony's in Denver."

"Yes." She picked up her fork and stabbed it in the air. "Boy's so driven he puts me to shame. Barely makes time for anything else. His instructors think he'll be a surgeon before he's thirty-two. Isn't that something?"

"Something."

"Becky Wheaton thought so. Blake said she was very impressed with how he was doing."

Becky Wheaton would never love anyone the way she'd loved Josh, Annie told herself. She poured a cup of coffee. She would need it to get through this night. Once she had it steadied on a saucer she looked at Babette again. "You must be proud."

"I am. I mean, my son was always driven, you know? Schoolwork, sports, the debate team. You name it."

"Definitely. That's Blake."

There was an uncomfortable pause. The familiar pause that told Annie exactly what was coming next. Babette consumed the rest of her cheesecake. "Like I said, I was thinking about Josh and . . . So, how's he doing, anyway?

I mean, the whole recovery from the accident and everything?"

"Actually, he's doing very well." Annie didn't hesitate, didn't give the woman anything but her most practiced answer. "He's in rehab for his back, and making progress. He's talked about starting his own business once he gets his settlement from the accident."

The woman smiled in a way that fell just short of condescending. "That's the Josh I remember. Always resourceful. And that Lindsay of yours—she was a smart one. Saw one of her feature stories in the paper the other day and I told myself, 'That Lindsay, she'll have books in our library one day.' She's quite a writer." She paused just long enough to refuel. "But then sometimes girls are more ambitious than their brothers. I read that in a *Cosmopolitan* article, and I stopped right there and thought of all the cases where that was true. Girls more successful than their brothers and the brothers never really—"

"Babette, I'm sorry." Annie held up her hand. She couldn't take another minute. "I need to slice the second cheesecake. Nate doesn't want his librarian friends leaving here hungry." She turned toward the kitchen and sipped hard on her coffee. "If you'll excuse me."

"Definitely. Go ahead." Babette turned back toward the dessert platter. "If the rest of you haven't tried this cheesecake you better grab a piece now. Best cheesecake in the Springs."

Annie let the double doors swing shut behind her and she steadied herself against the kitchen island. Why did they have to ask? *Dear God, isn't it enough that everyone knows about Josh's failures? Do they have to make me talk about the details?*

Conversations like the one with Babette made her feel like Josh was a piñata hanging high above the party while everyone took swings at him. Even her. Because the truth was she shouldn't work so hard to defend Josh. Just once, at one of these parties with people they'd known all their lives, Annie wished she had the courage to look a person like Babette in the eyes and say, "Josh is struggling. He moved here from Denver and he lives in a low-income, one-bedroom apartment. He's addicted to pain medication, he's trying to lose the last forty pounds of a significant weight gain, and his days are taken up waiting for a call from his lawyer saying that his settlement check is finally in the mail. But even then he'll probably spend the rest of his life in chronic pain."

Her heart hurt and she hung her head, blocking out the party chatter from the next room. He'd had so much potential, so many ways he could've succeeded. Her precious youngest child, her only son. The deeper truths Annie didn't want to admit to herself, let alone to a crowd of acquaintances. Josh had intentionally done things his way. He'd walked away from the faith he'd been raised with and made one poor choice after another.

And now he was paying for it with an existence that troubled Annie every waking hour.

She sensed someone behind her, and then felt a touch on her shoulder. "Annie?"

No need to find her happy hostess smile with Nate. She turned and let herself draw strength from his eyes. "Babette Long is driving me crazy."

"You?" He kissed her forehead. "I get e-mails from the woman every day, keeping me posted on the needs of the public libraries."

Exhaustion strained Annie's sense of control. "I don't envy you."

"What'd she do?"

Her eyes softened. "She asked about Josh."

Nate studied her for a few seconds, then he went to the fridge and pulled out the second cheesecake. "Not everyone who asks about Josh is trying to upset you." He set it on the counter next to the knife. "You know that, right?"

"How am I supposed to feel?" She kept her voice low. "The woman tells me about Blake, and 'Weren't Blake and Josh in the same graduating class?' and how Blake is breezing his way through med school."

A deeper pain flickered in Nate's expression, and for the slightest moment the last ten years of heartache showed in the lines around his eyes and the creases in his forehead. "You were smart to walk away." He sliced the cheesecake and grabbed another twelve plates. "Let's get this out there. They'll leave when the dessert's gone."

Nate was right, and not just about the dessert. Annie stayed away from Babette the rest of the evening, making her rounds and working the crowd—the way she was used to doing. This was their life, and Nate needed the support of every librarian in the Springs. That was the purpose of tonight, the reason she'd driven to Marigolds for two raspberry cheesecakes on a summer afternoon when she'd rather walk through their neighborhood or play tennis with Nate or sit on their spacious deck and watch the deer through the grove of trees that made up their backyard.

"The election isn't a sure thing," Nate reminded her often. "A position of influence comes with responsibility."

Annie knew the drill well. She worked her way around the room telling each group of librarians the same thing. "Nate's compelled to carry your needs before the board," or "Nate's always been passionate about public libraries." Nate enjoyed his position on the school board, and when she took a magnifying glass to her heart, she enjoyed it too. Maybe not her husband's monthly trek to Denver, but the sense of prestige that came with an elected position.

If people were busy looking at Nate and her, at their efforts toward another winning election and their position as part of Colorado Springs' social elite, then they were less likely to notice the fact that Josh wasn't doing much with his life. That's what Annie told herself, anyway.

The party ended and Annie moved into the kitchen. Even over the kitchen tap water she could hear Nate saying good-bye to the last librarians. "An increased budget for new books," he was saying, "that's what I'll be bringing up at the next meeting."

Annie rolled her eyes, and then felt bad for doing it. Nate's promise wasn't an empty one. Her husband really did care about librarians and public libraries, and whether the Springs was competitive on a statewide and national level with other progressive cities when it came to academic standards and testing.

It was just that on a night like this, when Josh was all she could think about, every line felt practiced and forced—like the plastic cheesecakes in the windows of Marigolds.

Finally, she heard the door shut, and silence. Wonderful, delicious silence. Nate joined her in the kitchen, grabbed a dish towel, and moved to Annie's left. She could feel him unwinding, relaxing—releasing the extra bit of air he'd kept in his lungs all night long. "That went well."

"Yes." She didn't look at him. She didn't want to spend another minute thinking about librarians. "Very well, dear."

He dried a handful of silverware without saying anything. Then he turned toward her, the way he did when he had something profound to say. "Not every kid grows up to be a doctor or a lawyer or a writer." There was an edge to his voice. "Everybody doesn't make the all-stars, Annie. Not in Little League and not in life. That doesn't mean Josh is a failure."

"What are you saying?" She didn't want to get mad at him. They got nowhere when they let their frustrations about Josh come between them.

"I don't know, I feel guilty." He tossed his hands in the air and then leaned back against the counter. "What if he could hear us talking about him? How would he feel if he knew we were disappointed?"

"I'm not disappointed." She hated that word, hated the finality of it. She turned back to the sink full of dishes. "I'm *concerned* for him and sorry for him because he never asked to be hit by that car." A catch sounded in her voice. "Lindsay's off making a name for herself at the paper, and where's Josh? Hooked on pain meds, sitting around his apartment." She gritted her teeth. "I ache for that boy because if he hadn't been injured, who knows what he'd be doing right now." The futility of it surrounded her, suffocated her. She threw the sponge into the sink and grabbed hold of the edge of the counter. "That isn't *disappoint-*

ment, Nate. It's just . . . why did that woman have to make Josh sound like a failure when he's only twenty-eight?"

"Annie." Nate put his hand on her shoulder. His voice was calmer than before. "It's okay to be disappointed." Before she could respond, he gave her a final look, picked up one of the clean pitchers, and began drying it. The conversation was over.

She studied him for a minute. In the past at a time like this she might've kept talking—just to make her point, or to get the last word in. But a long time ago she learned there was no point adding to a dialogue that had already ended. It was one of those understood aspects of their marriage—like how going out to dinner was assumed when he came home from work and found her curled in a chair reading a new novel or lost in the pages of her Bible study, or how a paper Nordstrom bag of his dress clothes left by the front door meant she was supposed to take them to the cleaners.

They finished the dishes in silence. Before Nate moved on to their bedroom, he leaned close and kissed her cheek. "I love you," he whispered near her ear. "Josh is going to be fine."

"I hope so." She responded to his touch, not angry with him. They needed each other more in this season of life than ever.

Nate slouched, his posture proof of what had to be an inner battle with defeat. "Josh is a good boy." His smile barely lifted his lips. "Some kids take longer, that's all."

Annie nodded and stared at the empty sink. "We'll keep praying for him."

"Yes." He touched her shoulder once more and then left.

She waited, listening to his feet leave the tiled floor and transition onto the carpet and up the stairs to their room. She dried her hands and went into the living room, to the bookcase next to the piano—the one with a dozen framed photos. She looked at them and then reached for the largest on the center shelf, the one of Lindsay and Josh in high school. By then Lindsay was shorter than her brother, but she was a senior, with confidence in her expression and the way she held herself.

Annie looked hard at Josh, at his eyes. He had that impish silly grin, the one he wore often in his early years at Black Forest High School. Like he didn't have a care in the world except one—his friendship with Lindsay. He looked up to her from the time he could crawl, chasing after her and beaming whenever she paid him attention.

Annie smiled at the picture, the way they had their arms around each other's necks. Their friendship had always been mutual—Lindsay adored Josh and saw him as her personal source of entertainment. While she was busy conquering one school year after another, Josh was less serious. He could make his sister laugh no matter what tests or projects she had pending. And up until his senior year in high school, Josh followed in Lindsay's footsteps, writing for the yearbook and newspaper and getting nearly straight A's in school.

But that was the year Lindsay fell in love with Larry, and after that she had less time for Josh. He had Becky Wheaton, of course, a bright, intelligent, beautiful girl who saw only the best in Josh. The two had been inseparable ever since they met at the beginning of their sophomore year. Josh loved her like he'd never loved anyone else in his life, and had even talked about marrying her after they finished college. But as she racked up one success after another, Josh began to flounder. He drank with his buddies on the baseball team and was kicked off the squad his senior year. They broke up, and though he tried junior college for a couple of years, he eventually lost interest in school. When he decided to tow cars in Denver instead of continuing at a university, Annie and Nate figured the job was only a phase. Give him a year, they agreed, and he'd be ready to get serious about his future again.

But that never happened.

Annie squinted hard at the photograph. Everything used to be so easy, so certain. Lindsay and Josh, best friends, with the whole world ahead of them. Becky, forever a part of Josh's life. Annie sighed. She had the ending all written, but somehow the story line changed.

Lindsay was busy now, married with two kids and a full-time job as a feature writer at the local *Gazette*. But even so, Lindsay was closer to Josh than she or Nate. Annie set the photo down, but her eyes lingered. Funny, she thought, how an entire lifetime can be summed up with one framed picture.

She let her eyes drift to other photos: Lindsay and Josh in an oversize raft catching white water on the Truckee River, Josh at age three dancing in six-year-old Lindsay's arms, the four of them at SeaWorld the summer before Lindsay started high school, Josh and Becky at their senior prom, a month before they broke up. The memories were like a balm to her soul, taking her back to a time when the questions were few and the answers easy.

A yawn caught her off guard and she checked her watch.

It was after eleven, time to turn in. But she couldn't pull herself from the pictures. Her eyes fell on a photo of Josh standing beside his tow truck the week after he'd been hired in Denver. Heartbroken over the loss of Becky Wheaton, he took a trip to Las Vegas and came back with a confession. He'd met a young woman, inadvertently promised her a life of luxury, and been intimate with her. Eleven months later he drove to the Springs, sat both her and Nate down, and admitted something else.

The woman was married—though Josh hadn't known that at the time—and now she'd given birth to a baby girl.

"She tells me the baby is mine. She wants child support." Josh looked devastated. "I don't know what to do."

Annie had been too stunned to speak, but Nate had calmly helped him sort through his options. "You need a paternity test." He worked to hide the pain in his voice, but it weighed heavy on his tone, anyway. "After that you can talk about the next step."

The paternity test never came. The woman found out Josh didn't have a hundred dollars in savings let alone money for child support. After that she wasn't willing to subject her daughter to the test, and Josh couldn't afford a lawyer. Over the years, though, Josh talked about the girl as if she were a very real part of his life. His daughter. He charted her birthdays and sent gifts to the woman without knowing whether they ever reached the child. And he talked about bringing her home one day, where she would become fast friends with Lindsay's kids—her cousins.

Only Lindsay listened. She would let him talk about the girl and always agreed that once Josh had his settlement money he should hire an attorney and force a paternity test. "What if she's really his?" Lindsay only asked the question a handful of times in the years since the family had learned about the child.

"Impossible." Annie always dismissed the possibility. "The dates don't line up—the woman didn't even tell Josh about the baby until almost a year after the Las Vegas trip." She hated even talking about the situation. The fact that one of her children would be in such a quandary broke her heart. The woman was married, after all. The child almost certainly belonged to her husband.

"She wanted quick cash," Annie once told Josh when the subject came up. "Let the matter go. Besides, what about Becky?"

"Becky moved on." A deep pain filled Josh's eyes. "I wasn't enough for her."

"I heard she broke up with that last guy." Annie always thought Becky and Josh would get back together. "At least give her a call."

"This isn't about Becky. It's about a little girl who belongs to me. I'm a father now, Mom. I need help figuring out how to connect with her."

"Don't be ridiculous, Josh. You have no way of knowing whether that child is yours or not."

The conversation came up again several times, but always Annie dismissed the idea and eventually Josh mentioned her less often. The child would be seven now, and he sometimes voiced what he called his greatest fear—that if his settlement didn't come soon he would miss her childhood entirely.

Another sigh filled the quiet room and Annie left the room, turning the lights off as she went. Josh had compromised his faith, walked away from regular church attendance, and managed to ruin his credit rating with one bad loan after another. He drove a beater pickup truck and could barely afford rent each month. He didn't drink anymore, but he had no real friends and no girlfriend in the picture. As if his entire life was wrapped up in his back pain, on hold for the day his settlement would arrive in the mail.

And then what? An expensive paternity fight? The sorrow of finally having to admit the truth—that the girl wasn't his in the first place? So what if he could finally buy a modest house somewhere in the Springs? The money wouldn't take away his back pain or make it easier for him to find a job.

She slowed her pace as she neared her room and all at once a reality dawned on her. She had no right getting angry at Nate for what he'd said earlier. Whatever she wanted to tell herself, Nate was right, and an image came to mind. A month ago she'd been caught in traffic on I-25 only to come across a disabled semitruck. The truck's trailer was extraordinarily high and hadn't cleared an overpass. There the truck sat, the overpass collapsed across the top of it.

That's how Annie felt now, like an entire overpass had given way and fallen around her shoulders. Because no matter how badly she wanted to believe otherwise, the truth wouldn't let her move out from beneath it. Yes, she was worried about Josh and frustrated for him and sad about his place in life. But there was no denying the other obvious truth.

She was disappointed in him.

THREE

Saturdays were tough because lawyers—for all the money they made—didn't work weekends. Josh understood. His attorney, Thomas Flynn, was one of the good guys. If the courts were open on the weekend, Flynn would be there fighting for him—Josh had no doubt.

But since he was still days away from his next deposition and moving his case one small step closer to settlement, Josh's plans for Saturday involved other jobs that needed tackling. He slept in and took the usual ten minutes to lie in bed, savoring that half-awake phase when the pain was still a spectator. His back hurt whether he was awake or sleeping, standing or lying down. But in the bliss of sleep, at least he wasn't aware of the pain. Not until ten minutes after he woke up.

Josh opened his eyes and, in as much time as it took him to look out the window and note the blue skies of another beautiful September day, the first deep ache tugged at his middle back. He shifted and winced and a crisscross of sharp, searing pains sliced one way and then another from his shoulder blades and hip bones across his spine.

You can do this, he told himself. *Please, God. . . . Help me get out of bed.* The getting out was the worst part—sometimes worse than any other pain he'd face all day. Something about moving around always made the pain lessen. He held his breath and swung his feet out over the edge of the mattress. The pain doubled and he cried out, panting, trying to find enough air to fill his lungs.

Please, God. . . .

He remembered the pain pills at his bedside. Strange that it usually took trying to move before he remembered the OxyContin, maybe because in his mind he was still the same Josh Warren he'd been for the first twenty-five years of his life, limber and mobile and athletic, able to move without giving his body a second thought. But the limitations he lived with were a quick reminder each morning that he didn't dare try a single hour of life without the help of his medication. Not until something could be done for his back.

Using all his effort, he swung his legs back onto the bed and slid himself up toward the headboard. The bottle was open, and he tried to remember. Had he taken another pill sometime in the middle of the night? Eighty milligrams every twelve hours—those were his doctor's orders. But sometimes he had to count the pills before breakfast to make sure he wasn't taking too many. And if he did, well, then sometimes he had to admit to himself that he was doing the best he could. Too many pills or not.

He took hold of the plastic bottle and his fingers felt stiff as he tapped a single pill into the palm of his other hand. The glass of water he kept by his bedside looked stale. Josh didn't care. He downed the pill and set the glass back on his nightstand. *Work,* he ordered the little round pill. *Start working.*

Ever since his music video encounter with Wynonna Judd more than a month ago, he'd used this time to pray. Talking to God took the edge off the way his whole body screamed for relief, and he couldn't do anything else, anyway. He let his head drop back on the pillow and he closed his eyes.

Dear God, be with my parents. I know they're disappointed in me. He exhaled and tried to sink back into the mattress. He grabbed a quick breath and held it. *The thing is, they don't understand the pain. I can't look for a job until I feel better, so help them not to worry about me. Not to be disappointed.* He grabbed at a handful of his comforter and clenched his fist. "Work . . . start working already." He remembered his prayer. *Also, God, I pray for Cara and Carl Joseph and Daisy and Cody . . . for Ethel next door and Keith in Ohio. For Becky, that she's finding the happiness she wanted. And that maybe she might be ready to love me again when I'm the person I want to be. Also for all my friends, God. Be with them and draw them close the way*—he cried out again and rolled partially onto his side—*the way You drew me close with that music video.*

For Lindsay and Larry, and Ben and Bella—my sister's husband and kids; Lord, keep them safe. He felt the first wave of relief pass over him and he wiped the perspiration on his forehead. *And please, God, be with Savannah. One day I want to be healthy and whole and bring her home here where she belongs. Please, God, let her come home. I want her to know her grandparents and her aunt Lindsay and her cousins. I want her to know me.* He felt himself relax. *That's all, God. Thanks.*

He opened his eyes and swung his feet out over the edge of the bed once more. This time the pain was bearable and it didn't cause him to cry out. The pill was working. He clenched his teeth as he drew himself to a sitting position and put his feet on the floor. His head spun a little, the dizziness a regular part of his mornings—at least for the first few minutes after he sat up. A side effect from the medication, his doctor had told him.

He stared at the amber bottle of pills. One day soon he would have surgery and the doctor would fix his back, and then, with a lot of rehab and sweat, he would be his old self again. He'd seen the surgeon again last Wednesday and the report looked good.

"Another forty pounds," the doctor had told him. "You get that weight down and we'll do the operation."

He looked down at his gut, the way it hung over his sweatpants. Weight had never been a problem before, but sometime after high school the pounds piled up. He was seventy pounds overweight when the accident happened. After the accident, he ate out of frustration and boredom and added another thirty. Now he'd lost all but the last forty, but still the doctor wanted to wait.

"Some of your injury is still trying to heal itself," he explained more than once. "As you lose weight, your back is bound to work better and feel better. We can probably schedule the surgery sometime next month."

Josh rubbed the back of his neck. He grabbed a white T-shirt from his second dresser drawer and slid it over his head. At least he could fit into his old shirts now, and Cara had complimented him on a recent picture he'd sent her. "You're looking hot," she'd told him. "Now just get yourself well."

He used the bedpost to pull himself up onto his feet. That was the goal. Get himself well again. He walked slowly into the kitchen, careful to keep his knees slightly bent so he wouldn't trigger a spasm. A single spasm in his back could lay him flat in bed for a couple hours or more, pain medication or not.

Josh was making himself a bowl of instant oatmeal—maple and brown sugar, his favorite—when there was a knock at the door. A quick survey told him the apartment wasn't as neat as it could be. Magazines were strewn on the couch and coffee table, and the blanket he kept along the back of the sofa had fallen onto the floor. Two half-full glasses of water sat on one of the end tables, on either side of a stack of unopened mail. When he got his settlement, after he started his own business and placed that first call to Becky Wheaton, he would have to make a habit of keeping things neat. Becky liked life to have an order about it, and Josh did, too. He only had to make time for that order. For now, this was usually how the place looked. Whoever was at the door, they weren't paying him a visit because of his clean apartment.

He moved as quickly as he could and opened the door. Bright sunshine met him on the other side, and standing on the front porch were his neighbors—Carl Joseph Gunner and Daisy Dalton. "Howdy, neighbor!" Carl Joseph grinned and pushed his thick dark glasses a little higher up the bridge of his nose.

"Howdy." Josh used the doorknob to steady himself. "Looks like a nice day out there."

"Another beautiful day in the Springs." Daisy looped her arm through Carl Joseph's. "Today's a bus trip to the movies. Saturday date day, right, CJ?"

"Right." Carl Joseph puffed out his chest. "Me and Daisy have a date day after a late breakfast."

Josh absently wondered if the two had come for a reason or just to say hello. They stopped by often—nearly every day—for one reason or another. "A late breakfast, huh?" He smiled, and the pain in his back dimmed in light of the distraction. "What's on the menu?"

Carl Joseph exchanged a frown with Daisy. "That's the problem." He shrugged big and shot a forlorn look at Josh. "The market trip was yesterday and we forgot."

"We forgot eggs." Daisy nodded. She pointed past Josh. "Can we borrow six eggs, Josh? Six eggs should be enough."

He chuckled quietly and the sensation felt wonderful. He stepped aside and motioned for them to come inside. "You bet. I can round up six eggs."

"Because, well"—Carl Joseph furrowed his brow, as if he was thinking very hard on the matter—"we could get by with five, but then maybe we'd be hungry at the movie."

"And hungry at the movie means too much popcorn." Daisy gave Carl Joseph a knowing look. "Not a very healthy choice."

"No." Josh patted his middle. "I know all about that."

Carl Joseph hesitated, but then he laughed out loud, as if Josh had just told the funniest joke ever. Again, Josh kept his own laughter quiet. The two were as guileless and transparent as any friends he had. He led them into the kitchen toward the refrigerator. "Let's see. We need something so you can carry them home."

"Not a basket." Daisy waved her finger, her concern genuine. "Mom says never to put all your eggs in one basket."

Carl Joseph's eyes lit up. "But maybe two baskets."

"Here." Josh pulled a square Tupperware container down from one of his cupboards. His back was loosening up, allowing him the ability to look almost normal as he moved about his kitchen. "This should hold all six eggs."

"I like that." Carl Joseph pushed his glasses up again and smiled at Daisy. "Plastic is good for eggs."

Josh placed six eggs carefully into the container and handed it to Carl Joseph. "What movie are you seeing?"

"It's an older one." A silly grin played across his face. "But Cody says what do you expect for three dollars on a Saturday."

"You expect a good time." Daisy cast a proud look at Carl Joseph. "Because that's a good use of money, CJ. It's a very good use."

The theater was an old one downtown, in a building that would have closed except for its decision to show old movies on the weekend at discount rates. Lindsay had written a piece on the theater for the *Gazette*. Low prices were filling the place and popcorn and candy sales were keeping it in business. Carl Joseph and Daisy were regulars.

"We're seeing *Flicka*. It's a movie about a horseback rider." Daisy must have realized that neither of them had answered Josh's question.

"A horse rider like my brother." Carl Joseph couldn't keep the pride from his tone. He thought the world of Cody, and Josh understood why. The guy came around all the time and Josh liked him. Back when they first met, Cody had shared with Josh his own story of heartache and pain. Somehow Cody's story gave Josh hope that maybe he'd come out happy in the end. The way Cody had.

"You can go with us if you want." Daisy took the container of eggs and held it to herself. She raised her eyebrows at Carl Joseph and her shoulders lifted a few times. "That's okay, right, CJ?"

"Sure." He tossed his hands. "Three people can take a movie date. Three or two, it doesn't matter."

For a few seconds Josh actually considered taking them up on the idea. He'd gone two or three times before, saving them a bus trip and spending the afternoon with them. But he needed to clean his apartment. "Not today, guys. I have plans."

Carl Joseph nodded. "Plans are good. Brother says a day with plans can't be half bad."

"Well . . ." Josh smiled. He thought about Cara and the plans they'd talked about just last night. "I'd say your brother's right. Planning is always good."

Josh was walking his neighbors to the door when Carl Joseph stopped and took a detour to the fireplace mantel. He squinted at the photos lined across it and pointed to the picture of the two girls. "Tell us the story again, okay?"

"Yeah, tell us." Daisy clapped her hands. "That's a very good story."

Josh didn't mind telling the story. Other than his neighbors, no one knew what really happened with the accident. The story hadn't been even a mention in the Springs paper. Josh gripped the mantel and leaned into it, buying a little added relief for his back. "Where should I start?"

"At the beginning." Carl Joseph took the photo down and held it close so he and Daisy could see it better. "I always like the beginning."

"Okay." Josh knew how to tell the story in a couple

minutes. "It happened on New Year's Eve nearly three years ago."

"In Denver, right?" Daisy's eyes were wide with antici- pation.

"Right. I was towing cars away from a no-parking area along one side of a busy street."

"Which is dangerous." Carl Joseph nodded his concern.

"Definitely dangerous." Josh hesitated, thinking back. "I was hooking up my sixth car of the night when those two girls came up and asked me a question."

"They were best friends." Daisy told the detail to Carl Joseph, as if she were the owner of that part of the story. "The very best."

"Right, and at that time there weren't any cars coming, so the girls were standing in the road. They were trying to find State Street and they needed directions."

"So you told them." Carl Joseph stared at the framed picture. "They seem like nice girls."

"They were. They hadn't been drinking, and they didn't want to get home too late. Too many bad drivers on the road on New Year's Eve." Josh ran his hand through his dark hair. He was feeling stronger than before so he re- leased his hold on the mantel and crossed his arms. "I was giving them directions when I saw the drunk driver."

Fear lined Carl Joseph's forehead. "It's against the law to drive drunk."

"Yeah." Josh uttered a quietly sarcastic laugh. "I don't think the driver was very concerned about the law."

"Because he was passed out." Daisy nodded emphati- cally.

"He was." Josh could still picture the guy, his head slumping forward onto the steering wheel as his car veered off the road. "And he was headed straight for the girls."

"This is the scariest part." Daisy partially closed her eyes, the way a person might in anticipation of a frightening scene in a horror movie. "I hate this part."

"Me, too." Josh imagined the accident all over again. "Everything happened so fast. The girls couldn't see the drunk driver, but he was headed straight for them. I pulled one of them out of danger, and as I reached for the other one the car slammed into us."

Carl Joseph and Daisy were silent, gripped by the story.

"I had time to throw the second girl onto the grass, out of harm's way, but at the same time the car hit my left shoulder and knocked me to the ground."

Daisy put her hand over her mouth. "That's terrible."

"He broke the law for sure." Carl Joseph's tone was hushed. "That was a very bad thing he did."

"Very bad." Josh felt the impact again the way he'd felt it that night, how the front grille of the Mercedes sedan had barreled into him, knocking the wind from him and leaving him in a heap on the ground. For the first few minutes he thought he was dead. He couldn't breathe, couldn't move, and as people surrounded him and sirens sounded in the distance he wanted only one more chance to tell his parents and Lindsay and Becky he loved them, to somehow get word to Savannah that he had tried to be her father, always he had tried.

Daisy allowed the hint of a smile. "The story has a happy ending, right?"

"It does." Josh had never told Carl Joseph or Daisy

about his back pain. They wouldn't understand, and it would only mar their visits with unnecessary concern. There was nothing they could do to help ease his pain or heal his back, so why complain to them about the way he hurt? Better to let them focus on the girls. He drew another breath and finished. "The car didn't kill me, and the two girls weren't hurt at all." He grinned at his friends.

"A happy ending for sure." Carl Joseph raised his fist high in the air. "I love that story." He smiled at the two girls in the photo and then at Josh. "That makes you a hero."

A hero. The words cast a ray of sunshine across his cloudy heart. All the pain was worth something, even if few people thought he was a hero. The girls did, certainly. And the people who read the article, and his neighbors. But he hadn't shared the story with his parents, not yet. He remembered the way his mother had received the news of his accident when he called her late that night.

"I was hit by a car," he told her, his voice flat. "I'm in the hospital, but I'm okay." He intended to go into the details, tell her how he'd pulled the girls to safety before taking the hit, but his mother was already talking.

"Josh, what happened? Are you hurt?" Then she called for his father. "We're on our way, son. We'll be there in an hour."

"Mom, wait." Josh was already on pain medication by then, and the scope of his injuries was still being realized. "I'm fine. I'm going home tonight and I'm coming down tomorrow."

"Oh, Josh." His mother's relief came in short breathy gasps. "You scared me to death." She wasn't mad, just worried about him. Afraid because he could have been killed. But what she said next stayed with him still. "Now maybe you'll see why I want you to get your degree, do something with your brain for a change. Towing cars, Josh? Every day I worry about you, and now this. Why don't you take some time and think about getting back in school. Not one good thing comes from your work as a tow truck driver, son. Not one good thing."

So he hadn't told her or his father or Lindsay. Not because he wasn't proud of his role in saving the lives of the girls, but because it wasn't enough. He loved his family, and they loved him—their feelings for him were all that kept him going some days. But they hadn't spent more than a rare few minutes at his apartment, and none of them had noticed the small photographs on the mantel. One day he would explain it all. He would get his settlement—half a million dollars or more—and he would open his own garage, and then, when his back was healed and life was good, he would tell them the truth about how he was hurt.

Daisy took the photograph from Carl Joseph and set it back on the mantel. "I love hero stories." Adoration made her eyes sparkle as she looked at Josh. "You and CJ and Cody are the only heroes I know." She looked at her friend. "CJ because he protects me from the rain, and Cody because he made my sister, Elle, love again. And you, Josh, because you saved the lives of those two girls."

Josh liked being a hero for these two. It seemed to give them hope about the world in general, and if it did, well, then that was another good thing that had come from the accident. No matter what his mother thought about his job as a tow truck driver.

"What about this one?" Carl Joseph picked up the photo of Savannah and studied it. He pushed his glasses back into place again. "Can you tell us this story, Josh?"

"Not today." Josh kept his tone easy, his smile in place. "That one's not a happy story."

"Oh." Daisy frowned. "Then let's not talk about it. I only like the happy ones."

"Me, too." Josh could feel the OxyContin holding his pain at bay, making it bearable for him to be on his feet this long. "You two better get home for your late breakfast."

Daisy gasped and looked down at the eggs. She'd been holding them in one hand, clutching them to her chest. "I almost forgot about late breakfast."

"Yeah, we better go." Carl Joseph took charge and grabbed hold of Daisy's free hand. "We have our movie date." He waved to Josh as they reached the door. "Thanks for telling us the happy story."

"Anytime." Josh followed them and waited until they were down the walkway. "Have fun today."

They both turned around and waved one last time. When Josh closed the door and went into his living room, he took a minute to sit down and catch his breath. He hadn't stood that long at one time for a week at least. From where he sat, he looked at the photos on the mantel again and his eyes fell on the one of Savannah. Maybe one day their story would be a happy one, too. When he could finally prove that the reason her eyes looked like his was because she was his daughter. He stretched his back and tried to find a comfortable position. He agreed with Daisy. The happy stories were the best.

Even if he was the only one who knew how much the happy ending cost.

FOUR

Maria Cameron held tight to her daughter's hand and together they trudged down the cement steps to the subway that ran beneath the streets of Manhattan. She had panhandled her way through another Sunday afternoon and now she needed the red line north along Broadway to 145th Street in Harlem. She and Savannah rented a room from a guy she'd met in the park three months ago. Freddy B, he called himself.

She paid her rent one way or another—with the money from tourists in Central Park or by spending the night in his bed when he wanted her. He lived in a one-bedroom apartment in a brownstone in the part of Harlem that had yet to experience urban renewal. But it was a home, and it would do for now.

"I'm hungry, Mama." Savannah's strawberry-blond hair was pulled back in a ponytail, and her cheeks were smudged with dirt—the way Maria had smudged them earlier that morning.

"We'll eat when we get home." She gave the girl a look intended to quiet her. She didn't need people scrutinizing them on the subway. "Keep quiet, now."

Savannah nodded and bit her lip. She pushed the sleeves of her sweater up, but as she did she exposed a series of small bruises. Maria reached over, jerked her sleeves back in place, and gave the girl a look that told her to be more careful. Strangers didn't understand bruises on a seven-year-old. But sometimes Savannah walked too slowly, and she had to be pulled along. It wasn't Maria's fault the girl's skin was fair, or that she bruised easily.

She paid the fare and led Savannah to the first two open seats. The subway always smelled the same—a faint mix of sour milk and old urine. Maria took stock of the car. An old lady at the far end, half asleep. Otherwise they were alone. She pulled a wad of bills from her pocket and counted them. September was a good month. Lots of tourists around the zoo entrance, less heat and humidity. Everyone in a good mood. She sorted through the bills and came up with an amount that surprised her even for September. A hundred and forty-two dollars. Not bad for a day's work.

"How much?" Savannah crossed her ankles and put her hands on her knobby knees. "Enough for rent?"

"More than enough." She eyed her daughter. "Don't ask so many questions."

Maria tucked the money into the back pocket of her baggy jeans, leaned her head back against the window, and closed her eyes. Good day or not, this wasn't how life was supposed to turn out. She was so far from those days that sometimes on the long subway ride home she forced herself to go back. Otherwise she would forget where she'd come from, and that wouldn't be good. Because if she couldn't remember the past, how was she ever going to find her way back there.

She and Raul had married ten years ago with dreams of opening their own pizza shop on the Lower East Side. Raul had business partners who were shady, but Maria didn't ask a lot of questions. It wasn't her deal where Raul got his money or how he spent his time when he came home late at night.

The trip to Vegas was his idea. "Go meet a guy with money. Get yourself knocked up and we'll be set. Regular money coming in first of the month till the kid's eighteen."

Maria hadn't liked the idea, but the fact that Raul suggested it made her just mad enough that she decided to go. Could be fun, spending a week away from Raul, playing in the bed of a new man, someone rich and mysterious. She let Raul book her plane and hotel, and she took the trip two weeks later. Josh Warren was the first guy she met, sitting at a bar in the Mandalay Bay casino. He had dark hair and fair skin and blue eyes that caught her attention across the room. She had fifty dollars in her pocket and instructions to find the highest roller in the hotel. A nearby restroom gave her the chance to freshen her red lipstick and adjust her blouse so her cleavage was more prominent. Then she ambled up to the man and took the bar stool beside him.

"Hi, there." She played with a strand of her red-blond hair. "What's a pretty boy like you doing all alone in a place like this?"

He didn't seem interested at first. He pulled a cigarette from a pack of L&M lights and offered one to her. She took it and held it out while he lit both of them. "I came alone." He took a long drag from the cigarette. "Haven't had a vacation in a year."

"Me, either." She wasn't sure the guy had money, but she was willing to take a few minutes to find out. "Buy me a drink?"

Josh studied her and exhaled a mouthful of smoke with a series of surprised laughs. "You're bold."

"Yes, sir." She crossed her legs and adjusted her short skirt in a phony show of modesty. "My mama taught me you get nothing in this world unless you ask for it."

"Touché." Josh held his cigarette up as if he were toasting her boldness. "Name's Josh Warren."

"Hello, Josh." The cigarette helped her voice sound velvety. She leaned over so he'd have a better view. "I'm Maria Cameron. Alone, same as you."

"Vacation?"

"Sort of." She willed herself to look the victim. "Old man used to beat me." She shrugged one dainty shoulder. "Finally left the jerk. Came here looking for a change in luck."

Josh didn't exactly look interested, but the glass of whiskey in front of him was half empty and he seemed pleasantly relaxed. "You a gambler, Maria Cameron?"

"Sometimes." She let her eyes move slowly down his frame. "Depends on the prize."

He laughed and they finished their cigarettes, flirting and making conversation. The part that caught her attention came just as he leaned across her to kill the cigarette in a nearby ashtray. Their shoulders brushed against each other and he whispered near her ear. "I got a million reasons why you should go out with me tonight."

"A million?" Maria's heart beat harder. What was he saying? That he was a millionaire? She leaned closer. "Tell me about it."

"I got plans." He ordered another whiskey for himself and one for her. When the drinks came, he grinned at her in a way that sent chills down her arms.

"Tell me." Maybe she'd fall in love with this Josh Warren. That would serve Raul right for sending her here in search of a one-night stand.

"I work out of a garage in Denver, but in a year I'll own the place. Then I'll open a chain of garages up and down the state of Colorado. I'll be a millionaire in no time, baby." He clinked his glass against hers. "That's the plan."

Maria wasn't sure just how much money Josh had right now, but with plans like that she had to believe she'd found her guy. "I have plans, too." She looked over her shoulder and lowered her voice. "But I don't like talking about them in public." She felt the corners of her mouth curl up. "Know what I mean?"

Josh paid their tab and without asking what she meant he led her to the elevator and up sixteen floors to his room. They spent most of the next four days in bed, and she never even bothered to check in under her own name, never spent a dime. If Josh wasn't a high roller, he certainly played the role that week. He told her he was a Christian and that he'd never done anything like this, and he tried everything he could to sell her on Denver.

"We can get married and get a place together." He had stars in his eyes from the time he first brought her to his room. "We'll find a church and raise a family and I'll take care of you the rest of your life." As an afterthought he asked about her age.

She was a well-kept thirty-two, but he didn't need to know that. "I'm twenty-seven." She studied him across the table at breakfast one morning. "What about you?"

"Just turned twenty-one." He was smoking again. "But that's in style. Guys with older girls."

With every passing day Josh seemed to fall harder for her. He talked about his family, his sister, Lindsay, and how his parents wanted him to continue college. "But my plans don't need a degree," he told her. "Everything's falling into place just like I hoped it would."

Josh made her feel things Raul never made her feel, and after three days she was thinking about going home with him to Denver and never looking back. It wasn't until the last day that Maria made sense of the plans Josh had been talking about. Sure, he planned to own the garage at the end of the year, but right now he was living on a tow truck driver's salary.

They'd been in bed, and as the details fell into place, she climbed out and got dressed in a hurry. "You mean, you're not a millionaire?"

He leaned on his elbow and let out a nervous laugh. "Not yet. Not for a year, anyway."

She gathered her things. "This can't work, Josh." She was shaking by then, attracted to him but scared about Raul. He'd left her a message at the front desk asking her to call. If she left with Josh now, Raul would hunt her down. He had friends who frightened her, friends who could find her. And if Josh wasn't the high roller Raul had ordered her to find, then why would she go with him, anyway? More than that, when she got home he'd be furious with her. She shook her head. "Not yet, not now." She had his phone number and address, and she'd given him hers. She backed up until she hit the hotel room door. "Besides, I'm married, Josh. I—I should've told you." She reached for the door handle. "I'll call you. Maybe then you'll have your plans worked out and I'll be single again and . . . and . . ."

Josh sat up. "You're married?" His cheeks lost their color. "How could you do this?"

Maria left without answering, angry and in tears. He shouldn't have exaggerated the truth. If he didn't have a million dollars coming, then why say so? Pretty boys with a tow truck driver's salary were a dime a dozen. Raul was better than that, after all. Josh followed her out into the hall, but she didn't look back. Once she exited the elevator she made her way to the front desk and called Raul.

"I found the high roller." She swallowed the lie and pressed forward. "I'm ready to come home."

Raul praised her and gave her instructions for catching a flight home to New York the next day. She spent the night with a stranger from Australia and flew home a few hours later.

"Think you're knocked up?" Raul asked her when he met her at LaGuardia.

Maria wanted to spit at him, but instead she glared with piercing eyes. "I had a good time. Let's just say that."

Her answer ticked him off. He beat her bad that night, punishing her for having a good time on a trip he had forced her to take. The bruises and screaming were the beginning of the end, and by the time she found out she was pregnant, her marriage was over. She moved in with a girlfriend and began a series of bad relationships, all the while waiting until the baby was born.

One look at Savannah and she was pretty sure who the father was. The infant didn't have Raul's dark skin or the Australian's light blond hair. And by then Josh was the only person she knew who could help her financially. Raul's words came back to her.

"Get yourself knocked up and be set for life . . . a regular paycheck every month."

She made the call to Josh when Savannah was two months old. "How are those plans coming along?" That's how she started the conversation, and on her end she crossed her fingers. "You a millionaire, Josh Warren?"

"You gotta be kidding me." He sounded hurt, like he was still angry at her for walking out that day in his hotel room. "Listen, lady, if I were a millionaire you're the last person on earth I'd tell."

"Unless maybe I have news that might interest you." Lying on a blanket next to her, little Savannah began to cry. "You're a father, Josh. I had a baby girl and she looks just like you."

On the other end, he said nothing for half a minute. "You're serious? You had a baby?"

"I did. I want to share custody with you, Josh." She waited a deliberate amount of time. "But I'm out of money. I need monthly support."

Whatever emotion Josh had experienced with the news, he buried it quickly. "How do I know she's mine? You're married."

"Not anymore. The baby's yours. I'm positive."

Josh's voice softened a little. "How can I believe anything you say?"

Savannah's cry grew louder, loud enough that Maria was pretty sure Josh could hear her over the phone lines. "That's your daughter, Josh. Send us some money and you can come see her for yourself."

"You're still in New York City?"

"Yes. I'm serious. Help me out and you can call her your own."

Josh paused. "What are you looking for?"

"Three thousand, maybe four. Enough for me and Savannah to get by."

Josh breathed in so loudly she could hear it. "Three or four thousand?" He released an angry laugh. "I'm still a tow truck driver, Maria. My plans haven't come together yet." He pushed ahead. "What if I come out there and meet you. For a weekend or so, something like that. If I could see her for myself then I'd know if she—"

"No." Maria was furious. "What are you saying? You have no money?"

"Not right now, but . . ." He sounded angry and shocked, not sure what to say or believe. "Let me book a ticket. I'll come in a few weeks and we can talk in person."

"Forget it." Maria raised her voice. She had a baby to feed and a life to figure out. The last thing she needed was a guy without money. "Call me when your plans come through. Otherwise, I'm not interested." She hung up the phone and didn't hear from him again for a year. He called with just one question. Did she still think he was the baby's father?

"Of course." She wasn't any kinder to him than she had been the last time they talked. "Did your money come through?"

"It will. I need you to do a paternity test, okay?"

"Not without money." Again she hung up on him.

Three summers passed, and he called again and this time he told her things were looking up. "My plans are working out. Tell me what you need."

Maria was still single, still trying to make things work out in the city. But she needed money more than ever. "Four thousand. Not a penny less."

"Okay." He sounded nervous. "I can do that. But I want something first."

"What?"

"A photo. I'll give you an address and you send me a picture of her. I won't write a check until then."

Maria agreed, and she kept her word. The next day she placed a picture of Savannah in the mail. She called Josh a week later. "I told you. She's your daughter."

"She—she has my eyes."

"Right, so when's the check coming?"

"As soon as I can pull the money together." Josh's tone took on a desperate quality. "I'll get you money, Maria, I will. Maybe not four thousand dollars, but something. I want to take responsibility. I want to meet her."

"Are you kidding?" Maria considered ripping the phone cord from the wall and throwing the receiver across the room. "You don't have the money? You lied to me?"

"Come on." He was pleading with her. "I needed to know. Now I only need to—"

Maria slammed the phone back on the base and cursed him for being a failure. A few weeks later she found a package from him in the mail. In it was a plastic-framed photograph of Josh, and a hundred-dollar bill. Tucked in the envelope was a note in which Josh promised to give more money, only if she would let him come for a visit. The hundred came in handy for a few days, but Maria tucked the package in a dresser drawer and when she moved a few months later she didn't give Josh her forwarding information. Since then, she hadn't talked to him, hadn't taken his phone calls. Once she could have sworn she saw him in Central Park, but she left before she had time to find out.

The subway ground to a stop and Maria opened her eyes. Savannah was still sitting beside her, still watching her with those big blue eyes. Josh's eyes. "We're almost home."

"I guess." She yawned and sat up a little straighter. Savannah's father never had any plans at all. He was like all the rest. The subway reached 145th Street and she took firm hold of Savannah's hand. They were home, and with this much money maybe she could get a good night's sleep in her own bed for a change and try to forget about the past and Savannah and a blue-eyed dreamer named Josh Warren. A guy who wasn't so much a high roller as he was like every other guy.

Just another loser.

❧

Savannah didn't really have her own room, just a corner halfway under a desk in the place where her mama sometimes slept. She wasn't allowed on the bed, in case her mama slept there. But even when Mama didn't, Savannah's place was on the floor. Her head beneath the desk, feet sticking out. She had a soft sleeping bag and a nice pillow, and anyway, she sort of liked sleeping beneath the desk because the little area was dark and private, like a tent or a fort.

Under the desk she kept all her treasures. There was a book called *Heidi* that some lady gave her when she was six and they were in Central Park, and a little plastic cross she got from her grandpa Ted before he died. Her grandpa told her about Jesus, but no one else ever talked about Him. It made her feel safe to think that someone like Jesus would care enough to listen.

But her favorite thing under the desk was the picture of her daddy. It wasn't very big and the black frame was cracked in two places. Savannah found it one morning in a box of things under her mother's bed. "Who's this?" She had held the picture up close to her mama's face.

Her mother smelled like beer, and her eyes didn't open very wide. "That?" She laughed, but the sound wasn't very funny. "That's your daddy. He's a real Prince Charming."

Later that day when her mama caught her looking at the photo, she grabbed it and threw it in the trash. But that night when Mama was drinking again, Savannah snuck outside and saved it. Mama didn't know she still

had it, but she did. And it was her most favorite thing because someday she was going to find him and that would
make everyone happy. Mama told her all the time that
life would have been better if she didn't have Savannah.

"I'm not a very good mother," she would say.

Some nights—though Savannah wouldn't have told
anyone but Jesus—she had to agree with Mama. Because some nights Mama grabbed her and shoved her
under the desk earlier than her usual bedtime, and sometimes there was no dinner because there was no money
from the people in Central Park. But the daddy in the picture gave her a reason to believe that Grandpa was right.
Jesus had good plans for her.

After all, her daddy was a real Prince Charming, if
only she could find him.

And what could possibly be better than that?

FIVE

Lindsay Warren Farrell was sorting through old magazines in a corner of her kitchen when the phone rang.
The kids were at school and Larry was at work, so she
didn't expect the call to be from one of them. She looked
at the caller ID and smiled. Josh. She hadn't talked to him
in a week, and she needed to catch up.

"Hello?"

In the background of wherever Josh was calling from,
a familiar song was playing so loud Lindsay could hear
it clearly. "Josh?" She could hear the words now, and she
sat on the nearest kitchen bar stool. What was going on?
Before she could ask whether it was really him or not, he
spoke up.

"Do you hear that?"

"Yes." She managed a confused laugh. "It's loud."

"I know it is." Josh sounded happier than he had in
years. "You won't believe what happened, Linds. Six
weeks ago I found the greatest song. Wynonna Judd was
performing something live on country videos, and—"

"Wynonna Judd?"

"Yes! She was singing this same song, 'I Can Only Imagine.' So, I thought it was her song and I've been looking for it when I stop by the market—you know, in the CD section at the back. But then I had this idea to look online and sure enough . . ."

"You found it by MercyMe?" Her smile spread down into her heart and soul.

"Just now!" He sounded amazed, almost breathless. "Today I can honestly say my back pain isn't the first thing on my mind. You know why?"

"You're too busy singing?"

"Sort of. I mean, I've been playing it all day." He rested for a few seconds, and when he started up again his pace was more controlled. "When I watched the video, I made a decision. Right then and there I gave my life back to Jesus and told Him I was sorry for every wrong decision I'd made without Him. I've been praying since then and, well, you know, just sort of thinking about how different my life should be at this point."

Lindsay could already feel the tears in her eyes. Sometimes Larry would see Josh's name on the caller ID and walk away from it. "He's always asking for money or needing some sort of handout," Larry told her once. "He's *your* brother, you deal with him."

But now Josh was proving why people could never, ever give up on someone they love. She'd prayed for Josh all her life—especially in the decade since he graduated from high school. Neither Josh's choices nor the circumstances that came with them had ever brought him closer to God, but now maybe he was finally ready to stop running his life on his own. "Josh . . . I'm so happy."

"Me, too. It's like I finally get it about God, about Jesus

going to the cross and how He opened the gates of heaven for people like you and me. If we let Him, He'll give us life here and forever. So now this is my song, you know? 'I Can Only Imagine.' "

Lindsay's heart was so full she couldn't speak.

"Anyway, I called for a reason. Can I go with you and Larry and the kids to church this coming Saturday? Don't you go in the evening?"

"Six o'clock." Lindsay felt like one of the townspeople watching Ebenezer Scrooge run around handing out gifts on Christmas morning. "You're serious, right? You wanna go with us?"

"Definitely." He laughed and it was the laugh of a big kid, not a troubled young man in chronic pain. "Truthfully? I've been attending a Christian church with a few of my neighbors for the past five Sundays. I love it. Makes me not think about the pain so much, you know?"

"Yes." She felt hot tears on her cheeks and she dabbed at them. A picture came to mind: herself, Larry, Ben, Bella, and Josh sharing a pew near the front of their church on Saturday evening. "I'll save you a spot."

"Come on, Lindsay." He sounded like his old self, the way he was before the accident. "I know you better than that." Another laugh. "My sister, Lindsay, on time? I'll save *you* one."

The song was still blaring in the background, and Lindsay struggled to find her voice. "You know what this is, right?" She couldn't wait to tell her mom about this phone call. Her parents went to the more traditional Sunday morning service, but this was one Saturday evening they needed to attend.

"It's a miracle." Josh didn't hesitate. "I could feel God doing something in my heart, changing me. But finding this song today—it's like the whole world looks different."

A sound came from Lindsay, but she wasn't sure if it was a laugh or a cry. She put her fingers to her lips. "I've prayed for this moment for so long." She walked toward the kitchen window and stared out at Pikes Peak in the distance. "With all your pain and the accident and the struggles you've had, I knew only God could bring you relief. And now—now look at you."

"You're right. A week of days like this one and maybe my back will heal itself." He sounded beyond upbeat, like he actually believed such a thing was possible. "If not, then I'll wait for the surgery, but at least I won't be walking under a dark cloud. Not anymore. I remembered this afternoon what Mom and Dad always told us: God has great plans for His people." He laughed one more time. "Isn't that great, Lindsay, because guess what? I finally believe it."

Lindsay told him again how happy she was for him and how she'd prayed for him and how different he sounded now that his faith was back in place. "The kids have a lot going on the rest of this week—piano, dance, football practice. Then there's parents night at the elementary school. Bella won't let me miss it. But Friday's open." Lindsay walked to the family computer and pulled up her iCalendar. "Come for dinner?"

"I'm in court that day." He didn't sound weary or defeated the way he usually did when he talked about the hearings and depositions associated with his car accident. "Dinner would be perfect."

"Then on Saturday you can come to Ben's football game. Mom and Dad will be there and we can go to church after."

"You might even be on time."

"Yeah." She laughed at that. "Now that would be a miracle." She was about to hang up when a thought hit her. "Hey, I'm running out to do a few errands. I have to take a dish by Mom's house. Care if I come by? I'm not sure I can wait until Friday to hug you."

"I'll be here."

Lindsay ran a brush through her hair and checked herself in the mirror. She and Larry worked out nearly every morning, sometimes running the hills around their home. Her hours at the *Gazette* were manageable, eight to four with Sundays and Tuesdays off. If she needed more time at home, the editors were flexible, as long as her stories were in by Saturday at five. Life was good and healthy and it ran like clockwork.

Only Josh kept Lindsay awake at night, wondering how she could help her brother, and whether he would ever turn back to the faith they'd shared as kids. And now . . . She grabbed the baking dish from the kitchen, a bag of clothes for the cleaners, and a few packages for the mail and hurried to her Tahoe parked in the garage. Now Josh was finally having the turnaround they'd all wanted for him.

She stopped at his place first. She couldn't wait to see him. His eyes would tell her how deeply he was affected by this revelation that God was on his side, that He still had plans for Josh even if they'd been derailed for a season. Her brother's eyes.

The apartment complex where he lived wasn't the finest, and the few times Lindsay had been here she'd always looked over her shoulder to make sure no one was lurking in the shadows. She'd talked to one of the news reporters at the *Gazette* once about whether the Garden Terrace Apartments were involved in higher crime than usual, and she was surprised when his check came back negative. "It's in a questionable area," the guy told her. "But that complex houses some physically disadvantaged adults. Most of them have been there for years, and that kind of stability usually makes a place safer."

Lindsay walked quickly, anyway. Fresh graffiti was spray-painted on the garbage Dumpster at the center of the parking lot, and one apartment had a broken window. But whatever she thought of the complex, she would need to spend more time here. Usually Josh discouraged her from coming, complaining that he was too tired or not ready for company. He seemed to prefer their visits take place at their parents' house. But maybe that would be different now, too.

She knocked on the door and he opened it more quickly than usual. Was it her imagination or was he standing taller, straighter? "Josh . . ."

The song was still running from his stereo system, but it wasn't as loud as earlier. His eyes met hers and he held out both arms. "Everything's going to be okay, Linds." His voice was soft, full of the emotion he rarely showed. "It really is."

Her brother had been taller than her since her second year in high school, and at six foot four he had nine inches on her, easily. He'd lost a lot of weight, but he still hadn't found the svelte athletic build he'd had as a teenager. Lindsay didn't mind. She put her arms around him and pressed her head to his chest. He was a mountain of a man, and his extra padding made her feel small and safe in his arms.

When she pulled away, she let her eyes linger on his and she saw it, the sparkle that hadn't been there for three years. "You're really back, aren't you?"

He nodded. "Like I just woke up from a nightmare." He stepped aside and motioned for her to follow him into the apartment.

She had a little time. The two of them moved into his living room. She set her purse down on his cleaned and polished coffee table and as they sat on the couch facing his fireplace, he grinned. "See, Linds. Not a single dish or piece of mail." He gestured to the clean room. "Proud of me?"

"I'm trying not to pass out." She giggled. Her brother had always kept a messy room, even when they were kids. *"Life takes too much time,"* he used to say. But since his accident, the rest of the family worried that his dirty apartment was a symptom of his pain and possible depression. She surveyed the room, the way the furniture was in order, the clean windowsills, and she patted his knee. "I might have to hire you for mine."

They fell into an easy conversation and Lindsay turned the topic back to his renewed faith. "So you actually feel better today? I mean, your back doesn't hurt as much?"

Josh shifted, probably trying to find a comfortable position. "Before, I let the pain control everything I did, my entire day. Sometimes my back hurt so bad I could almost picture the pain like a living, breathing being, like the devil had me surrounded and there was no way out. You know?"

Lindsay reached for his hand. Her heart hurt to hear her brother talk about his situation that way. So what if he hadn't wanted company. If he'd been that down and discouraged, if the pain had felt that overwhelming . . . "You should've said something. I could've come by after work more often and at least brought you dinner."

"No." Josh's forehead was damp, proof that he was still hurting even now as he talked with her. But the peace in his eyes went deeper than whatever he was feeling. "Don't worry about it, Linds. I was fine." He looked at the photos lined across his fireplace mantel. "I had to reach this place by myself. Just me and God."

She stood and moved closer to the three photographs. The one of the little girl caught her attention first and she took hold of it. "Were these here last time I came by?"

"Probably." He sounded sheepish. "It's not like I usually ask you to sit with me in the living room. Anytime you've been here I'm usually in a hurry to get you out."

"Why?" She still had the picture in her hand, but she looked back at him, hurt by his admission.

"Because." His expression begged her to understand. "I didn't want you to see me like this. My back . . . it can be a challenge getting around. When I'm here alone I don't have to act like everything's okay. I can lie down on the floor or stay in bed if that's what makes me feel better." He smiled. "But, I don't know. Today's been so weird. The pain's still there, but it's distant now. Like someone shouting at me from across a football field."

Her heart broke for him, her brother who had always been so happy and easygoing. To think he hadn't wanted her to stop by because he was embarrassed by his pain.

The reality was awful. Lindsay sighed and turned her attention back to the photograph. She'd seen the picture just once before. "How old was she here? Four or five?"

"Four." Josh stood and walked to the spot beside Lindsay. "I keep thinking that a year from now I could have partial custody of her. I bet she's just perfect, you know?"

Lindsay smiled at him. "I can't wait to meet her." Never mind that their parents didn't think the girl was really Josh's daughter or that years had passed without any word from the girl's mother. The child honestly did bear a resemblance to Josh, so the possibility of her being Josh's daughter was a very real one as far as Lindsay was concerned. Besides, why argue the idea? Josh believed she was his daughter, and Lindsay believed in Josh.

She set the photograph down and looked at the one beside it. The picture showed two teenage girls dressed in jeans and sweaters, standing in front of the snow-covered front yard of a two-story home. "Who are they?"

"It's a long story." Josh's answer was quick. "They're best friends. I met them on a job."

Lindsay looked at the girls again and she knew without asking that her brother wasn't interested in either of them. They were ten years younger than him, at least. Whatever the story behind them, it must've mattered greatly to Josh for him to keep their photo where he could see it every day. "Did you take the picture?"

"No." Josh turned away and walked to the kitchen. "I'm not sure who took it." He pressed his hand to his lower back, but he didn't slow his pace. "It's no big deal, really. I just keep it there to remind me of the good that can come from towing cars." He reached for the cupboard near his sink. "Want some water?"

"Sure. Thanks." She was still thinking about the teen-age girls. If Josh needed a reason to believe in his job, then whatever he had come up with, Lindsay was happy for him. Especially since his work had cost him his health, and, in the last three years, his employment.

Lindsay took a glass of water from him. "Tell me about these neighbors of yours, the ones you're going to church with."

"They're a great group. Carl Joseph and his girlfriend, Daisy, live in separate apartments in my building, and then there's Carl Joseph's brother, Cody, and his wife, Elle, who is Daisy's sister. The four of them go every week together, and ever since I told Carl Joseph about that Wynonna video and how I felt God calling me back to Him, they've included me in their group." Josh's eyes were full of light. "I really have a very rich life, Lindsay. The settlement has nothing to do with that."

She made a point to remember how he looked in that moment, sunshine streaming in through his small kitchen window, standing there in his tiny apartment, his back no doubt killing him, and believing with all his heart that no amount of money could make him any richer. Happy tears made her eyes damp. "I can't wait for Friday dinner. And Saturday, too." She hugged him one more time and held on longer than usual. When she eased back, she looked straight into his heart, the part that would always belong to her. "I think maybe you're just starting to live again."

"I am." He breathed in deep and stood straight again. "I can hardly wait to see what God has for me next."

"Me, too. I mean—I have my brother back." She took her purse from the coffee table and slipped it up onto her shoulder. Then she kissed her brother's cheek and headed for the front door. "Friday night."

"I'll be there." They were at the door and Josh leaned into the frame. "Oh, and that six hundred dollars you loaned me?" He pulled a check from his pocket and handed it to her. "You can cash it on Wednesday."

Lindsay hadn't thought about the loan since she gave him the money a few months ago when his doctor bills were too high for him to pay the rent. "Josh, you don't have to do that." She tried to hand the check back to him, but he wouldn't take it. "Consider it a gift."

"I can't." His tone was still light, but Lindsay knew he was serious about the money. "I told you I'd pay you back and I meant it. I have my bills figured out for next month." He smiled. "Thanks for being there. I didn't want to get behind, and because of you and Larry, I didn't."

"Well . . . you could've waited for your settlement."

"I owe Mom and Dad almost a year's wages." He gave her a funny look, the way he used to on a Saturday when they had just one afternoon to clean the entire garage. "That will definitely have to wait for the settlement." He touched her shoulder. "Yours I can repay now, so let me, okay?"

"Okay." She held his eyes a few seconds longer before she folded the check and put it in the pocket of her jeans. "I love you, Josh. I'm so happy you found your way back."

"Love you, too." His eyes danced. "Tell Ben to look for me in the stands."

With that Lindsay ran lightly to her car and as she pulled

out of the complex she saw Josh standing on his porch watching her, his smile visible from across the parking lot. She waved one last time and then made a quick decision. She would do her other errands first, then go by her mother's house last. That way she wouldn't feel rushed. Today the two of them needed to talk about more than the schedule for the coming week, or who Ben's team was playing in Saturday's game.

She walked through her parents' front door an hour later and found her mother on the phone out back in the garden. Lindsay was practically bursting with the news about Josh, but her mom motioned to her to wait a minute. She had a pile of pulled weeds at her feet and a small box of gardening tools nearby. Lindsay leaned against the back wall of the house and looked beyond her mother to the acreage that made up the backyard. She and Josh used to play games out here every afternoon, and in summer their parents would set up an aboveground pool for them and their friends. So many happy memories.

"Like Nate always says, the election isn't a sure thing, so we have to be careful. We had the librarians here on Friday and this week it's another group of representatives from the teachers union. I think we're serving cheesecake again." She made a face in Lindsay's direction and drew small circles in the air with her free hand, as if to say she was trying to wrap up the call. "Right, well, maybe you should be here. You're a friend of ours and a friend of theirs. That's always good for Nate."

Lindsay worried about her mom. Before her dad ran for the Board of Education, her parents were involved with a Bible study at church and bringing meals to the homebound. Now it seemed like nearly every hour of the day was dedicated to helping her father get reelected. Maybe the talk about Josh would help get her mind off the dinner parties and political posturing that took up so much of their time.

Another two minutes and finally her mother's call ended. She exhaled hard and made a mock show of exhaustion. "That woman is more connected than anyone in the Springs, but boy, can she talk." Her mom looked at her watch. "The garden will have to wait. We have a dinner tonight with her and three other people." She dusted her hands on her navy cotton pants and smiled at Lindsay. "You brought back the baking dish?"

"I did, but I was sort of hoping you might have a few minutes."

"Oh, honey, I'm sorry. I need to get ready." Her mother breezed past her. "Come into the kitchen for a minute. I have to wash up."

Lindsay had no choice but to follow her. "I stopped by Josh's apartment earlier. He was playing this song—"

Her mother flipped on the water, tapped a few squirts of soap into her hands, and began rubbing them together. She raised her eyebrows in Lindsay's direction as if to say she was still listening. But over the sound of the water, Lindsay knew her mother couldn't catch every word, so she waited.

After a minute, she turned off the water and reached for a paper towel. "So he was playing Christian music, is that what you're saying?" She dried her hands and tossed the damp paper into the trash compactor. The sound of the container opening and shutting added to the noise, and Lindsay waited.

Her mother seemed to understand that this conversation needed more of her attention, so she stopped short, her eyes on Lindsay. "Sorry, honey, go ahead."

"Anyway, yes. He was listening to 'I Can Only Imagine.' You know that song, right?"

"Hmmm." Her mother shook her head. "Doesn't sound familiar."

"It's a song about heaven, and when he called me this morning he was playing it so loud I could barely hear him over the phone, and he said it was like he finally—"

"He has to be careful of the neighbors. It's not like he has many friends, Lindsay." She looked at her watch again, and then folded her arms. "Loud music isn't going to endear him to anyone."

Lindsay stared at her mom. Why was she doing this, making it so hard for her to share the good news about Josh? *Be patient,* she told herself. *God, please give me patience. Mom doesn't know what's coming.*

"Anyway, the point wasn't the neighbors. It's that Josh seems changed by the song, by the message in it. He was talking about God today, and how he's going back to church, and . . . even his pain didn't seem as bad as usual."

Her mother took one of the oranges from the fruit bowl, grabbed another paper towel, spread it on the counter, and dug her fingernail into the fruit's skin. "You don't mind if I eat, do you? I completely forgot lunch, and breakfast was something small left over from yesterday."

Lindsay wanted to scream at her. This was outrageous. "Did you hear what I said? About how he wants to go to church with us and how his pain seems more manageable?"

"I hate that pain medication he's on." She took a section of the orange, ripped it in half, and put one small piece into her mouth. With her free hand she dabbed at the corners of her lips and focused on her next bite. "That OxyContin can kill a person." She chewed and swallowed another piece. "I was on the Internet looking it up the other day and it actually said if you chew the tablets instead of swallowing them, the release of the drug could be strong enough to kill you." She waved another section of orange in the air. "The doctor has him on way too high a dose, and sure he might not feel any pain today, but what about when he's addicted to the stuff? Then we'll all wish he would've lived with a little more pain and not said yes every time the doctor increased his dose."

When Lindsay's frustration left her without a response, her mother continued. "And yes, dear, he talks about church and God once in a while. I'll believe something's changed when I see it. Otherwise it's just a lot of talk, and you know Josh. Always dreaming about his plans for this or that—even before the accident." She ate a few more sections of the orange, and then slipped what remained into a ziplock bag.

"Mom, are you even hearing me?" Lindsay wanted to cry. This was a big day for Josh, and their mother wasn't connecting with anything she was saying.

"Of course I'm hearing you, dear." She put the orange in the refrigerator. "It's just that if we're honest with ourselves we've heard these stories from Josh over and over again." Her look was bathed in discouragement. "I really worry about your brother. Ever since high school he's struggled to put his plans into action." She closed the distance between them and kissed Lindsay on the forehead. "Thanks for being such a good sister to him. It's important that all of us keep encouraging him. That's especially true for you." She began walking toward the stairs and her bedroom. "I have to get ready, but we'll talk more about it later, okay?"

If Lindsay hadn't been so mad at her mother, she would have yelled at her. She would have told her no, it wasn't okay, and that no dinner party was more important than the changes she'd seen in Josh that day. But if her mom didn't care to listen, then so be it. She wouldn't ruin the good feelings in her heart by fighting with her mother.

By the time Lindsay was back in her car, her anger had faded and in its place was the pity she felt more often for her mother. Pity because her mother's focus wasn't on her faith the way it once had been, and because she wasn't only worried about Josh, she was embarrassed by him. Their mom was frustrated that Josh hadn't become an educator like his father or a writer like Lindsay. As she turned onto the main road toward home, she thought again about her brother and his renewed excitement for God and life and his determination to find his way despite the pain.

If she was honest with herself, honest about the ugliest places in her heart, there had been times when she, too, had been embarrassed by Josh's career decisions. He'd been capable of so much more than driving a tow truck. But at least her embarrassment hadn't lasted long. If towing cars was what her brother loved to do, then she would be glad for him—no matter what else he might have done with his life.

She still didn't know the story behind the photograph of the two teenage girls, but the next time they were together she would press him about it. Clearly, he kept the picture on the mantel for a reason—one that brought tears to her eyes as she pulled into her garage.

When no one in his family was proud of his work at the garage, when he couldn't find affirmation anywhere else, the photo probably gave him something that meant the world to her brother.

A reason to believe in himself.

SIX

Josh was about to pass out from the pain. He was on the witness stand, answering questions in a calm, deliberate tone, but on the inside his body was screaming for relief. *Where are You, God? I need You here. . . . Please. . . .*

The attorney for the insurance company was taking a minute with his associates, regrouping for the next round of biting questions. Josh closed his eyes for a few seconds and tried to adjust his position, tried to find even the slightest relief from the pain. The joy and hope and faith that had marked his world three days ago was still there, but it was harder to feel. That's all. *Please, God. Are You there?*

My child, I am with you always . . . even until the end. . . .

The answer wasn't loud, but it resonated in his soul and brought with it a peace that reminded him of the truth. This deposition wasn't the end of the story—no matter what it netted. His life was changed now, and no amount of pain could undo that. He heard the attorney clear his voice as he stepped back up to the microphone.

Josh opened his eyes and tried to look relaxed and professional. Thomas Flynn, his attorney, had told him a number of times how important this day in court would be to his final settlement. The judge could still decide on an amount anywhere between a hundred thousand dollars and a million dollars.

The lead attorney for the insurance company was William R. Worthington, of Worthington and Associates in Denver. He was in his early fifties with a head of gray-flecked hair. Everything from his dark designer suit to the way he carried himself told those in the courtroom he was a force to be reckoned with. The insurance company was hoping Worthington would save them hundreds of thousands of dollars when the battle was over.

Worthington held a half-inch-thick document, and he flipped slowly through the first three pages. His actions gave the impression that he was carefully sorting through something important—a pile of damaging evidence, perhaps—and that he was putting great thought into his next question.

Josh knew differently.

"Everything an attorney does is part of the act," Flynn told him. "The confidence, the appearance that they've already won the case, the pauses—all of it."

Now the attorney leaned close to the microphone. "Mr. Warren, you've had trouble with your weight, is that true?"

"Objection." Flynn was on his feet. "Question is vague, Your Honor."

"Sustained." The judge was a wiry man who seemed bored with the proceedings. "Counsel will rephrase the question."

"Very well." Worthington nodded his head slightly. "Mr. Warren, you're overweight. Is that true?"

"Actually, over the past couple years, I—"

"Yes or no answers, Mr. Warren. Are you overweight?"

Josh pictured the doctor telling him he only needed to lose another forty pounds. "Yes." He pulled a tissue from a box at the corner of the witness stand and dabbed it on his forehead. "Yes, I am."

Worthington flipped through another few pages. "More than one medical doctor has told you that your weight is a health risk, is that true?"

More than one doctor? Josh's mind raced through the possibilities, and then he remembered. The emergency room doctor who treated him in the hours after the accident told him he needed to deal with his weight. "However bad your injuries are, they'll be worse if you don't take care of your weight." Josh winced as a wall of pain slammed into his lower back. "Yes. Two doctors. That's true."

"Mr. Warren, do you need a break?" The judge's voice held more compassion than Josh had heard from him since the deposition began. "We can take a ten-minute break."

"No, thanks. My back hurts either way, and I'd like to get home. I have dinner plans with my sister tonight."

"Very well." The judge motioned to the attorney. "Carry on."

"Thank you, Your Honor." He looked at Josh. "I'm going to read a statement written by your current doctor, and you tell me if it's something you're familiar with. Do you understand?"

"Yes, sir." Josh hated how they talked to him, like he was a third-grader caught cheating on a math test. Did the guy really think Josh was making up the pain? That if he wanted to, he could drive down to the garage and start towing cars again tomorrow? He gripped the edge of the wooden desk in front of him and waited.

"Here's the statement: 'It is my opinion that my client, Josh Warren, age twenty-eight, could experience dramatic improvement in the condition of his back injury if he would lose weight.'" Worthington paused for effect. "'It is nearly impossible to determine how much of his current pain and disability is caused by his excess weight, and how much is caused from being hit by the car.'"

Josh remained calm. Flynn had warned him the insurance company attorneys might take this angle, accusing him of destroying his own health and thereby calling into question whether the accident had really been that damaging. "Don't worry about it," Flynn had said to him that morning. "Even if you'd walked away without an injury, if the only reason you couldn't go back to work was an emotional one—like you're too afraid to drive a tow truck now—a settlement would still be in the works. The insurance company's client was drunk out of his mind. He drove off the road and hit you, nearly killing you. Your weight isn't going to factor into the judge's decision whatsoever."

Josh blinked. "Yes, I'm familiar with that statement." Why didn't the guy ask him about the weight he'd already lost? He was down sixty pounds from the time of the accident. He was exhausted and ready for his next pain pill. *God . . . please get me through this.*

"And is it true that you've been told by your doctor that surgery on your back isn't advisable until you lose another forty pounds?"

"Yes. I've been told that."

Worthington ran his thumb across a section of text at

the middle of the page. "What was your weight when you graduated from high school, Mr. Warren?"

"One ninety."

"One hundred and ninety pounds, is that right?" He cast a knowing look at the judge.

"Yes, that's right."

"And your weight at the time of the accident?"

"Two ninety-five." Josh could hardly believe himself as he said the number. How had he let that much weight pile up over the years? More than a hundred pounds? No question the doctor was concerned about his weight. The fact that he'd already lost sixty made him determined to stay the course and get back under two hundred again.

Worthington raised his brow. "Two hundred and ninety-five pounds? That was your weight at the time of the accident?"

"Yes, sir." Josh felt the demons behind him again, poking a hundred pointy knives into his spine. *I need You, God. Make them go away.*

My strength is sufficient for you, My son. Trust in Me. . . .

I'm trying, God. . . . I'm really trying.

Worthington turned the page and hesitated. "I have here"—he held the document up for the judge's sake—"a study done last year determining that people with morbid obesity—more than a hundred pounds over their ideal weight—are more prone to injuries on the job. I'd like to admit this document into evidence, Your Honor."

"Objection." Flynn was on his feet, his eyes blazing with indignation. "Unless that study involves my client personally, it's only hearsay and has nothing to do with my client's specific situation."

"Sustained. Relevance." He peered down at Worthington. "You should be familiar with the rules of evidence in a case like this."

"Yes, Your Honor." The attorney didn't look too upset. He probably expected the admonition, but either way, the information was out there. Heavy people were more prone to injuries.

Josh looked at his attorney, and he could almost read Flynn's eyes. The report about overweight people wasn't something he needed to worry about. Again, he didn't fall off a ladder or slip at the coffee counter. His weight had nothing to do with the fact that he'd been hit by the drunk driver. He took a few short breaths through his nose, expecting the pain to prevent him from inhaling fully. But the pain seemed slightly less intense than a few minutes ago. *Thank You, God. . . . You're holding me up. I can't do this without You.*

I am with you. . . .

"You have no children, is that right? No dependents at all?"

Josh paused, but only briefly. "I have a daughter."

His answer seemed to catch Worthington off guard. Like Flynn had said, the insurance company preferred Josh to be single with no children. But Worthington covered his surprise well, barely hesitating to regroup.

He leveled his stare at Josh. "Were you considering a medical disability before the accident, Mr. Warren?"

The question seemed to come out of nowhere. "I'm not sure what . . ." He glanced at Thomas Flynn. "Could you restate the question?"

"At the time of the accident, were you planning to take

medical disability?" His words were fast, rapid-fire, and aimed straight at his motives for filing suit.

"No, sir. I had no such plans."

"But your weight was making it difficult to keep working, right?"

"No, sir." He kept his voice in check, but his anger was rising. Flynn had warned him about this, too, and at previous depositions the insurance company's attorney had tried similar lines of questioning. Planting doubts, that's all the guy was doing. Josh steadied himself, forced himself to keep his answers free of emotion. "I had no plans for a medical disability."

"And because of your weight, you were struggling to keep up your production with the other tow truck drivers at the garage, isn't that right, Mr. Warren?"

"No, sir." He adjusted his feet, but the move brought no relief to his back. He was pretty sure if someone walked behind him they would see flames where his spine was supposed to be.

"And after the accident you were almost glad to have a reason to go out on medical disability, isn't that right?"

Josh hesitated, his eyes locked onto the attorney's. Before he could answer, Flynn was on his feet again. "Objection. Counsel is harassing the witness, Your Honor."

"Sustained." Again the judge gave Worthington a look that told him he was in danger of crossing a line. "Change your line of questioning, Counsel."

"Yes, Your Honor. I apologize."

"Carry on."

Worthington kept the questions coming for another ninety minutes. He asked Josh about his days at home and whether he was able to sit for an hour at a time, and if so was he aware that a majority of desk jobs didn't require more than an hour of sitting at a time, and had Josh considered looking for a job, or was he content to sit back and let an insurance company take care of his needs. Thomas Flynn objected a handful of times, but at the end of the questioning the damage was done. If Josh had been a prize-fighter, at the final bell he would've been bloodied and battered on the ground in the middle of the ring—victim of a knockout by decision.

One thing was sure. Whatever settlement this case netted, Josh would have earned every dollar several times over.

Flynn called a brief recess and he talked to Josh in the hallway. "You look tired."

"I am." Josh's body was screaming for another pain pill, something that would give him relief from the fire in his back. But the pills could make him loopy, and he needed to stay sharp just a little longer. "My sister's counting on me for dinner."

Flynn was a family man, an attorney dedicated to seeing justice done. He liked to gamble, but he also believed in miracles. Both made him the perfect attorney as far as Josh was concerned. Flynn looked at Josh with compassion. "I'm sorry about your pain." He put his hand on Josh's shoulder. "But I need a few minutes in cross. Something to bring a little balance back."

"I thought you said the judge wouldn't consider that stuff—my weight and whether I wanted a disability or not. Which I didn't, by the way."

"I know, and I told you the truth. None of that should

matter." He folded his arms and released a frustrated sigh. "But at the end of the day, the judge is as human as the next guy. Deciding these cases isn't based on an exact formula."

"Okay." Josh could no longer draw a full breath. He would exist on short gasps and forced exhalations, the way he had learned to do when the pain was this bad. "I can last another few minutes." He still had the hourlong drive back to the Springs, and it was almost five o'clock.

The break ended and Josh took the stand again. Flynn was deeply competitive when it came to law. Josh knew that from the private conversations they held in his attorney's office. Flynn had taught him every way to win the case from the witness stand, training him with more care and detail than any of Josh's baseball coaches ever had. Now he donned a look of kindness and empathy. "You doing okay, Mr. Warren?"

Josh almost smiled. The tone of the question, the wording, was intended to make one very clear point: that Worthington had all but whipped and beaten Josh in the earlier session. "Yes, sir. I'm okay."

"Is your back hurting?"

"Yes, sir."

"On a scale of one to ten, on the pain scale used by doctors, where's your back pain right now, Mr. Warren?"

Josh didn't hesitate. "A nine, sir." A ten happened when he could barely breathe at all. He was close, but for now he was still at a nine. Flynn let that detail sink in for a few seconds.

"Okay"—he looked at his notes—"you said your weight

was two hundred and ninety-five pounds at the time of the accident. Is that right?"

"Yes, sir." Josh didn't worry about where Flynn was headed. His track record left no room for doubt, no matter what the line of questioning.

"Can you tell this court how many days of work you missed in the month leading up to your accident?"

They'd been over this a number of times, analyzing the actual employment records from the garage. "None, sir."

"Very well." He glanced down at the notepad in his hand. "How many days of work did you miss in the six months leading up to your accident?"

"None, sir."

Flynn looked impressed. "Okay, Mr. Warren, how many days of work did you miss in the year leading up to your accident?"

"Not one, sir."

"You were hired by the North County Police Garage four years and three months before your car accident, is that right?"

Flynn knew it was. Josh had worked at a smaller garage for a few months leading up to that move. Working for a police garage meant he had the chance to go out on police calls and tow cars from crime scenes and accident locations. The work was much harder than what he'd done before—towing stalled cars and parking violators from private strip-mall spaces—but it was more pay and more prestige. It hit him again, how much he'd lost because of the accident. "Yes, sir. I worked for North County for more than four years."

"And during that entire time were you morbidly obese—at least a hundred pounds overweight?"

The question no longer shamed him. He could do nothing to change the past. "Yes, sir, I was."

"And how many days did you miss work the entire time you were employed by North County Police Garage?"

"No days, sir."

"No days!" This time Flynn stepped just far enough out of his quiet, compassionate role that he could have won an Oscar for his show of surprise. Anyone in the courtroom would've guessed that this was new and shocking information to the veteran attorney. "Very well." He looked down at his notes.

Josh was ready to go. He felt his feet tense up from his effort to try to remain upright. *Help me survive this, God. . . . I need You.* He shifted again and this time he found a small pocket of reserve stamina. Enough to survive. *Thank You, Lord. This is temporary, I can feel it. I'll get through this deposition, and the next, and one day soon I'll have that surgery. You'll see me through it, I know You will.*

I am with you always, My precious son.

Josh felt a peace push back the demon of pain.

"Now, about your weight." Flynn lowered his notes. "You were two hundred and ninety-five pounds at the time of the accident, though you missed no days because of health issues in the more than four years you worked for the North County Police Garage. Is that correct?"

"Objection." Worthington stood sedately, adjusting his cufflinks. "We've been over this, Your Honor."

"Sustained." The judge gestured for Flynn to move forward. "Counsel is correct. You've established the information about the plaintiff's work history."

"Yes, Your Honor. Thank you." Flynn looked contrite. He paused to gather his thoughts. "What is your weight now, Mr. Warren?"

"Around two-forty."

"Two hundred and forty pounds?"

"Yes, sir."

"So you've lost a great deal of weight since your injury, is that right?"

"Yes, sir, nearly sixty pounds."

"Are you on a diet to lose weight?"

"Yes, I am."

"Would you please tell this court why you're on a diet to lose weight?"

"Because"—Josh pressed his hand into his lower back—"I need surgery on my back and the doctor thinks it'll be more successful if I'm at a normal weight."

Flynn hesitated. He lowered his notes and shot a piercing look at Josh. "Did you enjoy your job as a tow truck driver, Mr. Warren?"

"Yes, I did."

"Tell us in your words what being a tow truck driver meant to you."

Josh hadn't been expecting this question, and he was surprised at the emotion that welled up in his throat. "I think—I think my family wanted me to be a teacher or a writer, maybe a doctor. They wanted me to go to college after high school. But I've always liked the idea of driving a truck." He shrugged, and the movement sent a different pain down the length of his back. "As a tow truck driver I could help people. They might've been in an accident or the victim of a crime, and, I don't know, I liked being there for them." He worked to keep his composure. "I loved being a tow truck driver, sir."

"But you'll never be able to drive a tow truck again, is that right?"

The detail wasn't something he liked to think about. "Yes, sir. My back—even after surgery—will be too unsteady for that sort of work."

Flynn nodded, his eyes deep with compassion. "I have one last question for you, Mr. Warren, and remember you are under oath." He looked at his notes again, letting the drama build. "You stand to win a large sum of money in this case. Right now, if you had to decide between going back to the day before your accident and being a tow truck driver for life or winning two million dollars in this lawsuit, which would you pick, Mr. Warren?"

Josh's throat felt scratchy and his eyes stung. "I would go back . . . to the day before the accident. I would have my health and my job, which is all I ever wanted, anyway."

Flynn nodded slowly. Then he turned a grief-stricken face to the judge. "No more questions, Your Honor."

The deposition was finally over. Josh didn't know a lot about the field of law, but he had a feeling that if this were a football game, Thomas Flynn had just scored the game-winning touchdown. Out in the hallway he shook his attorney's hand. "You're good."

"You're better. Sitting up there and taking that garbage from the other side."

He needed to understand one thing before he could leave. "Two million? I thought we were asking for one."

"I filed an amendment. With all they've put you through, and with the new information from the doctor about the impossibility of you returning to your preferred line of work, I changed the amount." They started walking down the hall. "And you know what?" He stopped and gave Josh a sad smile. "I think we'll get it."

Josh was in the car five minutes later, sorting through the center console of his old Mustang for a bottle of Oxy-Contin. It was six o'clock and he wasn't due for another pill until he turned in for bed. But if he wanted to breathe on the drive home from Denver, he would have to take the medication sooner than later.

He found what he was looking for and dug around the floor of his car through a stack of legal documents and an old McDonald's bag until he found a warm bottle of water. He opened it and downed the pill before he could give the move a second thought. One day he'd have to figure out a way off the pain meds, maybe with some of that two million dollars Flynn was going to get him. He held his breath and prayed the OxyContin would work quickly. He had a court case to win, a surgery to schedule, an old girlfriend to find, and his God to fully reconnect with. Most of all he had a little girl out there who needed her daddy.

For now, an addiction to OxyContin was hardly on his list of concerns.

SEVEN

Lindsay was putting the final touches on a spaghetti dinner, watching Larry toss a ball with Ben and Bella out back and listening for the doorbell when the phone rang. She checked the caller ID. "Josh," she groaned. "You're late." She answered the phone with one hand and with the other she stirred the spoon through a pan full of noodles. "Hey, Josh—where are you?"

"I can't make it, Linds. Sorry. Maybe nex' time."

"Josh?" Lindsay's heart skipped a beat. She turned off the stove and walked to the back door, her eyes on her family. "What's wrong? You sound funny."

In painstakingly slow and slurred speech he told her that he'd been on the freeway for only ten minutes and that he'd taken a pain pill. "I had to, Linds. It's so bad today. But . . . I feel sorta funny. I can breathe better but I'm a lil' dizzy."

"Josh, that's terrible. Get off the freeway and get to a doctor."

"Linds." Josh's laugh sounded easy and untroubled. "I'm fine. I would pull over if I thought I couldn't drive."

"How would you know? You don't sound right."

"I'm tired, tha's all. I'm fine. The deposition went longer than 'spected. I'll be fine with a lil' sleep."

"I'm staying on the phone with you." The way he was slurring his words terrified her. "Keep talking to me or I'll call nine-one-one." She didn't want to be angry with him, but if he was having trouble talking then he couldn't possibly be driving well.

"Don't worry about me, Linds. I've felt this way before. I've been driving under the influence of pain medication for almost three years."

He had a point. "Okay." She still felt worried. "Don't worry about dinner. Maybe Saturday night—after Ben's game and church. Larry could barbecue."

"Yeah, Sis . . . that'd be great."

"So the deposition . . . how did it go?"

"Flynn's a' best. With him and God, we'll win this thing yet, you know?"

"Good . . . but Josh, I still don't like how you sound. Maybe you should go to the hospital and make sure you're okay."

"I'm fine. I tol' you, Linds. Jus' need a lil' sleep."

"Okay. I'm staying on the phone until you get home."

"I love you, Linds, you know? You're my best friend."

She closed her eyes. What if he'd been killed in the accident? She couldn't imagine losing him—especially not now when he'd finally found his way back to the Lord. The years ahead would be their best yet. "I love you, too, Josh. Now we need to get you better."

"I can always count on you, Linds."

They talked about his faith and he told her about praying for God to get him through his time on the witness stand. Flynn had doubled the amount he was asking for, but Josh didn't seem overly excited about the fact. "You know what?" He sounded a little better than he had earlier in the conversation. "I don't wanna get rich. I wanna get better."

"I know, and you will." She wished she could blink herself there, so she could take over at the wheel and get him home safely. "God has great plans for you, Josh. It's all just beginning for you."

"I'm gonna meet Savannah. That's the best part."

"Yes. You'll be able to afford a wonderful attorney."

"I already have him. Flynn can handle the custody case. It's next on his list as soon as the settlement comes through."

She stretched the call, talking about Ben's coach naming him the starting running back for tomorrow's game, and how Bella had designated herself as her brother's personal cheerleader. "She's three years older than him—just like you and me."

"I know. They're both lucky. Savannah will like having them as cousins."

Lindsay wasn't sure why, but tears filled her eyes. Her brother wanted so little from life, but somehow things had never quite fallen into place. Until now, anyway. If he could just get past his injury, get the surgery he needed, and be finished with the lawsuit. The best years for Josh really might be right around the corner. She was midway through telling him about a feature story on a local hiker whose hundredth birthday was next week when she heard him exhale loudly.

"I did it." He sounded relieved. "I'm home. Jus' pulled into the parking lot."

She breathed a silent prayer of thanks. "Okay, now go in and get some rest. Saturday's going to be a big day and you need to be feeling good."

"I will. Tell Ben and Bella I can't wait to see them." His voice broke, and she realized he was more emotional than he'd let on. "Thanks for talking me through that drive, Linds. I was a little scared."

"I love you. If you need anything, call. I'll be right there."

"Okay. Love you, too."

The call ended and Lindsay dabbed at her eyes. Why was she so sad now? Her brother was home safely, and after a good night's sleep he'd be the same cheerful guy he'd been a few days ago when MercyMe was blaring through his house. But she'd been looking forward to seeing him tonight, and without him her dinner plans suddenly seemed flat.

Lindsay sniffed and ordered her heart to change directions. She had no reason to be sad, nothing to be discouraged about. Josh was making his turnaround. Everything was going to be fine for him. Besides, they had Saturday to look forward to. Lindsay found her smile again as she finished dinner and called her family in to eat. That night at the table, six-year-old Ben said the blessing. He thanked God for the food and for family and for the football game tomorrow. And he asked God for a special favor.

"Please, God, be with Uncle Josh tonight. He's too tired to be here, so help him feel better. In Jesus' name, amen."

And as the meal began and the conversation shifted to Bella's fourth-grade reading assignment, Lindsay felt a peace she hadn't known since Josh's phone call. Because God had certainly heard the prayers of her little Ben and that could only mean one thing.

Josh would feel better in the morning.

❧

Annie called her daughter's house to find out how Josh's deposition went.

"He's not here." Lindsay was helping Larry with the dishes. "He was too tired. But he said it went well. I told him we'll do dinner Saturday night."

Too tired? Annie had talked to Josh that morning and he'd been full of energy, ready to face the attorney for the insurance company. "He was looking forward to having dinner with you." Immediately, Annie's concern turned to worry. Josh's medication was bound to have an effect on him. "Did he talk about the pain pills?"

"He said he took one before he drove home." Lindsay's voice fell. "Honestly, Mom, I was worried about him. He didn't sound right, like he was half asleep or drunk or something. I've never heard him like that."

"I have. It's not good. He has to be so careful with those drugs." Annie wrapped up the conversation quickly and immediately dialed Josh. It was just after eight o'clock, so even on a day when he was tired, he would normally still be awake. Annie stepped out onto their covered front porch and paced the length of it. The phone rang once . . . twice. . . . "Come on, Josh," she whispered. It was still in the seventies outside but a chill ran down her bare arms. "Pick up the phone, son."

He answered just after the fourth ring. "Hello?"

Annie pressed her hand to her chest. "Thank God." She dropped to the glider swing and sank back in the cushion. "Your sister said you were too tired for dinner."

"I was. But I'm feeling better now." He sounded tired, but sharp. None of his words were slurred as far as she could tell. "The deposition was terrible. The worst ever."

On days like this, when some hotshot lawyer had dragged her son through a day of emotional torture, when he'd been forced to drive an hour each way to give yet another round of answers in a game designed by a big insurance corporation to avoid paying Josh his settlement, Annie could only picture one thing: a trip they'd taken to Yellowstone National Park the summer before Josh started middle school.

They were about to leave their tent when they heard a barking dog. Annie was closest to the tent flap and she peered out in time to see the drama unfolding in a field across from the campground. A baby black bear had wandered away from his mother and now the barking terrier had backed him up against a tree. The baby bear looked one way and then the next, searching for an escape route, but the dog quickly closed off his options.

In a blur of motion, and with a bellow that rang through the campground, the mother bear tore into the clearing, picking up speed. The dog never knew what hit him. He was still barking at the bear cub when the mother reached him from behind and sent him ten feet in the air with one swipe of her massive paw. The dog flipped three times and landed on his back, but injured or not, he had the sense to run for his life.

The danger to her baby behind them, the mother went to her cub and licked his face, nuzzling him and hovering over him until the two of them returned to the forest.

That's how Annie felt now, like the mother bear ready to tear into any attorney who would put her son through the rigors of demeaning questions, hearing after hearing after hearing. She thought about going to see Josh now, so she could hold him and will away his suffering.

"Mom?"

"I'm sorry." She leaned against the porch railing. "You shouldn't have to go through that." She breathed in slowly. *Positive,* she told herself. *You have to stay positive for him.* She pulled herself up a little straighter. "So tell me about it. Are they any closer to settling?"

"I think so." Josh was clear-minded and deliberate as he told her about the questions. "The insurance company wants the judge to think I was on the verge of a medical disability anyway, because of my weight."

"That's ridiculous. Besides, you're almost back to your normal size already." Annie pictured her son on the stand, the insurance company's attorney embarrassing him, humiliating him. "Is it worth it, son? I mean, what does Mr. Flynn say?"

"He thinks we'll have the judge's decision in a few weeks. The insurance company is running out of reasons to delay." Josh explained how his attorney had done a brilliant job at the end of the deposition, and how Flynn was asking for twice the settlement. He was still talking when Nate stepped out onto the porch and gave her a curious look.

"Josh," she mouthed.

Her husband nodded and hesitated. He must've seen her concern because he came and stood beside her. He kept his voice low. "Is he okay?"

Annie nodded, but tempered that with a worried shrug.

"So, I'm almost finished with these hearings. Maybe one more, and Flynn says we'll be finished."

The news landed in Annie's gut like a bucket of rocks. One more deposition was like knowing her son would be exposed to one more beating. "Maybe I'll go with you next time."

"That's okay." He laughed lightly. "I'll get through it. Then I can pay you and Dad back, and move on with my life."

"And you're feeling better? Now that you've been home for a while?"

"Yes." Josh rarely complained about his pain, and to-night was no exception. "Hey"—his voice grew tender—"I talked to Flynn about helping me find Savannah. Once we have the settlement, you know?"

Annie opened her mouth to shoot down the idea. There were a hundred more important things Josh should take care of once he got his settlement—including his back surgery and figuring out whether he should go to college now or, if not, what line of work he was going to get into since driving a tow truck was no longer an option. Chasing after the child of a woman he'd spent a week with in Las Vegas couldn't possibly be good for him. Just another dead-end road.

But whether it was the concern in her husband's eyes or the whisper of God, she felt suddenly compelled to agree with him. "I'm sure Mr. Flynn would be a big help in whatever you need after the settlement comes."

"Yes." Josh seemed like he wanted to push the issue, talk more about Savannah, but he exhaled instead and he sounded more tired than he had before. "You still don't believe she's mine, do you?"

Of course not, she wanted to say. "There's no proof. The woman—she wasn't reputable, Josh. The photo could've been of someone else's child for all you know."

Another slow sigh filtered across the lines. "I understand that. But when I look at her eyes I see my own. I have to find out the truth. At least pray for me about that."

"I will." She was grateful to have something they could agree on. She nodded at her husband. "Your father and I will both pray that when the time is right, you'll find your answers, okay?"

"Good enough." He must've been at his computer because she could hear the rapid click of his fingers on a keyboard. "Listen, I'm online but I'm going to turn in early. I'll see you tomorrow at Ben's game."

"All right." Annie couldn't explain it but she was almost desperate to keep the conversation going, to reassure Josh that she cared about him more than he could ever know.

Nate tapped Annie's hand. "Tell him I love him," he mouthed.

"Your father loves you. And I love you. You'll get through this."

"I know. I love you both."

She could hear the smile in his voice and it made her feel better. "Good night."

" 'Night."

Annie clicked the off button and set the receiver on the porch railing. What was the ache in her heart, the longing to drive across town and hold her son the way she'd done when he was a little boy? She went to Nate, leaned into him, and listened to the steady thud of his heartbeat. "I just want the whole court thing to be over."

"Long day?" Nate led her to the glider and they sat down together.

"I guess the deposition was very difficult. Intense questions from the insurance company's attorney. More harassment." She lifted her eyes to his. "I'd like to drive down to that man's office and tell him a thing or two."

"It won't be long now, right? A few more weeks?"

"I hope so. After three years it's hard to believe the case will ever be settled."

"It will." He kissed the top of her head and set the swing into a soft, subtle motion. "Josh will land on his feet and he'll find his way. I believe in him."

"I do, too." Her answer was quick, and she remembered her thoughts from last week, how she could do nothing but admit her disappointment where their son was concerned. She leaned her head on Nate's shoulder. "It was so much easier when he was little, when his bike was stolen from school or he didn't get a part in the middle school musical. I could hug him and pray with him and make him a plate of cookies." She blinked back the beginning of tears. "The world would always look brighter in the morning."

"He's still young, Annie. The accident was a big setback." Nate's voice was calm, full of the confidence Annie only wished she had when it came to their son. "Tell you what." He angled himself so he could see her better. "Let's pray for him right now. While he's so heavy on your heart."

Nate started and Annie finished, and after ten minutes of talking to God about her son, Annie felt better. Enough that she went inside and found the flour and sugar and chocolate chips and made Josh a plate of cookies. As she took them out of the oven, she smiled thinking about how happy he would be when she gave him the gift at Ben's game, and how good it would feel to hug him, to remind him he was loved, no matter what his circumstances. As she cleaned the kitchen that night she wanted to believe that hugging him, and praying for him, and baking him a plate of chocolate chip cookies could only mean one thing.

Tomorrow, the world would look brighter.

⸎

EIGHT

Josh had only been online with Cara for ten minutes and already he felt himself rebounding from the ugliness of the deposition. He was still exhausted and a little dizzy, but his pain was tolerable, at least. He leaned against the desktop and waited for Cara's next message. As he did, he remembered the strange way he'd felt in the car earlier. The trip home from Denver had been a little hairy, and Lindsay was right. He should've pulled over. But if he fell asleep in his car in some parking lot or on the side of the road, then what? The OxyContin could knock him out for eight hours or more and he would have been a target for anyone who happened by. Instead, he prayed constantly and took Lindsay up on her offer. Their conversation helped him stay focused and alert.

So . . . didn't you have a court thing today? Cara's message flashed in the box at the bottom of his screen.

Cara didn't know how much he stood to win in the settlement. Money had no place in their friendship, which was good. Especially after the mistakes he'd made with Savannah's mother. He clicked open his iTunes library and pulled up his list with the MercyMe songs. His fingers flew across the keyboard. *Yes. It's not worth talking about. . . . I came home, had dinner, and went back out to the grocery store.* He didn't tell her the part about picking up a bag of groceries for Ethel, the old widow in the apartment above his. It wasn't something he talked about, just a regular part of his week. Ethel was ninety-two and her hips hurt. No surgery would ever help at her age, so Josh saved her the trip to the market. It was the least he could do. He added to his last message, *Did I tell you my latest plan?*

Cara's answer was immediate. *Tell me.*

With all this healthy eating I've been doing, next summer I want to play football again.

Uh . . . on a real team, you mean?

No. LOL. At the park with my sister's son. The boy loves to play catch and since the accident I haven't touched a ball. All that's gonna change. And you know what else?

What?

I'm gonna play with my shirt off. I'll have my surgery and hit the gym the way I used to do, you know?

There was a slight pause before her next message. *If anyone can make that happen it's you, J. I mean, come on . . . you've lost almost sixty pounds. What's your secret, by the way? You never talk about it.*

No secret. Josh leaned back in his chair as a sudden searing pain shot through his lower spine. He winced and kept typing. *I cut out the junk, sugar and stuff. That's it. No more three-a-day root beer Big Gulps.*

LOL . . . good for you, J.

He yawned and wondered again whether Becky would ever want him back or if he should push things with Cara, talk to her about the future. The answers would come eventually, he had no doubt. He would call Becky and if she wasn't interested, he could fly out to see Cara once his health was right. He could stay at a nearby hotel and they'd have a few days to find out if what they shared on-line could translate into real life. *I have other plans,* he typed. *But if I tell you it'll spoil everything, so . . . they'll have to wait till later.*

☺ *Now you've really got my interest.*

Let's just say I plan to keep it, you know? Your interest.

Ah . . . you're my best friend, J.

And you're mine. The pain in his back was intensifying. *Oh, and pray for Savannah, okay? I feel like she's not doing that great.*

I will, I'll pray. . . . Hey, listen to me! A month ago the word "pray" wouldn't have been in my vocabulary. But you, J, you've changed me.

He had an answer as soon as he read her message. *God changed you. He changed me, too—isn't it great?*

Anyway . . . why do you feel funny about Savannah?

I don't know. He moved his mouse back to iTunes and double clicked the song that started him on the path back to God. The words filled the small spaces around him and he sang along. Cara must've been waiting for more of an explanation. He centered his hands on the keyboard and tried to get in touch with his feelings. Slowly, his fingers began to move. *Maybe it's because I haven't seen a photo of her in so long. . . . Sometimes I wonder if she's still alive or if she knows about me at all.*

Cara's answer came slowly, one sentence at a time. *That's*

sad. And it's wrong. You've got to get your lawyer to help you find her.

I will. And she's out there, I know it. I just feel like I'm supposed to pray for her. Until I meet her, it's the only thing I can actually do for her, you know?

The first time you meet that little girl, I want a front-row seat, J. It's like a movie or something. That's the kind of happy ending it'll be.

Josh thought about his conversation with Carl Joseph and Daisy last week, how the best stories were the ones with happy endings. He began typing. *That's what I'm asking God for . . . a happy ending for me and Savannah.* He moved forward in his chair and waited a few seconds, but the pain was gaining ground on him. At this rate he wouldn't last another few minutes at the computer. The song was ending and he started it over again. One more time through and he'd turn in for the night. *I need to turn in soon,* he typed. *Sorry.*

That's okay. I'm tired, too.

I might sleep a little longer tonight. I want to feel good for Ben's game tomorrow. We're all going to church after, and then to Lindsay's house for dinner.

Sounds wonderful. Wish I were there.

He smiled. *Me, too . . . you'd really like Lindsay.*

They talked about their siblings for a few minutes, but the fire in Josh's back was relentless. *Hey, gotta go. I'll check in with you tomorrow, okay?*

I'll be waiting. Sleep well, J.

Thanks. He flinched at another shot of pain. *Don't forget about Savannah.*

Josh powered down his computer and opened the top

desk drawer. Inside was a picture of him and Becky from their senior prom. Was it all just a dream, the idea of contacting her after so many years, maybe asking her out for coffee, and seeing if there were still feelings there for both of them? Sometimes Becky seemed more like a fantasy, the perfect girl waiting for him to become the perfect guy.

But on nights like this he could still smell the shampoo in her hair, still feel her in his arms as he waltzed her across the prom dance floor. He could hear her laugh and feel the way his heart connected with hers. He doubled his determination as he set the picture back in his desk drawer. He would make something of himself and he would call her. God could take care of the rest.

Until then, he was grateful for Cara.

He yawned, and even that small action hurt his back. He wanted to head straight for bed, but lately he'd added a brief side trip to his bedtime routine. He pushed back from the desk, struggled to his feet, and then walked to his fireplace. Every step hurt worse than the last, and by the time he reached the mantel with the photographs, sweat was dripping down his forehead. *Dear Lord . . . I can't get through this without You. Please. . . .* He closed his eyes and held his breath, looking for even a small window of relief. Two pain pills a day, those were the doctor's orders. But sometimes—when he'd been to Denver for another hearing, especially—he would take three. The increase wasn't much, not compared with the stories he'd seen online of some out-of-control people. Three was more than he liked to take, but it wouldn't kill him.

He exhaled and opened his eyes, opened them to the picture of Savannah. *I don't know where she is, Lord, but*

I know she's mine. I know it with everything inside me. He grabbed another excruciating breath and steadied himself against the mantel. *You can see her right this minute, so please . . . be with her and comfort her. Keep her safe, God, so that when I'm better I can have a chance to be her daddy. She's all that keeps me going sometimes.*

I am with her, My son . . . and I am with you . . . always.

The holy reminder seemed to come whenever he was at his lowest. Josh released his hold on the mantel, kissed his fingertips, and pressed them to Savannah's picture. *Thank You, God. . . . Now, if You could please help me get some sleep.*

He gave his daughter a final look, turned, and shuffled to his room. The pain had become a spasm ricocheting from his shoulders to his lower back. He'd have the rest of the weight off by the end of February and then he could finally have the surgery.

He brushed his teeth, washed his face, and fell into bed. The haze of pain was making him nauseous, so he moved quickly for the bottle of pills on his nightstand and took one in the palm of his hand. His water glass wasn't even half full, but he didn't have the energy to get out of bed again. He'd have to down it quickly, making the best use of the water he did have.

For a moment he let himself imagine a life like the one he used to lead. Heavy or not, he could flop into bed and find instant sleep without so much as a thought of pain medication. He put the pill in his mouth and swigged the rest of the water, but the liquid slid down his throat leaving the pill behind. On impulse, he chewed the pill and swallowed it.

Not until he set the glass back on his nightstand did a thought flash in his mind. The doctor had said something about chewing the pills, right? How he had to be careful because a chewed pill could release the medication too quickly into his system or his bloodstream, or something like that. Panic flooded his veins and made him sit straight up despite the pain. His heart pounded hard, faster than usual. What if chewing the pill would hurt him? Maybe he should call 911, or at least contact his mother to ask for her advice.

But even as he sat upright sorting through his options, sleep came over him. Thick and heavy and sweet, the pain in his back faded and he felt his body relax. Slowly, he slid down until his head was partially on his pillow. In the farthest corner of his mind a nearly silent alarm was still sounding. He was okay, right? He had to be okay because God had great plans for him. *Lord . . . help me.* The sensation of sleep intensified and for the first time since the accident, Josh's pain all but subsided.

The relief felt wonderful, intoxicating. *Everything was going to be okay. You're with me, right, God?*

Until the end of the ages, My son . . .

Good. Josh smiled and let himself be dragged under, pulled into a sleep deeper and sweeter than any he'd ever known, even before the accident. God had great plans for him and for Savannah, so there was no reason to be afraid. And as he let the darkness close in around him, he released every care, every pain. The sensation of relief was so strong he felt like he was sleeping in the palm of the Lord's hand. The last thing Josh experienced was something he hadn't known for a very long time. Maybe not forever.

Complete and utter peace.

❧

Savannah didn't know the big man talking to her mama, but his dark eyes made little chill bumps up and down her arms. They were in Central Park begging money, that's what Mama called it—begging money—and a big man in nice clothes stopped and talked to them. Well, not to them, but to her mama. He had bushy dark hair and a little gold cross on a skinny chain and three big gold rings. At first her mama and the man laughed and talked loud about having a good time and what about plans for the night. But then Savannah saw the man show her mama some money. A lot of money, because there were zeroes on the dollar bills and Mama said zeroes were good.

That's when Mama told Savannah to sit on the bench and wait and she and the man walked toward the pond and their talking changed to quiet indoor voices. Savannah felt a little scared sitting there by herself, but she swung her feet and kept her eyes looking at the ground. Mama said it was always better to keep her eyes pointed to the ground so people wouldn't get the wrong idea. Savannah didn't know what that meant, but it sounded serious so she looked at the ground. Also she talked to Jesus, whom her grandpa Ted taught her about when she was five and they met for the first time in his hospital room. Grandpa Ted was her mama's daddy, but Mama said she didn't get along with him. She told Savannah they had to go to the hospital because Grandpa Ted was dying. That's the only reason.

"I don't have long, Savannah," he told her. Then he talked to her about Jesus—how He was God, but you couldn't see Him, and how He made all things and even how He wanted to be in her very own heart. Grandpa Ted took her hand that day and smiled the nicest smile anyone had ever given her. "If you love Jesus, if you talk to Him and trust Him, then one day we'll be together forever."

"Where is that place?" Savannah liked Grandpa Ted. She wished her mama had taken her to meet him before he got so sick.

"It's called heaven, sweetie." Grandpa coughed a lot and it took him a few ticks of the clock before he could talk again. "Sometimes life isn't so good this side of heaven. But, ah"—his eyes lit up and got a little bit of tears in them—"heaven will be absolutely perfect, Savannah. Like a birthday party that never, ever ends."

"A birthday party that never, ever ends."

Those words made the most beautiful picture in Savannah's head and that picture made her smile. She thought about it again and again, especially after her grandpa Ted went there a few days later. There were a lot of scary days with Mama, so what Grandpa Ted told her sounded like a good idea. Trusting in Jesus. Yes, it was a much better idea than anything her mama had thought of.

Jesus, I'm looking at the ground so no one gets the wrong idea. She held on to the edge of the bench, but it was sticky, so she let go and folded her hands in her lap. *I'm glad You're in my heart because I feel a little scared about that man Mama's talking to. Maybe she knows him from our room in Harlem. Or maybe not, and that means he would be a stranger, so Mama shouldn't talk to him.*

She lifted her eyes for just a quick look, and finally her mama and the man were coming back. They were laughing and whispering and the man had his arm around her shoulders. Savannah felt a sick feeling in her stomach, because she didn't think her mama knew the man, which meant she was letting a stranger put his arm around her. Anytime that happened, her mama ended up hurt or crying or angry at the stranger.

Savannah sighed and looked at the ground again. Where was her daddy right now? *Do You know, Jesus? 'Cause if You do then could You tell me, please? He's a Prince Charming and he loves me, I just know it. So if You find out where he is, please . . . tell me, okay?*

"Savannah?" Mama's voice was different, all sweet, like there was a song inside her. Not the way she usually sounded, which was sad and mostly angry and frustrated.

She looked up. "Yes?"

"This is Victor." She smiled at the man and blinked a few extra times. "He's going to take us to his house by the park today."

"For a sleepover." The man winked at Savannah's mama. Then he raised his hairy eyebrows at her. "Sound like fun?"

Savannah's heart beat harder, faster. Jesus didn't like lying, that's what Grandpa Ted told her. But just then her mama's look told her, *Listen, young lady, you better tell the stranger yes or else trouble for you!* She gulped at the man and answered him in her most quiet voice. "Yes, sir. But I like my own spot on the floor, thank you."

"That right?" The man laughed hard from deep in his round belly. "Don't worry, little one. We'll have a good time. All of us." He elbowed Savannah's mama. "I hope you have half her spunk."

"Spunk." People used words like that to talk about her.

Spunky. Feisty. Spirited. Mama said it was because her hair was red and she had freckles. They all three started walking toward the pretty buildings on the edge of the park. Savannah couldn't read yet, because her mama said school could wait. But the building where the man took them had the letters R-I-T-Z, and a man in a fancy costume was waiting for them out front.

Victor took them through a pretty room to a restaurant and they ate dinner at a table with a white sheet over it and pretty glasses and plates and forks. Savannah didn't dare say anything, but she couldn't stop looking around. The people and the furniture and the carpet and the ceilings— none of it looked anything like their room back in Harlem. More like something from a movie. *This*, she thought, *is a place where my daddy would live*. She knew exactly what he looked like so she started checking to see if he was one of the people who walked by.

Victor talked mostly to Mama. They ordered steak and potatoes and Savannah got a hamburger and French fries with a tiny little bottle of ketchup. Savannah kept looking for her daddy while they ate, which took a long time because her mama and Victor had two bottles of wine.

After that Victor took them into an elevator up to his house. "His room," he called it. Savannah's mama and Victor were laughing loud and walking very crooked. But when they reached Victor's door, inside was a whole house with a living room and two TVs and big giant windows that showed the park across the street. Savannah had never seen anything so beautiful in all her life. Victor turned the TV on for Savannah and he found a show with kids singing. "Wait here, little one. Your turn will come later." He grinned at her, but the way his eyes looked made her feel scared.

Then he and Mama went into another room and Savannah heard the click of a lock. They stayed in there a long time until it was almost night. Savannah got tired of watching TV. She walked to the window and stared at the park and the sidewalks that went along the edge. So many people. Sometimes she wondered if she would ever find her Prince Charming daddy.

A thought, or maybe a wish, filled her heart. That maybe right this minute, wherever he was, her daddy was thinking about her, too. That made her feel safe and sleepy inside. She went back to the couch and stretched out.

"Savannah?"

The voice belonged to a man and Savannah sucked in a quick breath as she blinked her eyes open. She pushed herself into the corner of the couch. She must've fallen asleep. This wasn't her place on the floor in their room in Harlem, so where was she? From the window she could hear pouring-down rain and a little bit of thunder. She blinked fast and then she saw him. That strange man, standing close by her. Light came into the room from the street outside and she could see his grin. The same grin as before.

"No," she whispered. She tried to move farther into the corner of the couch.

Please, Jesus. . . . Please keep me safe.

The man took a step closer, but just then Savannah's mama stepped out of the room. "Victor, come back. . . ." She still sounded funny from the wine. "I wanna show you something."

Victor looked once more at Savannah and touched a

piece of her hair. "No loss." He spit a little when he said the word "loss." "I don't care for redheads, anyway." He did that belly laugh again. Then he winked at her and went back into the other room with Mama.

Once the door closed, Savannah breathed hard and fast, and her heart pounded like the rain against the windowsill. She wasn't sure what the man wanted or why he had come to her, but deep inside her she knew that God had heard her prayer, and that He had just rescued her from something very bad. *Thank You for my red hair,* she told Jesus before she fell asleep again. Because maybe that helped her be safe.

Two days later her mama and Victor got in a fight. He yelled and she yelled and then Savannah saw him slap her mama across the face. Savannah ran for the door and covered her face, but before Victor could do anything else bad, Savannah's mama took her by the hand and they left. In the elevator, Mama touched her hand to her cheek and she started crying.

Savannah thought it was because her cheek was red, and because Victor didn't want to be her friend anymore.

"Men are pigs." She closed her eyes. "How could I believe him?" She sniffed and then she rolled her eyes. "I'm a terrible mother, Savannah. I don't even like children. I should take you to CPS and drop you off. We'd probably both be better off."

"Is that where my daddy lives?"

Her mama looked at her with the strangest look. "Is that what you want? To live with your father?"

Savannah opened her eyes wide. "Yes, please. At least for a little while."

Her mama cried harder then. "Fine, Savannah. You'd be happier with him, anyway. And I could do whatever I wanted."

Mama said that all the time, that both of them would be better off if Savannah went to CPS or to live with her daddy and that then she could do what she wanted. But her mama never took her there. Savannah figured that was because her mama loved her, even though she said she didn't like children a lot. She probably just didn't know how to act around children. That's what Grandpa Ted whispered to her when they talked that time in his hospital room.

Savannah stayed quiet while they walked to the subway and climbed down the stairs. She wasn't sure where CPS was, or if her daddy was there, but she had a feeling that this time maybe her mama would really do it—take her to be with her daddy. Until then she would keep praying for that to happen, since her mama thought it would be better for both of them. As they got onto the subway and found two seats, Savannah pictured her daddy one more time. God had kept her safe and now God was going to let her find her wonderful Prince Charming daddy. She could feel it. And that must mean her daddy was doing more than just thinking about her. He must've been talking to Jesus about her, too.

And that thought made Savannah smile for the first time in two days.

NINE

Carl Joseph took one egg at a time from his new carton in the fridge and set them carefully in the same plastic container Josh had given them. Along the way he lost track of how many, so he counted them twice. When he was sure he had six eggs, he closed the fridge.

"A good neighbor returns things they borrow," he said out loud. "And so I'm a good neighbor." He held the eggs tight against his body, put his apartment key in his pocket, because an independent person always has his key in his pocket, and then he locked the door behind him and walked down to Daisy's apartment.

He knocked on the door two times fast, then two times slow. That was his special knock just for Daisy and only he used that knock, no one else. Not even Brother or Elle. He looked up at the sky and smiled. Blue skies meant Daisy would be happy all day long. He whistled a song about somewhere over the rainbow, and after the "dreams come true" part, Daisy opened the door.

"Hi, Daisy." He held the eggs with one hand and pointed to the sky. "Blue means dry, and dry means good."

Daisy smiled at him and her eyes were sparkly like sunshine on a lake. "Thank you, CJ. I love blue skies."

"Well." Carl Joseph pushed his toe around in a few shy circles. "Actually God gave 'em to you." He laughed at that joke. "But you already know that."

"Of course." She tapped him once lightly on the shoulder. "Silly, CJ. Of course I know blue skies are from God." She looked at the eggs in the plastic container and her eyebrows went up. "Good idea, CJ. We have to take the eggs back to Josh."

"Because that's what a good neighbor does."

"Right." She pointed her number one finger into the air, which she liked to do whenever Carl Joseph had a good idea. "Good job, CJ." She linked her arm through his, grabbed her big blue purse, and they walked across the parking lot toward Josh's apartment. "Remember Disneyland, CJ, and how I pretended to be Minnie Mouse?"

Carl Joseph pushed his glasses a little higher up on his nose. "And remember I bought you a pair of Minnie Mouse ears for that day?"

"Right." She walked a few steps without saying anything, which meant she was thinking. "I have an idea, CJ. How 'bout I wear my Minnie Mouse ears next time we have a date day?"

"We could go to the mall!" Carl Joseph could picture what a fun time that would be.

"To the Disney Store." Daisy pointed at Josh's apartment just ahead. "We could ask if Josh wants to come, too. Because maybe he could buy a Minnie Mouse dress to go with this. . . ." She reached into her purse and pulled out a brand-new pair of Minnie Mouse ears. "Tammy and

I stopped at the mall on the way home from work yesterday. I bought these for that little girl in the picture on his fireplace."

"That's very nice, Daisy." Carl Joseph smiled, but only halfway. "Except Josh said that story doesn't have a happy ending."

"But God gave us a happy ending at Disneyland, remember?"

He thought about that. "And Disneyland is the happiest place on earth. . . ."

"Right." She pointed with her number one finger again. "So let's give these Minnie ears to Josh and ask if he should come with us next time and get that little girl a Minnie dress." Her smile got softer. "Maybe with these Minnie Mouse ears that story will have a happy ending, too."

"Yeah . . . maybe that, Daisy. Maybe that." They reached Josh's apartment. He had Daisy on one arm and the eggs in the other, so he used the tip of his foot to knock on Josh's door.

They looked at Josh's door, but Josh didn't come to open it. "Maybe your tennis shoe didn't knock loud enough."

The sunshine felt warm on Carl Joseph's shoulders. "Yeah, maybe." He put the eggs down carefully on the ground, because all his eggs were in one plastic container. Then he knocked real hard with his hand, the right way. He put his lips up close to the door. "Hi, Josh. It's your favorite neighbors!"

Daisy giggled beside him, and she twirled the new Minnie ears and they waited some more. A car pulled into the parking lot and dropped off two girls. A mom in the car told them good-bye and then she pulled away, and still . . . still Josh hadn't opened the apartment door.

"You think maybe he's sleeping?" Carl Joseph looked over his shoulder at Daisy.

"If he is, we should probably wake him up."

"Yeah, right." Carl Joseph pushed his glasses up on his nose again and tried the door handle. It wasn't locked, so the door opened right up. A nervous feeling came over him, but he tried to smile, anyway. "I guess he was expecting us."

Suddenly, Daisy's smile was gone and she shivered a little. "What if he isn't here? It might be breaking the law to go inside if he isn't here."

"He's here." Carl Joseph turned halfway around and pointed to the old Mustang in the parking lot. "See that, Daisy? That's his car, so he's here."

"Okay." Daisy didn't sound that sure of herself. "Let's go in together."

Carl Joseph picked up the eggs and went inside a few steps. He faced toward where Josh's bedroom was. "Josh . . . it's your favorite neighbors. Are you awake?"

"Josh?" Daisy put her hands around her mouth so her voice would be louder. "Josh, wake up, okay?"

The sounds in Josh's apartment were his refrigerator and his clock on the kitchen wall, and a buzzing fly near the sliding patio door. But not Josh's voice. A strange feeling started to grow in Carl Joseph's stomach. It was the same feeling he had when he took the bus one time before he graduated from Elle's class on independent living. That day he took the wrong bus and he almost got lost forever, except Brother and Elle found him. How he felt that day was how he was starting to feel now.

"Come on, Daisy." He walked into Josh's kitchen and Daisy followed him.

"I'm scared, CJ. Where is he?"

"I don't know." He thought about opening the fridge and putting the eggs away but then he remembered his manners. It wasn't his fridge, so probably only Josh should put the eggs away. He left them on the counter in their plastic container. "Daisy"—he put his hands on both her shoulders—"don't be afraid. Let's just go to his room and wake him up. Because that's what good neighbors should do."

Her eyebrows were all scrunched together. "Are you sure?"

"Yes." Carl Joseph didn't listen to the scared feeling inside him. He held out his hand to Daisy. "Come on."

Together they walked down the small hallway to Josh's room and Carl Joseph knocked again. Still no answer. "Josh?"

"He's asleep," Daisy whispered. "Go on, CJ . . . go in."

Carl Joseph opened the bedroom door and there was Josh, lying on his bed. "Josh?" He used a regular inside voice because he thought Josh would wake up if he heard his bedroom door open. "Wake up, Josh."

They walked up to his bed slowly, and halfway there Daisy stopped. "He—he doesn't look right, CJ."

"He's very sleepy." Carl Joseph didn't want Daisy to say that, because what if . . . He walked right up to the side of the bed and gave Josh's shoulder a little shake. "Josh!" This time he used his loudest voice because maybe that's what it would take to wake him. "Josh, wake up."

"CJ, I'm scared again."

"It's okay. Let's say his name at the same time really loud. Maybe that'll wake him up."

"All right." She was shaking very much, but at the same time they said the numbers.

"One . . . two . . . three." Then, they both yelled Josh's name and Carl Joseph gave his shoulder another shake. But Josh didn't blink or move or anything. He just lay there, frozen still.

That's when Carl Joseph thought that maybe Daisy was right. Maybe something was wrong with Josh, and he needed emergency help. On the wall of his apartment and Daisy's, too, there was an instruction sheet of paper that told about how to get emergency help. Carl Joseph pushed up his glasses and swallowed hard. "Daisy?" He took a step back and turned to her. "Maybe we should get emergency help for Josh. Maybe emergency help could wake him up."

"Oh, no!" Daisy put her hand with the Minnie ears to her mouth. "Emergency help is for very bad problems."

"But if he can't wake up"—Carl Joseph looked back at Josh—"then this is a very bad problem, right?"

"Right." Tears came to her eyes. "Hurry, CJ, call for emergency help!"

Carl Joseph felt his heart pumping hard against his chest because this was more scary than being lost on a bus. He picked up the phone next to Josh's bed and tried to remember the numbers. It was nine something—nine-nine-nine, was that it? He put the phone back down and closed his hands very tight. *Please, God. . . . Help me remember the emergency help number. Please. . . .*

"What are you doing?" Daisy was crying. "CJ, call emergency help!"

"I'm praying. Because that's the first emergency help for me." He didn't yell at her, but he said it in a certain way so she'd understand.

He saw in the corner of his eye that she was walking a few steps away from Josh and then back again, nervous and scared. "Hurry, CJ."

Just then God gave him the right number, because he could see it in his head. He picked up the phone and dialed just like he saw it. "Nine-one-one, that's how to get emergency help."

In no time a woman said, "Nine-one-one, what's your emergency?"

Carl Joseph looked at his favorite neighbor. "Josh won't wake up."

"Excuse me, sir?"

"Josh!" *Stay calm,* he told himself. Because he wasn't really feeling very calm. *Stay calm. Help me, Jesus. I need You.* The first rule in emergency situations was to stay calm and pray. "He lives in the apartment across the parking lot. He's our favorite neighbor and he won't wake up."

"Is he breathing?"

Was he breathing? Carl Joseph hadn't thought about that. His heart was running fast inside him now. "How can I tell?"

"Sir." The woman sounded a little impatient. "You check if his chest is moving and if air is coming out of his nose or mouth."

"Okay . . . okay, I'll check." Carl Joseph put the phone on the edge of the table next to the bed and he stared real hard at Josh's chest. But no matter how hard he stared Josh's chest wasn't moving anywhere. Then he put his hand up in front of Josh's nose, but no air was coming out. Behind him Daisy was crying harder, so when Carl Joseph picked the phone back up he had to talk loud so the lady could hear him. "His chest isn't moving and no air is coming out." He began to take fast breaths because that couldn't be good. No chest moves and no air. "Help us, please!"

"An ambulance is on the way, sir. Are you the only one there?"

"Me and my girlfriend, Daisy. We live in the independent living apartments, but we were here because good neighbors return things they borrow."

"Yes, sir. Wait there until the paramedics come, okay?"

"Yes, ma'am." He hung up and he looked at Josh. Maybe a person could stop having his chest move and air come out if he was very, very sleepy. So he tried one more time to wake him up. "Josh!" he yelled. "Wake up right now!"

Still nothing.

"He isn't okay, CJ. Let's go." Daisy sounded very scared now, like when the rain came and she was afraid she would melt. "Let's go outside."

"We have to wait for the paramedics." He put his arms around Daisy and rocked her one way and the other. "That's what emergency help told me."

So Daisy pressed her head against his chest and they waited that way until they heard sirens. *Please help us, God. . . . Please help our neighbor.* Carl Joseph said the same prayer over and over and over again until he heard someone knock at the door.

"Paramedics. Anyone inside?"

"Carl Joseph and Daisy," he shouted. "We're back here in the bedroom."

Two men in blue uniforms hurried down the hall and into Josh's room. The first one looked at Josh and then at Carl Joseph. He was in a very big hurry. "Step out of the room, please." Then he yelled something to the other man about a cart and paddles.

Carl Joseph took one more look at Josh and then, together with Daisy, he left the room. He wasn't sure how far to step out, but he could hear more sirens, so he decided they should step all the way out to the sidewalk. He took the plastic container of eggs on the way, because he wanted to be sure Josh got them. Then he remembered that anytime he needed emergency help he was supposed to call Brother. He could hear loud sounds coming from Josh's apartment, and a horrible thought came to him.

What if Josh—what if he was dead?

"CJ, what's happening?" Daisy was still crying and some of her tears were falling on the new Minnie ears. She needed to be somewhere else, somewhere away from the sirens and police cars and the fire truck coming into the parking lot.

"Come on, Daisy. Let's go to my house." He took her there, and then he called Brother.

"Carl Joseph, how are you?" Brother sounded happy. "We're still on for dinner later, right?"

"Brother, something's very wrong with our favorite neighbor, Josh."

His brother's happy sound left right away. "What is it?"

"He won't wake up. We went there to take back six

eggs because a good neighbor returns what he borrows, and Josh won't wake up." His words all ran together the way his breaths did. "He won't wake up and so I called emergency help and now paramedics and an ambulance and firemen and police are all here."

"Okay, buddy . . . don't worry. I'm on my way."

"Thank you, Brother." Carl Joseph held on to Daisy until Brother came through the front door. "Buddy, I'm going over to Josh's apartment. Do you want to come or stay here?"

"Come." Carl Joseph was still breathing too fast and he still felt sick, but he had to go back to Josh. Josh was his favorite neighbor. He released Daisy. "You, too? You wanna come?"

"No . . . yes." She held on tight to his arm. "Yes, if—if you stay with me."

"I will." They hurried out the door with Brother and by then there were other people in the parking lot looking at Josh's apartment, old Ethel from right upstairs over where Josh lived and the two teenage girls who had gotten out of the car earlier and some other people, too. No one was laughing or talking or doing anything but waiting and watching.

When they got as close as the police cars, Brother stopped and turned to him. "I'll be right back."

Carl Joseph felt like he might stop breathing. His face was wet across his forehead and his heart was still running hard inside him. "Brother," he tried to whisper so Daisy wouldn't hear him. "I'm very scared for Josh."

"Listen, buddy." His brother put his hands on either side of Carl Joseph's face. "Everything's going to be okay,

no matter what happens to Josh." Brother sounded serious, but calm. "Josh loves Jesus, remember?"

"Yeah, I remember that now." Carl Joseph nodded a lot of
times. "Josh loves Jesus." And for people who love Jesus, everything would be okay in the end. That was always true. His
heart slowed down just a little. "Thanks for that, Brother."

Daisy was still holding the Minnie ears, but Brother's
words seemed to make her feel better, too. He jogged from
them to the front of Josh's apartment just as a police officer was coming out. Brother said something to the policeman and they talked back and forth for a minute. Then
he looked down at the ground and rubbed the back of his
neck and that made Carl Joseph feel bad all over again.

Because Brother only did that when something was very,
very wrong.

≈

Cody had no idea how he was going to go back to his
brother and Daisy and tell them the truth about their favorite neighbor.

Josh Warren was dead.

The officer stopped him at the door and told him the
news. "How? What happened to him?" Cody could hardly
believe it. Josh was only in his late twenties, healthy but
for a few pounds and his injured back.

"Died in his sleep. . . . I'm sure they'll do an autopsy."
The officer had a cell phone in his hand. "This was in his
room. Do you know the names of any of his family?"

"Not the names." Cody tried to think what Josh had
told him. "His parents are in Black Forest, I think."

The officer was scrolling through the contact list in Josh's phone. "Mom and Dad." He sighed and gave Cody a sad glance. "If you'll excuse me."

Cody took a step back and then walked slowly toward his brother and Daisy. Somewhere across town Josh's parents were about to get the news no mother or father ever wants to hear. He stopped for a few seconds and stared into the blue sky. Death was never easy, but especially not the death of a young person. *I know You're in charge, God. . . . But I don't get it. Josh Warren? What did he ever have? What good ever happened to him?*

His thoughts weren't irreverent, just honest. The way he always was with God. When Ali had died, her loss shook him to his core, almost made him give up on living. But by some miracle, God had brought Elle into his life, and with her he'd found a way to live again, a way to believe.

But Josh? He hadn't found love or the settlement he was waiting for. And most of all he hadn't found his daughter. A heartsick feeling dragged at Cody's heart. That little girl would never know her dad, or what a nice guy he was. He swallowed hard against the lump in his throat.

Carl Joseph was waiting.

TEN

Annie was eating breakfast with Nate on the back porch, watching a pair of deer maneuver through a grove of pine trees when the phone rang. Lindsay, she figured, telling her exactly where they were supposed to meet for the football game and how excited Ben was that everyone was coming. Lindsay called often—at least once a day—so she smiled at Nate, excused herself from the patio table, and went inside.

Some people talk about having a premonition, how in the minutes or hours or days before a car accident or a drowning or before getting that certain report from a grim-faced doctor, there was a nudging, a small, slight certainty that something very bad was about to happen. Later, no matter how long the road of years or how many summers separated that event from current-day living, the premonition would remain. "I had a feeling," people would say as they looked back. "I just knew."

That wasn't the case for Annie.

As she walked into the house she noted that the sky was spilling rays of blue sunshine between the trees and the house smelled like the fresh, hot cinnamon rolls she'd just taken from the oven. Her only thought about the coming day was that God must have been happy with her for Him to allow a Saturday in early fall to feel this perfect. Her whole family was going to be together. A football game, a church service filling up nearly an entire pew, and dinner at Lindsay's. This would be the sort of day, she told herself, they would look back on years from now and relive over and over.

A smile was already on her lips as she answered the phone. "Hello?"

"Mrs. Warren?" The voice wasn't familiar.

"Yes?" A slight frustration buzzed at her. She glanced back out at the porch, at Nate eating by himself. The deer had moved on, and she had missed them. For a sales call.

"Mrs. Warren, this is Sergeant Daniel White with the Police Department."

He hesitated, and in that single hesitation, Annie felt her world turn upside down. Because why—why would a police officer call her at home on a Saturday morning? And at the same time, his tone of voice told her the answer. She braced herself against the kitchen counter.

"Ma'am, do you have a son named Joshua David Warren?"

"Yes." *Get on with it,* she wanted to yell. *Tell me why you're calling.* "Is something wrong?"

"Please come to his apartment as quickly as you can, ma'am. There's been a problem."

"There's been a problem?" Adrenaline screamed into her veins and her heart responded by trying to burst from her chest. "A problem?"

"We'll be here waiting for you, Mrs. Warren. Please hurry."

She hung up the phone and her feet somehow took her back through the house toward the porch. She hadn't said good-bye to the officer, or thank you, or any of the usual polite things. She hoped the police officer wouldn't think her rude, or assign the impolite behavior to her husband where it might hurt his reelection bid. She allowed the crazy, irrational thoughts because they held back the avalanche waiting to crash in around her.

"Nate." Her tone was flat. She stood in the doorway gripping the frame. "We have to go."

Immediate concern lowered his eyebrows. He pushed back from the table, his eyes locked on hers, still chewing his cinnamon roll. "Annie . . . you're white as a sheet." He came to her, put his hand on her shoulder. "What is it?"

The police officer wouldn't blame Nate. Not when he had the chance to meet them in person and see for himself that she wasn't rude or ungrateful or impolite. Not really. "The officer said to hurry." She turned and walked back into the house, grabbed her keys from the drawer near the refrigerator, and held them out to Nate.

"Annie . . . talk to me." He was following her, his face still frozen in alarm. "What officer? Who was on the phone?"

She blinked and her strange trance cracked just enough to let her say, "Something's wrong with Josh." The adrenaline kicked into another gear and she dropped the keys. Before they hit the floor she was in Nate's arms. "Dear God, no." Her words were wrapped in panic. "Not Josh . . . not my son."

Nate allowed the embrace for only a second or two, then he took firm hold of her arms. "A police officer called about Josh? Is that it?"

"Yes." Annie couldn't allow the first few rocks to tumble down the hillside of her heart, couldn't let her mind go where the events of the last minute wanted to take her. She locked eyes with her husband and implored him with her eyes. "He's fine. He has to be fine."

Nate grabbed the keys from the floor and took her hand. "I'll drive."

"Thank you." There. She'd remembered her manners. "We need to pray."

"I am. I won't stop." But he did three times along the ten-minute drive to ask the same question each time. "The officer didn't say what was wrong?"

"No." She took her eyes off the road only for a second or so each time. "Just keep praying." But each time she let her tongue hand out that answer, a voice in her soul shouted at her that maybe it was too late to pray. All of existence as she knew it was about to change, because this was how other people's lives changed. A phone call or a knock at the door, the mile marker of a life that would forever more be divided into two parts. Before that single moment and after it.

Her prayer was a cry for help and she silently uttered it with every few breaths. *Lord, be with Josh. . . . Comfort him and give him peace. Whatever's happened to him, don't leave his side, please, God. . . . I can't do this without You.*

Daughter, I am with you always. . . .

The answer anchored itself within her and allowed her to draw her next breath. *Lord, be with Josh. . . . Comfort him and give him peace. Whatever's happened . . .*

Not until Josh's apartment parking lot came into view

did Annie know for certain the gravity of the situation. An ambulance was parked at an angle not far from Josh's front door, and next to it a fire truck and two police cars. People stood in small groups and Annie wanted to yell at them. *Don't just stand there. Do something. . . . Help my son.*

"Please, God. . . ." Nate spoke the words out loud as he slammed the car into park. This time there was no confusion or question mark in his voice because the answer was obvious. The emergency vehicles told them what the officer had not.

They climbed out of the car and then suddenly Annie had the most desperate feeling to be with her son, with her youngest. Her baby. She began to run toward his front door and she kept running, even when she tripped over the sprinkler head. A police officer appeared in the entryway, and he stopped and waited for her. But why wasn't he in a hurry? Why wasn't he helping her son?

She picked up her pace and behind her she could hear Nate running, too. Josh was in trouble, but they were there, so everything would be okay. *Please, God, let it be okay.* Josh had been through enough without this, but if she could reach him and take him in her arms and cradle him close the way she'd done when he was little, then he would be okay, because her love was that strong. Strong enough to change this trouble around.

"Excuse me." She motioned with her hand for the officer to step aside, but he moved right into her path. "I need to see my son!" Her voice was so filled with terror, she didn't recognize it.

"Ma'am, I'm Officer White."

"Thank you for calling." Her mouth was dry. "We need to see him."

Nate was a step ahead of her now, talking at the same time. "Is he inside?" He was breathing fast, and he barely glanced at the officer. "What happened to him?"

"Sir, I need you to stop." The officer held out both hands, partially blocking the doorway. "Please. . . . You can't go inside."

Annie opened her mouth to say something or scream or cry, but she felt suddenly paralyzed. Nate put his arm around her, and the officer's words mixed with the sound of a radio coming from one of the emergency vehicles behind her, and the traffic on Elm Street that ran alongside the apartments, and the fast, relentless beating of her heart. Every noise intensified so it was hard to hear what he was saying. Something about not knowing the cause of death and finding the open bottle of pain medication beside her son's bed and wondering if Josh ever took more OxyContin than the regular dose. And Nate was asking how long Josh had been dead and . . .

Annie's knees buckled and she grabbed on to her husband. Her son was dead? Her youngest child was gone and she hadn't said good-bye? It wasn't possible. She held her hand straight out, as if maybe she could touch him or reach him somehow. "Josh!" The cry that came from her was like that of a crazy person, a scream that begged God to turn back the clock, to give her a chance to come here and hold him the way she'd wanted to yesterday after his deposition. "Josh, no!" She screamed his name again and Nate pulled her into his arms.

"Please." He was shaking as he stared at the officer,

his voice shrouded in fear and disbelief. "We need to see him."

The policeman hesitated. "You don't want to go in there." He looked back into the apartment and then at Annie. "Remember him the way he was."

The way he was? This wasn't happening. She was just talking to him on the phone, telling him he should get some rest and making plans to see him at today's football game. If she could only go inside and see him, maybe the paramedics hadn't done a thorough check, maybe he was only sleeping hard, the way he sometimes did when he took an extra pain pill.

A paramedic came out, stopped at the doorway, and spoke in a low voice to Officer White. "The coroner is on his way."

And just like that, the avalanche gave. It caved in around her and buried her, in suffocating layers of pain and grief. "Not Josh, please, God!" The scream wasn't as loud as before but it was heavy with a fear Annie had never known.

Nate drew her close again and soothed his hand over her arm. "Shhhh, baby . . . it's okay. Hold on to me."

Annie wasn't sure how they walked from the front door back ten feet to a spot near the end of the sidewalk, or how long they stood there. But at about the same time, a white van pulled up and two men with a stretcher walked quietly past them. Annie stared at the ground, at a crack in the asphalt near her feet. She wanted to run back to the car and tell Nate to drive as fast and as far from here as possible, so the scene playing out before her wouldn't be real.

If she looked down long enough, she could convince herself she wasn't here in Josh's parking lot, but at the football game. Standing outside her car, walking to the bleachers, a blanket under one arm, a bag of water bottles on the other. None of this was real. She was at the football game and Ben was warming up on the field, and Lindsay and Josh and Nate were saving her a place in the bleachers. And she was thinking how just yesterday Josh was the one in the uniform, the one waving to them from the forty-yard line, and she and Nate were saying how with Josh's height and strength, maybe he'd play football in high school and even college. She blinked and she could see all of Josh, each first day of school, each long, endless summer, and every rushed morning trying to make it to the bus on time

Nate leaned his head against hers and a quiet groan came from some broken place inside him. "Not Josh," he muttered, and his grip on her grew tighter, more desperate.

She kept her eyes down, glued to the crack in the asphalt, until she felt something wet on the side of her neck. *Don't look up*, she told herself. The stretcher would have to come out eventually. *Don't look up*. But she wanted to see whether the tears on her neck were hers, so she lifted her gaze just enough to find Nate's. His anguished face a twist of sorrow and disbelief, tears streaming down his face. "He's gone, Annie . . . our boy is gone."

Annie shook her head. He wasn't gone. He was twenty-eight years old. He had his whole life ahead of him. She noticed the crowd of people. A handsome dark-eyed man standing next to a young couple with Down syndrome. A woman with two teenagers huddled close on either side of her. An old woman standing a few feet away by herself, arms crossed in front of her chest, squinting at Josh's front door.

Annie wondered if they were her son's friends, and a

realization hit her at once. She didn't know any of Josh's neighbors. She wasn't sure if Josh knew them, for that matter. But since they were here and they cared enough to watch, she thought about introducing herself and thanking them for coming. The way she would if this were one of Nate's dessert parties.

But this wasn't . . . this wasn't . . .

She squeezed her eyes shut and pressed her cheek against Nate's. The police officer's voice was saying something about clearing the way for the stretcher, and all Annie could think was that someone was hurt. Josh. Yes, that was it. Josh was hurt and he was coming out of the apartment on a stretcher, and the people had to make way because he needed a doctor.

But for every ounce of effort she put into convincing herself of this, the real details screamed at her from all sides. The sound of wheels against concrete came from his front door and she did what she never should've done. She opened her eyes and looked straight at the sound, and that's when she saw it.

A memory flashed in her mind, of her and Nate reading the paper one morning a decade ago, and Nate sharing the story of a family hiking Pikes Peak when their teenage son slipped off the path and tumbled to his death. Paramedics were summoned, but they could do nothing to help, and the boy's parents and sisters were forced to watch while his body was retrieved and carried away.

"What a horrible thing," Annie had told Nate. "No mother should have to watch her son's dead body being taken away. I'm not sure I could bear it."

And now she was that mother.

With the two men from the coroner's office at either end, the stretcher came into view. The body was covered with a white sheet, and Annie knew without a doubt that the form on the stretcher was Josh. First, the feet nearly hung off the stretcher, the way Josh's feet could sometimes hang over the edge when he came for a visit and he stretched out on the living room sofa.

And second, because the sheet was part of a set Annie and Nate had given Josh last Christmas. White with a thin brown stripe near the top.

"Josh!" Her voice could barely be heard. "God, help him. . . . Please help him." She gripped Nate's arm tighter. "He can't breathe." She moved to take a step toward him, but Nate held her back.

"Annie, don't. . . . We need to call Lindsay."

Don't? She wanted to scream at them to stop, because Josh could hardly get medical help with a sheet over his face. But then someone was crying, and Annie looked over her shoulder. It was the young woman with Down syndrome. She was covering her eyes and sobbing, and her friend had his arm around her and he was saying, "Josh is in heaven now, Daisy. Heaven's a good place, remember?"

The reality hit her full force.

The phone call . . . the police officer . . . the coroner's van . . . the quietly grieving neighbors. All of it provided a truth that she could no longer deny. This wasn't a dinner party for Josh's neighbors, and no, her son wasn't sick or asleep or struggling to breathe beneath the Christmas bedsheets.

He was dead. Her baby was dead, and she hadn't had

the chance to tell him good-bye. She remembered something Josh had told her after his accident, how he was glad he hadn't died that night because he would have been without family.

"Whatever happens to me, I don't want to die alone," he'd told her. "There's nothing more awful than that."

But that's just what had happened. Her only son had died without any family at his side. "Josh . . . no! Not Josh, God . . . please. . . ." Annie started to cry again, and her cry became a wail. Her Josh was gone, and she would never draw another breath without feeling his loss, brushing against her ribs and hurting her insides like a permanent injury. The suffocating avalanche of pain shut out any glimmer of light, and beneath the weight of it, Annie closed her eyes and felt herself begin to fall.

Nate caught her. It had to be Nate. But she couldn't stop the dizzy swirling in her brain or the way her arms and legs and even her hands hurt from the loss. Josh was leaving and she couldn't will herself to stand up and go to him, to tell him a proper good-bye. Black spots mixed with the blurred images in her mind, and around her the sounds began to dim. *Josh . . . not Josh, God.*

She was fainting, and she couldn't stop herself no matter how badly she wanted to move, to take the walk from where she was standing to wherever Josh was. But he wasn't here at all, because he was in heaven. She couldn't breathe right, couldn't open her eyes. She had just witnessed two men wheel her son's dead body out of his apartment and toward a coroner's van. Nate was holding her, but she was falling harder, losing control. The last thing she remembered was the terrifying truth that Josh was dead, and the certainty that she would be next. She'd been right that day when Nate read her the article about the family on Pikes Peak. This was a pain she could never, ever bear.

Even if God Himself held her up.

ELEVEN

Thomas Flynn hung up the phone, pushed his chair back from his mahogany desk, and paced slowly to the oversize window in his office on the twenty-third floor of the Markham Professional Building. He stared out at downtown Denver and let the futility of the situation wash over him. Josh Warren was dead.

The message was waiting for him when he came in this morning. An urgent call from Josh's mother, Annie Warren. Somehow Thomas knew even before he placed the call that something was very wrong. Josh hadn't been himself at the deposition. His skin had paled to a sickly shade of gray and he shook from the pain. At the time, Thomas thought his client's appearance could actually be good for the case. Anyone in the room could see the damage the accident had caused him, because he wore it like a second set of skin, tight around his body without the possibility of ever taking it off.

He'd told Josh the truth—they were close to a settlement. A month, maybe two. Three at the absolute most. The judge was tired of the defense's attorneys, a trio of three overpaid suits who apparently made billing the insurance company something of a sport.

There were requests for delays due to scheduling conflicts and corporate meetings and the attorneys' inability to gather proper evidence. More delay requests came with the revelation of even the slightest new detail in the case—usually provided by Josh during a deposition. The idea that his doctor had asked him to lose weight before he could have back surgery, for instance. Something like that single detail could send the defense into a tailspin after which it would take four weeks to right itself.

The judge knew how the game was played. Deny a motion and the case could get thrown out on appeal. So he'd been patient, narrowing the window of extension as much as possible. If the defense asked for six weeks to examine and prepare for a response to some new detail, the judge would generally grant them three.

But the game was winding to a close—all parties could feel it, and Thomas had been through enough of these to know the signs. Already the defense had agreed that there was liability on the part of its client, the insurance company. The admission meant the judge would decide the settlement amount, which was far better for the defense than the alternative. No culpable deep-pocket client wanted a jury trial. Not when its insured was a drunk driver who hit a guy in the act of being a hero.

The determination that there would be no jury was, in theory, intended to make the process simpler. For that reason, the defense could only push the process so far without making a mockery of it and angering the judge. And the defense definitely didn't want an angry judge when it came time to determine the settlement amount.

Even so, on this Monday morning Thomas had expected

to find a copy of yet another motion on his desk. After all, Josh had revealed something fairly dramatic in Friday's deposition.

Josh had an heir, a daughter.

He raised his right arm over his head and leaned it against the cool glass window. Annie Warren didn't know how her son had died, just that he'd gone to sleep Friday night and never woken up. Some of his colleagues could hear this sort of news about one of their clients and be laughing over coffee and doughnuts in the break room ten minutes later.

Not Thomas.

Josh mattered to him, same as every client he ever represented. He handled personal injury cases because he enjoyed breaking stereotypes. Not all attorneys who looked for victim settlements were ambulance chasers. Some, like him, took on clients who really had been hurt by the misdeeds of someone else. Thomas liked to think of himself as a modern-day Robin Hood of sorts, taking money from the rich and guilty and putting it in the hands of the poor and damaged.

But now that would never happen for Josh, and Thomas asked his secretary to hold all calls. He would need a day to regroup, to figure out what to do next in Josh's case. Thomas squinted against the glare of the late September morning. If he'd known something was this wrong with Josh, he would have driven home with him or taken him to a hospital.

What happened to him, God? Josh's weight was down, and mentally he seemed more able to handle the deposition than on past trips to Denver. So how did he die in his sleep? Thomas turned and leaned against the windowsill. As he did, his eyes fell on a small plaque that stood on his desk. His wife had given it to him because it contained one of his favorite Bible verses.

In all things God works for the good of those who love him, who have been called according to his purpose. Romans 8:28.

He read the words three times over, but still he wasn't sure. All things? He had loved God all his life, and Josh had come into a stronger faith in the last month or so. But how could his death now work to the good for anyone? Especially Josh's parents. Thomas sighed and the action slumped his shoulders some.

He returned to his desk and stared at the documents spread out before him. Josh's deposition from Friday's hearing. The page that troubled him in light of the news was toward the end, the place where Josh was asked whether he had an heir. The question wasn't a surprise to Thomas, of course. He had prepped his client that the topic was bound to come up the way it always did in a settlement case.

"You don't know the girl, and you can't be sure she's your daughter," Thomas had advised Josh every time the subject arose. "If they ask you about having an heir, I'm suggesting you tell them the truth—that as far as you know, you have none."

"But that isn't the truth." Josh had always seemed genuinely baffled by the recommendation. "I *have* a daughter, and most likely she lives somewhere in New York City."

"Just because you sleep with a woman and she has a baby doesn't make the baby yours." Thomas never wanted to sound cruel, only factual. "The woman wasn't trust-worthy. She was married and she was looking for an affair. Now, because there's a child involved, it's become an emo-tional issue for you. Take your feelings out of it and see the situation for what it is."

The reason Thomas was concerned, and he'd ex-plained this to Josh, was because of his parents. Josh owed them just over twenty-five thousand dollars, and since the accident they had taken responsibility for him, sometimes driving him to appointments when he was in too much pain to move, following up with Thomas after a hearing or decision by the judge on one or another motion by the defense, and being his sole emotional sup-port system.

If by some terrible series of events Josh were to die be-fore the settlement came through, his parents deserved the money. Thomas even spelled that out for Josh, but he was still adamant. "If one of their attorneys asks me on the witness stand if I have a daughter, I'll tell them what Maria Cameron told me. Savannah is mine. That's what I believe, and so that's the only truth I can give."

Thomas read over that part of Josh's deposition again and the beginning of a headache started near his temples. He had no choice but to find the woman, to let her know about Josh's death and the pending settlement. If the search panned out, and if Savannah really did belong to Josh, then his parents would be repaid everything he owed them but not a penny more. The rest of what could be a two-million-dollar settlement would go to Savannah, by way of her mother.

Thomas pictured his client, the sincerity in his eyes.

Kind, loyal Josh. For him, giving an answer in favor of Savannah was never about losing his settlement money to the girl's mother. Rather his testimony was a public validation of his love for the child, his determination to find her one day and share custody of her. In Josh's mind, he was Savannah's father. Period. He would do anything for her.

But what about Annie and Nate Warren?

The scenario raised the temperature in the room and made Thomas anxious to find out the truth. He stared at the deposition and shook his head slowly. The odds of Josh being the girl's father had to be slim. A woman like Maria Cameron could have slept with ten men that week and her husband, too. She wanted money, nothing more. That's why she'd called Josh looking for child support when the baby was a few months old. But she'd given up too easily, in Thomas's opinion. If Josh were really the girl's father, Maria would have checked in at least once a year to see if Josh had come into a better financial picture.

Thomas turned his chair so he was facing his computer. Josh's parents didn't know about this twist in the case yet, but eventually Thomas would have to tell them. Especially if somehow Josh's suspicions turned out to be true. Thomas remembered something Josh had told him about his parents and their opinion of Maria Cameron. "They don't believe I'm Savannah's father." Josh's disappointment had sounded with every word. "They'd like to forget I ever went to Las Vegas."

Thomas felt the same way. He signed in to an online service his law firm subscribed to, one that allowed access to information that could help locate a person of interest. In the search line he typed Maria Cameron, and for city and state he entered New York, NY. In almost no time the search turned up six women by that name. But the one that interested him was several years older than Josh, with a criminal record.

He double clicked that entry and a host of information appeared. Thomas scrolled through it slowly. The photo was taken during a booking for prostitution, and it showed a woman who might have been attractive at one time. Strawberry-blond overprocessed hair, pronounced cheekbones, and sunken eyes.

According to the file, she'd been arrested six times over the last several years for charges ranging from drugs to bad-check writing and sex for sale. He pulled up the most recent report, from over a year ago. At the bottom it showed the details of the woman's arrest.

```
Suspect is female Caucasian, age 38. She
was booked for suspicion of offering
sex for sale, and at the time of
arrest it was discovered that she had
a minor child with her, a six-year-old
daughter. Suspect was brought to the
precinct, booked and fingerprinted, and
held overnight pending formal charges.
Minor female child was turned over to
suspect's roommate, Freddy B. Johnson.
```

Below that the document listed Johnson's address and phone number—the only phone number the suspect gave, according to another paragraph written by the arresting officer. Thomas jotted down the number and did a quick check on the other five women named Maria Cameron. Each of them was married and without any sort of police record. Thomas had a strong hunch he'd found the right Maria Cameron with his first guess.

With everything in him he wanted to rip up the piece of paper with Freddy Johnson's phone number and explain that he'd tried to find the so-called heir of Josh Warren, with no luck. But all his life God had dictated his decisions, and that was especially true in his law practice. Josh claimed to have an heir, and it was the responsibility of Thomas and his staff to see that the claim was checked out, one way or another. Even if the news would be crushing to Josh's parents.

He picked up the receiver, dialed the number, and leaned on his elbows. After four rings an answering machine picked up. "Leave a message at the beep," was all the gruff voice said. The beep came quickly and Thomas hesitated. "Uh . . . This is Thomas Flynn, attorney for Josh Warren. I'm looking for a Maria Cameron and need her to call me back. Her daughter may be the sole heir and recipient of a settlement from a pending lawsuit." He rattled off his office and cell numbers twice, and then hung up. He'd done what he needed to do.

Now he could only pray that what happened next would fall in line with the Scripture on his desk, and that all things really would work out to the good of those who loved God.

Especially for the grieving parents of Josh Warren.

TWELVE

It was a perfect day for a wedding, a beautiful fall Saturday bathed in cool blue sunshine and framed in green leaves with a hint of orange and yellow. That was the only thing Annie could think as she slipped into her dress and applied a second coat of mascara. Thoughts like that helped her stay sane, made it possible for her to get through the day without breaking down and never getting up again.

She repositioned a few loose strands of hair and lifted her gaze to the bathroom window and the blue skies far beyond. Back when Josh and Becky were serious, they had sometimes talked about wanting an early fall wedding. Annie could hear her son now, the timbre of his voice, the sparkle in his eyes when Becky was near.

"October," they used to say. "That's the perfect time for a wedding."

Annie had to agree. The dry heat was behind them and snow was still a month or more away. Resorts and cruises gave great deals in October and beaches were warm and empty, with schoolkids back in class. Annie spritzed hair spray on her long bangs. Becky Wheaton had arrived yesterday, still single and lovely, and she was staying in their downstairs guest room. Family had flown in from Maine and San Diego and Atlanta, and everyone was meeting at the church in an hour. Only this wasn't the wedding Josh had looked forward to.

It was his funeral.

Annie had survived the last week on God's strength alone, she had no doubt. But she did her part by keeping busy. Josh was her baby, her only son. She wasn't going to tell him good-bye without creating a movie of his life and a printed program that people could take home to remember him by. The program was first, and Annie got it off to the printer on Tuesday. The movie took longer.

Annie used the iMovie program on her Mac and mixed short video clips of Josh's life with still photos and occasional titles or bits of text until she had a seamless production nearly an hour long. Then she dubbed in music where it applied, using songs that spoke of a life gone too soon and the sadness of saying good-bye.

Late last night, Annie and Nate had previewed the movie through teary eyes and Annie found herself thinking of Babette and the others who had the nerve to look down on Josh. Whatever his situation at the time of his death, the movie had enough highlights to leave a stunning, poignant picture of Josh's life. His blue medal in the fifth-grade all-area track meet, the trophy for his Pinewood Derby car the year he was a Boy Scout, the time he emceed the talent show for the eighth-grade graduation party.

One memory after another combined to tell a story other people might've forgotten: that Josh had been a success at one time. Never mind the fact that there were only a few photos and no video after he began working as a tow truck driver. This was how Annie wanted to remember him, and it was how she hoped everyone at the funeral today remembered him. The way he was before he lost sight of his dreams.

Nate found her in the bathroom still messing with her hair. "You ready?"

She took a last look at herself in the mirror. Wasn't this how it felt when Lindsay got married, everyone in town for the occasion and the rush of getting ready for a meeting at the church? She swallowed back her tears. "I don't want to do this."

"Me, either." He put his arms around her. "I can't believe he's gone."

It was the sort of thing they'd been saying all week, even as they met with the funeral director and purchased a casket and made plans to bury Josh in a cemetery at the base of his favorite mountain. How could he be gone? What was this crazy chain of events they were caught up in, and why did it still feel like they could pick up the phone and call him or hear a knock at the door and find him standing there, looking for time with his family?

The walk to the car, the trip to the church—all of it passed in a blur. The service was set to start at eleven o'clock, and in the minutes before, Annie looked around and felt pierced with disappointment. The church was barely a quarter full, forty-five, maybe fifty people in attendance. Mostly family and a few of Josh's friends—Becky, Keith and his wife, and a handful of people Annie vaguely recognized from the horrific minutes spent in Josh's parking lot a week ago. Two more were signing the guest book at the back of the church.

Keith was a pallbearer as were Nate and Annie's two nephews, Josh's cousins from Maine. Again there was that uncanny similarity. The flowers marking the front of the church, the candles, the guest book. The dark suits for the pallbearers and the boutonnieres for the lapels of the men's jackets. It was the party Josh always hoped to have one day, with everything but the bride and groom.

Annie glanced over her shoulder again. There should have been more people than this, more lives touched by her only son. Where were the people they entertained? The ones whose kids had gone to school with Josh? Were they too busy to come, or had time created that much of a chasm between their lives and Josh's?

Tears stung Annie's eyes and she leaned closer to Nate. *I loved you, son. Your father and I loved you. Lindsay, too. That's all that matters. And God, You loved him, too, right? You loved Josh?* Annie suppressed a wave of panic, because what if Josh didn't love the Lord? He'd loved Him as a child and even as a high schooler. But lately? Annie wasn't so sure.

She dismissed the picture of Josh missing church and seeming distant from God in recent years. That wasn't the Josh she remembered, and now she had to believe with every breath that he wasn't the Josh God remembered, either. *Please, God. . . . Remember him the way he was. No one can snatch Your people from Your hand, right? Let that be true for Josh, please. . . .*

Her eyes fell on the casket at the front of the church. It was covered with a spray of red carnations and next to it, propped up on an easel, was a framed photo of Josh in hiking shorts and a white T-shirt, a picture taken by Lindsay when the two of them climbed lower Pikes Peak a year before the accident.

The sound of quiet sobbing came from Lindsay, who was sitting on Annie's other side. Lindsay had her head on her husband's shoulder, and next to him, Ben and Bella sat quietly, with their eyes downcast. Lindsay tried to talk to her a few times this past week, something about a music video and Wynonna Judd, but the distraction of phone calls and the movie Annie had been making and the details of the service always stopped them from finishing the conversation.

Annie made a point to get the details later. For now she could only stare at her daughter. Her brother had been her best friend all her life. She would never be the same without him.

Music started, the haunting refrains of a pipe organ playing "Great Is Thy Faithfulness," and Annie tried to believe it. With everything inside her, she tried. But all she could think was if God was faithful, if there was no shadow of turning with Him, then how come Josh was in the wooden box and not in the pew with the rest of the family?

She closed her eyes and tried to imagine new mercies every morning, when every day for the rest of her life she would wake up and experience the same realization. Her only son was dead. *God . . . I can't do this. I can't live without him. Please, take me home so I can hug him one more time.*

The service was over quickly. A pastor from the college ministry shared a brief message because he was the last person Josh ever connected with at the church, back when it looked like he might finish college and become an educator and go the path of his parents.

"It's never easy when someone leaves us in the prime of their life," the pastor was saying. "At times like this we must lean on God more than ever before."

Annie leaned harder into Nate. She couldn't remember the pastor's name. Aaron or Andy . . . She opened the program and scanned the list of names at the front. The survived-by list and the pallbearers and there it was, Pastor Allen Reynolds. Of course. Pastor Allen had met with Josh several times the fall after he graduated from high school, trying to convince him to give higher education a chance and get more involved with the college group. But even during his two years of junior college, Josh had followed through on very little of what Pastor Allen suggested.

"God's ways are not our own." The pastor hesitated as he looked out over the congregation. "If they were, then what sort of God would we be serving?"

Annie blinked and two tears slid down her cheeks. *Good question,* she told herself. *What sort of God would take my only son before his life even had a chance to begin?* And why hadn't things worked out with Becky? The girl had spent all of high school in love with Josh, and the two of them talked about going to college together. So why didn't they? How come, like everything else about Josh's life, those plans had fallen apart?

One of her brothers read a section of Scripture from 1 Corinthians, but Annie wasn't really listening. She locked eyes on the casket and all she could think was that her baby was trapped inside that box. The newborn she had held in her arms in the hospital twenty-eight years ago, the one who at three months old smiled at her and captured her heart all in the same breath. The boy who toddled across the room in his daddy's shoes and who caught her a toad for her birthday the year he was four.

The child she had adored and dreamed about and planned a future for was in the casket and he wasn't ever coming out. Her body made a sudden move to stand, to cross the front of the church and close the distance between her and the wooden box. She might not be able to open it, but she could at least put her hand on it so Josh would know she was close by. But even as her legs tightened and she tried to stand, she ordered herself to stay seated. Pastor Allen was still talking. People didn't stand up in the middle of a funeral service, even if their only boy was trapped in a casket ten yards away.

After the Scripture reading there was another song. Finally, the pastor explained that people were welcome to follow the hearse to the cemetery and then back to the Warren house. His voice and the voices around her as the pastor dismissed the congregation sounded distant and small, like someone had turned down the volume on a distorted pair of speakers.

Somehow, she and Nate found their way back to the car, and Lindsay hugged her before she climbed inside. "It isn't fair." Lindsay was still crying just as hard as earlier. "I miss him so much."

Annie could hear the music coming from the church, another round of "Great Is Thy Faithfulness." She blocked it out and kissed her daughter on her cheek. "I miss him, too."

Nate hugged Lindsay. Then, they got into their separate cars and lined up behind the hearse. Again Annie was struck by the strangest, saddest thought. Since Josh stopped running track his junior year of high school, he hadn't been first at anything he did. Someone was always a little faster, a little stronger, a little more equipped for the right job or right break or right opportunity. But not here. Here he was in first place once again, the hearse leading the way in a procession that would cross town and end up at the cemetery.

When they arrived, Nate said a few words to the family and friends who followed them there. "We grieve the loss of our youngest child, our son, Josh. But we know we will see him again in heaven." The sincerity in Nate's expression was matched only by that in his voice. "Thank you for coming. We hope you'll come to the house when we're finished here."

There was little conversation as people quietly paid their respects and then made their way back to their cars parked along the private road that ran through the center of the cemetery. Becky was one of the last to leave. She walked up to the casket and touched her fingers to the wood. For what seemed like a long time, she stood there, her eyes closed, cheeks wet from her tears.

Maybe if you had stayed with him, Annie thought. . . . But she couldn't harbor bad feelings, not toward the girl who had been the love of her son's life. Instead, all she felt was a great ocean of loss and sorrow. Because if they'd stayed together, this day could've been so very different.

After Becky left for their house, a finality settled over the moment because they were alone—just Annie, Nate, Lindsay, and her family. One at a time they took a few moments beside Josh's casket, until it was Annie's turn. She barely moved her feet through the fresh-cut grass until she

was at his side. There she was struck by a sudden and profound thought. So many times when Josh was growing up,
he'd brought her flowers. Her son was quick with a hug or
a kind word, but often when he wanted to show his love
he'd give her flowers. She could see him running through
the door during the spring of his fourth-grade year, a handful of dandelions clutched in his fist. "Here, Mom. I picked
these for you."

And she could remember holding them and smelling
them and smiling at him and thinking, *I hope no one ever
tells him they're weeds.*

There were flowers for her birthday each year and on
the last few Mother's Days, a wild bouquet picked from a
field not far from his apartment. She stared at the spray of
carnations on top of the casket. Carefully, she eased three
from the display and brought them close to her nose. They
smelled of late summer and sweet sunshine, and Annie
thought about where she'd dry them and how she'd save
them forever.

Because these were the last flowers she would ever get
from him.

❧

Only twenty people showed up back at the house for
the late lunch spread Annie put together. The conversation was peppered with happy stories from Josh's childhood and wistful projections of what might have been if
he hadn't had the accident. Becky stayed until the end, not
saying much and keeping to herself. Before she left, she
pulled Annie aside and hugged her, really held on to her.

"I never stopped loving him." She whispered the words in a voice thick with tears. After another quick hug she was gone.

Annie still wasn't clear about what happened to end things between Josh and Becky years ago, but this wasn't the time to talk about it. Besides, it was too late to matter now. Josh had missed out on a life with Becky, and he'd missed out on the settlement he so badly deserved. He'd missed out on being a dad and having the life he dreamed about. His entire life seemed like one big missed opportunity.

When the last guest left, and after Nate turned in for the night, Annie went outside on the front porch and stared through the evergreen tops to the distant stars. Josh's funeral service had been like his life—small and insignificant. Just as well that Babette stayed away. The service would've given her one more way she could compare Josh with her son and find Josh lacking.

A breeze blew against Annie's brow and she thought of one more sad detail. The daughter Josh talked about, the one he was sure was his own, was also not at the funeral. She wasn't his daughter, definitely not. But still, something hurt deep inside her because the girl he'd thought about and prayed for and longed for didn't know he had died. But there was something even sadder than that. Whoever she belonged to, the girl hadn't only missed Josh's death.

She'd missed his life.

THIRTEEN

Freddy had saved the message for her, and by Sunday morning Maria had listened to it four times. Each time, the lawyer's words held a deeper reservoir of hope and potential. A settlement? From a big-time lawyer? So, maybe she *had* picked the right guy that night in Las Vegas. Josh hadn't been worth anything last time they'd talked, but he must have come into some kind of fortune, because now there was a settlement at stake.

And her Savannah was the guy's only heir. What kind of great luck was that?

The thought made her giddy with possibility. She had Savannah dress in her best jeans and T-shirt, the one with the flowers on it, and she took her downtown on the subway to Central Park. But this time Maria had no intention of begging money off people. Today was the turnaround Maria had been waiting for. They would walk the path through the park and talk about mother-daughter things, the way they always should have. And Maria would dream about all the ways she could spend the money.

Strange about the timing. On Friday night Maria had placed an anonymous call to Child Protective Services asking whether it was possible to turn a kid in if you couldn't handle raising her any longer. She wouldn't give her name, but the lady she talked to said it was definitely possible. First, they'd give the overwhelmed parent a class on child rearing and then they required the parent to take several counseling sessions and blah-blah-blah. But the bottom line was yes, CPS would take her. Maria was seriously thinking about taking Savannah this week and dropping her off for good.

Freddy was tired of sleeping with her, and a couple opportunities had come up with a pimp in the financial district. High rollers with big money and no one to spend it on. She could see herself in a penthouse suite, the kept woman of some bank manager or investment millionaire. But not with Savannah in tow, definitely not.

Late Friday she'd even told Savannah her plans. "My days as your mama might be just about over." She'd talked real nice, giving Savannah her most kind smile. "I care about you too much to let you live like this any longer. Plus, some big opportunities are showing up for your mama." Maria had drunk nearly a bottle of Freddy's burgundy wine, so she probably said more than she should've. "You understand, right?"

Savannah shook her head. "No, Mama. I don't wanna leave you."

But the girl had to know that her life was about to change. "Don't worry, Savannah. There's someone out there who wants you a whole lot more than me. Someone better for you."

"My daddy, you mean?"

Maria had only laughed. "Yeah, sure, baby. Maybe it'll

be your daddy." What mattered wasn't who took Savannah in, but that Maria could finally be free of her. At least that's how she felt Friday and Saturday. But all that changed the minute Maria listened to the message from the lawyer.

"Today's a celebration," she told Savannah when they stepped off the subway. She reached for her daughter's hand and realized how good it felt to connect with her this way. "Mama's ship has finally come in."

"What ship?" Savannah seemed confused, like she didn't know what to make of her mother's new attitude.

"The ship of good fortune."

"Is it in the harbor?"

"No." Maria laughed and she felt like other mothers for the first time, the ones she saw near the zoo and the playground and the fountain. The ones who were always walking and talking and laughing with their daughters. She smiled at Savannah. "This ship used to belong to your daddy, but now—now it belongs to me."

"To you?"

Maria suddenly worried about that answer. What if the attorney arranged a talk with Savannah and heard that Maria thought the money was her own? She cleared her throat and slowed her pace. "Actually, the ship belongs to—to both of us." She found her smile again. "Isn't that wonderful?"

Savannah shrugged one shoulder, but her eyes looked happier than they had in a long time. Maria could've burst into song. She still had a little money from her time with the high roller in Central Park, the one with the gold chains. At the hot dog cart, she pulled a ten from her pocket, bought chili dogs and pop for both of them, and together they sat on the nearest empty bench.

Maria savored every bite of her dinner and breathed in deep the air of change around her. She had been looking forward to the next chapter in her life, finishing her role as a mother and moving into the world of people with lots of money. But she could get used to this, being a mother without having to sleep with anyone just to survive. If the settlement was large enough, she wouldn't need to work her way into the world of the wealthy.

She was about to become one of them.

On Monday morning, Maria paced, checked her watch, and counted down hours until finally it was nine o'clock on the West Coast. At one minute after nine she placed the call to Thomas Flynn, attorney.

A woman answered on the first ring. "Flynn and Associates, how can I help you?"

Maria felt a little breathless. She stood straighter and leaned against the kitchen wall in Freddy's apartment. "This is Maria Cameron. I'm returning a phone call from Thomas Flynn."

"Just a moment, please."

Her heart beat hard, and she hoped this Flynn guy wouldn't hear it over the phone lines. Savannah was watching something on MTV, and Maria had turned the sound down so she could hear every detail of whatever good had come their way.

There was a click on the line. "Thomas Flynn here."

"Hello." Maria wasn't sure how formal she should be. "Mr. Flynn, my name is Maria Cameron. You left me a message on Friday."

"Yes." There was a pause and something changed in the man's voice. "I called about a client of mine—Josh Warren. Are you familiar with that name?"

"Yes, of course. We were—we were very close." Maria silently congratulated herself on her acting job. Besides, for those few days in Vegas, she and Josh truly were close. She would have moved in with him if he'd been honest about his financial status. She turned up the concern in her tone. "Has—has something happened to him?" Maria was pretty sure about the answer, otherwise there wouldn't be a need to discuss the fact that Savannah was his heir.

"Yes." The attorney let out a breath, as if the news was still difficult for him. "Mr. Warren passed away a week ago."

Maria allowed a soft gasp. "That's terrible. Was it an accident?"

"We aren't sure what happened. He died in his sleep."

"No." She pictured the virile young man who had shared a bed with her some eight years ago. His death truly was a shame. If he'd lived long enough to win the money coming to him, he would've been a great catch. She softened her voice. "That's just awful."

"Yes, well . . ." The attorney sounded disturbed by the fact, and maybe a little suspicious. "The reason I'm calling, Ms. Cameron, is because Mr. Warren was at the end of a major lawsuit when he died." He asked if Maria had a seven-year-old daughter named Savannah, and when Maria assured him that yes, she did, he went on. "His estate stands to receive a major settlement, and, well, he told the court that your daughter was his sole heir."

"That's true, at least as far as I know." Her contrite tone

hid the excitement starting to build within her. "Do you mind if I ask—how much is the settlement for?"

"That hasn't been determined." This time there was no doubt about Mr. Flynn's disgust toward her. "The point is, paternity needs to be determined before we can consider your daughter a rightful heir to Mr. Warren's estate. Would you be willing to subject your daughter to a paternity test?"

From the beginning Maria had known Savannah belonged to Josh. Her husband at the time rarely slept with her, and Maria suspected he was sterile because he'd never managed to get her pregnant. Not that she really wanted kids. She wanted the child support, and she'd figured a child wouldn't be too bad. Better than getting a job, anyway. When Savannah was born, she'd seen Josh in her from the beginning. The girl had his eyes and the shape of his face, and after a few months she was sure. Regardless of what people thought about her, she hadn't slept with more than a few men in the time frame when she'd gotten pregnant, and Savannah looked more like Josh than any of the others. She glanced at her daughter, sitting cross-legged in front of the TV. "Yes, sir, for sure. I don't have medical insurance, but if you set it up, I'll take her wherever you want for a paternity test."

"Very well." The man sounded tired. "I'll take care of the details and get back to you."

"Thank you, Mr. Flynn." She was still sounding the part of the grieving friend. "I'll share the news with Savannah."

"Let's wait. I think we should have test results first."

"Okay." Maria sounded hurt. "But I can assure you with

my whole being that Savannah is Josh Warren's daughter. If you want us to wait for the test to talk about it, I can do that."

"Thank you. I think it's the least we can do."

Maria hung up the phone and for a brief moment she felt sorry for Josh. He'd been a nice guy, a little heavy but good-looking. And in the few days they'd known each other he had fallen hard for her. There was something sad about the fact that he was dead—especially since he really was Savannah's father. But on the other hand . . .

For the first time in her life something good had come her way and she wasn't going to do a single thing to mess it up. Not this time. Once they had the results of the paternity test, she and Savannah would take the money and make the kind of life for themselves Maria had only dreamed about. The thought made her smile as she found a box of macaroni and cheese in Freddy's cupboard.

Poor Josh. He was just like any other guy until now. But once they had the paternity test, she and Savannah would ride this all the way to the bank, and in some ways that would mean Josh's death wasn't in vain.

All of which made Maria feel better about herself than she'd felt in a very long time.

∽

Thomas felt like he needed to take a shower after just five minutes on the phone with the woman. From the tone in her voice and her hurry to find out the amount of the settlement, he could sense that Maria Cameron was just like he'd imagined her to be. She couldn't care less about

Josh Warren—only that by some good twist of fate she'd managed to trick him into fathering her child. If she was right, anyway, and Josh really was the girl's dad.

The paternity test would be the deciding factor, and he would set it up through a clinic in New York City. She had no insurance, so clearly Josh's estate would be footing the bill. He allowed a heavy sigh. With the certainty in the woman's voice, he had no choice but to give Josh's parents a warning.

He dialed Annie's cell phone, and when she answered, he heard the same thing he'd heard each time he'd talked to her since Josh's death: the hollow emptiness of someone whose heart had broken, someone who would never be the same again. "Hello, Thomas. How are you?"

"Hi, Annie. I'm fine." He wished he could tell her he was just checking in with her, and that he had no news on the lawsuit. He wished he could tell her anything but the truth. "There's, uh, there's some new information that's come to light in the court case."

She uttered a sad laugh. "It's been three years. How could there be anything new?"

"It's nothing for sure yet, but I wanted you to know I'm working on the case and I've come across a few speed bumps." His stomach churned with the possibilities. "When I have more information I'll call or come see you."

"Is this about the settlement?" The word "settlement" sounded bitter on her tongue.

"Well . . ." He was still standing at the window, still looking out over downtown Denver and wondering how he could find some good news for the woman. "It's more about Josh's estate, how the settlement will be disbursed."

Thomas hated being evasive, but he had no choice. He had to raise the possibility of a problem, but there was nothing to tell her, not until the paternity test results were in.

"His estate?" Annie was a smart woman. Her voice told him that she suspected the news might not be good, even if she had no idea what the details involved.

"Yes." Thomas stood and paced to his window. How much heartache could the woman take? "I'll tell you when I know more, Annie. I promise."

There was a slight pause on the other end. "Can I tell you something?"

"Of course."

"My husband and I don't care about Josh's money, not in the way some people might care about a large settlement." Her voice sounded strained, like she was on the verge of crying. Each word was deliberate as she continued. "But my son lost his life because of that accident, because that driver drank himself into a stupor and got behind the wheel. Whatever this new information is, whatever's happening with Josh's estate, we're trusting you, Thomas, to see that justice is done." She hesitated. "The same way Josh trusted you."

Her words were like so many weights on his shoulders. "I appreciate that." He tried to imagine how she'd feel if the paternity test came back positive, and he put the possibility out of his mind. "Every day I ask God to give me the wisdom to do what's right by Josh's memory."

"Thank you." She sniffed softly. "Nate and I are doing the same, praying for you. No settlement will bring Josh back, but we have ideas about how to use the money he has coming to him. Charities and family members who can benefit from his legacy. A college fund for Josh's niece and nephew. That sort of thing."

"Right." Thomas swallowed hard. "Good. Well, like I said, I'll be in touch when I know more."

The call ended and Thomas lowered the phone to his side. He didn't know Maria Cameron but he could picture her, a single mom raising a lonely girl in New York City. What sort of married woman would go to Vegas alone and trap a man into sleeping with her? That's what she'd done, no question. He lifted his eyes to the hazy sky. He'd heard it said that when the haze didn't quite burn off over the city there was always sunshine just beyond the clouds.

But today he had to wonder.

Dear God . . . You know all things and I believe in You even when life doesn't make sense. But just know I'm struggling with this one. If the paternity test comes back positive, then everyone loses—even the little girl. She'll never see any of the money if her mother gets her hands on it. His head hurt again and he willed himself to trust. *If all things really work to the good of those who love You, then please work in this situation and let the right thing happen for Josh's family. Please.* As he finished the prayer, he didn't hear an answer or sense a Bible verse come to mind. But he had the undeniable assurance that he'd been heard by God Almighty—whatever lay ahead.

For now, that would have to be enough.

FOURTEEN

Lindsay was on her way to Josh's apartment and she couldn't shake the sick feeling surrounding her. She'd been in a fog since getting the news about her brother. Every hour of each day since his death, she'd walked through life like she was in some sort of trance, doing the next thing, breathing in and out and in again, but not sure whether she could make it through another day.

Her husband was being wonderful, taking care of the kids and giving her time to plan Josh's funeral with her parents. Now, this week, it was time to go through her brother's apartment and box up his things. Even the idea of such an action felt ludicrous. Her brother's life reduced to a few boxes of personal items?

Lindsay pulled into the apartment parking lot and took the spot closest to his front door. Her mother had given her one of the keys, and the apartment manager had told them to take the rest of the month to go through Josh's things. He'd already paid rent through the end of October. Lindsay wore jeans and a sweatshirt, and from the back of her Highlander she took out a stack of boxes and a dozen black Hefty bags.

She had no idea what she was about to encounter, but she had a feeling that over the next few weeks, they would learn more about Josh than they'd known before. The walk up to his front door felt strange, as though she were violating his privacy. Yes, she'd been here before—even recently—but to come here this way without him here . . . the whole trip made her uncomfortable.

Once she was inside, she was overcome by a rush of emotion. His cologne still filled the room, and there by the front door were his dress shoes, the ones he'd probably worn to Denver for his deposition. She had the saddest urge to call out to him, just in case everyone was wrong and he was still here, still sleeping off the effects of the pain medication.

Her mom was meeting her here, and Lindsay hoped she'd be here soon. This wasn't a job Lindsay wanted to do by herself. She picked up her brother's shoes and brushed off a light layer of dust before setting them back down. His kitchen was neat, the way he'd left it, and his mantel still held the three photos—the family shot, the one of the little girl who might or might not have been his daughter, and the other of the two teenagers. A heavy coat of pain fell across her shoulders as she stepped closer to that third photograph. She had asked Josh about it last time she was here, but he hadn't gone into detail. Something about how the photo gave him a reason to believe that good could come from driving a tow truck.

Lindsay had told herself she'd get more details about the story later, when she wasn't in such a hurry. Only now that conversation would never take place. She gripped the mantel and hung her head. *Lord . . . I want to know why these girls mattered to my brother. Please help me find the reason.*

I am with you, My daughter.

The response whispered to the hurting places inside her, and Lindsay took them as a promise. Somehow she would know the story of the girls. She moved across the room to Josh's computer desk. Two oversize file drawers made up the right side of the place where the chair sat. Lindsay took the chair and opened the top drawer.

At first, the files showed little promise of being anything more than old utility bills and auto loan statements. One file showed Josh's bank records, and Lindsay pulled them out and studied them, feeling guilty. She still hadn't deposited the six-hundred-dollar check from him. Even then, what the statements showed stunned her—Josh was living on barely any money at all, averaging a balance sometimes less than a couple hundred dollars through an entire month. All this time she thought he'd been bringing home his same salary through workmen's comp, but apparently not. The amount going into his account every month was less than a thousand dollars. He had a balance of just over seven hundred now—barely enough to cover the check he'd written her.

No wonder he'd borrowed money from their parents once in a while.

She returned the bank records to the file, and there at the back of the drawer was a thick envelope marked with a single word: Accident. Lindsay picked it up and pulled it onto her lap. The details inside this envelope told about the event that changed everything for Josh. The event that killed him. Her eyes blurred with tears as she opened the envelope.

Inside was a set of letters paper-clipped together that looked like his initial correspondence with Thomas Flynn, his attorney. Beyond that were notices of hearings and details of his lawsuit against the drunk driver's insurance company. At the back of the envelope was a clipped-together file of letters and a newspaper article.

She carefully slid the bundle free from the envelope and studied the last page of a three-page letter. It was handwritten to Josh by a woman named Karla Fields. Before stopping to read the letter, Lindsay thumbed through the next letter and saw that it was from a man named Bill Sedwick. The newspaper article was at the back of the stack. Lindsay carefully pulled it free from the others and set it on top.

It was printed from an online newspaper, and Lindsay felt her pulse quicken as she stared at the photos that anchored the article. One was of her brother, a head shot, probably the one on his work badge. But what caught her attention was the other photo. It was a staff photo taken at what appeared to be the scene of Josh's accident.

The faces in the picture were the same as those in the photograph on Josh's mantel.

Lindsay knit her brow and read the headline above the story. *Tow Truck Driver Hailed as Local Hero.* Her hands began to tremble. Local hero? What was this, and why hadn't she and their parents ever seen the article? She began reading.

```
A local tow truck driver pulled two
teenage girls out of the path of a
drunk driver Saturday night, flinging
```

himself in harm's way and taking the
hit instead, according to police.
Josh Warren, 25, was giving the girls
directions when he saw the drunk driver
careen out of control and head straight
for them.

The article named the drunk driver, and the fact that he'd been convicted three previous times for driving under the influence.

"No question that the quick-thinking
brave actions of Mr. Warren saved the
lives of those two girls," one officer
at the scene reported. "Josh Warren is a
hero by every definition of the word."
 The girls, Sarah Fields and Susie
Sedwick, both seventeen, were unharmed
in the incident, but Warren was unable
to get completely out of the path of
the vehicle. The blow knocked him to
the ground and caused severe damage to
his back and neck. He remains in the
hospital in serious condition.

Lindsay stared at the words and tried to imagine again why her brother hadn't told them these details. They knew he'd been hit by a drunk driver, but not that he'd saved the lives of two girls in the process. Why in the world would he keep a thing like that from them? The story hadn't made the Springs newspaper, and so without hearing about it from Josh, there had been no way any of them might have found out.

She found her place and kept reading.

```
Witnesses at the scene said that the
driver was slumped completely over the
wheel when his car veered off course
and hit Warren. Police at the scene
determined that the driver's blood
alcohol level was nearly three times the
legal limit. Charges are pending against
the driver, who could stand to serve up
to five years in prison because of his
previous convictions.
```

Lindsay blinked and studied the photos once more. So that explained the picture on his fireplace mantel. He'd lost his health, his mobility, his career, and his ability to earn a living, but two girls were alive and well because of his actions. The drunk driver had been sentenced to four years, but Thomas Flynn thought he could be out anytime. No wonder the picture of the girls was a reminder. Lindsay could imagine that even on the most painful days, the photo gave Josh a reason to feel good about himself, about his actions.

Tears fell down the bridge of her nose onto the article and she set it on Josh's computer desk so it wouldn't get any wetter. The clipping was the first thing she was going to show her mother. She picked up the letter from Karla Fields. It was long and drawn out, but Lindsay read every word.

She wouldn't be alive today if it weren't for you, the woman wrote. *I pray God blesses you mightily for your sacrifice. I will continue to thank Him for your act of service all the days of my life.*

The letter from the other girl's father was very similar. One paragraph read, *In our culture of self-serving, self-seeking young people, you give me reason to hope for our future. I've enclosed a photograph of the girls so you'll always remember what your act of heroism meant to all of us. Thank you will never be enough.*

Lindsay cried through the reading of both letters, touched to the core and yet not surprised that her brother would do such a thing. Hadn't he looked out for her through high school and the years afterward, even though she was older? He was always putting more care into the lives of the people around him than worrying about himself.

Of course he kept the girls' photo on his mantel.

She sat back in his computer chair and remembered a few conversations she'd had with her brother—especially the year after he started working as a tow truck driver.

"Mom and Dad aren't happy about it," he'd told her once when they met in Denver for dinner. "They want me to finish college and teach somewhere."

Lindsay had wanted to stick up for him, help him so he didn't walk away from the conversation feeling lesser because of his job. "They think you're going through a phase. You'll get back to school eventually."

"What if I don't?"

"Then they'll live with it." Lindsay covered his hand with hers. "Besides, you look great in a tow truck."

But the conversation came up a number of times, and always Josh couldn't be convinced that his parents were proud of his work towing cars, even for one of Denver's official police garages. His concern for what they thought only grew after the accident. Not only had the job failed to become something lucrative or successful, it had cost him his health.

Something else he'd said came back to her. It was after the accident, maybe six months or so. "After the settlement comes through I'll open my own business, something Mom and Dad can get behind."

Lindsay always felt sorry for him when the topic of his job came up, so she agreed with him, even tried to get excited for him. But it hurt her that Josh lived in the shadow of his parents' silent disapproval. Now the reason he hadn't shared about rescuing the girls seemed obvious. The act of pulling the girls from the path of the drunk driver wouldn't be enough to gain their respect for his job. That would have to wait until he found another line of work—at least by Josh's estimation.

The possibility that Josh was too embarrassed to tell his family about his rescue brought with it a fresh wave of tears. Her poor brother, suffering every day with his back pain and not feeling good enough about his heroism to share the details. Before she could look at the bottom file drawer, her mom walked in. She held on to the door frame and looked like she was being hit by a wave of the same emotions that had hit Lindsay half an hour ago.

"It's wrong, being here without him." Lindsay stacked the article and the two letters together and held them on her lap.

"I had the strangest thought that if I walked into his apartment he'd still be here." Her mother came in and took the seat closest to the computer. "Like it wasn't possible to be here without him."

"Exactly." Lindsay was about to hand her the information about Josh's rescue when there was a strong knock at the door. Lindsay set the stack of documents on the desk and answered it. Standing on the front step were Josh's neighbors, the couple with Down syndrome.

"Hi." The young man pushed his glasses up on the bridge of his nose. He had a plastic bowl of eggs and he held them out to Lindsay. "I saw your car." He leaned in and looked at Lindsay's mother. "Yours, too." He did a half bow. "I'm Carl Joseph. This is Daisy."

"Hello." Lindsay took a step back and welcomed the pair into the apartment. "You knew Josh?"

"He was our very best neighbor." Carl Joseph's eyes teared up.

Lindsay could see that her mother wasn't sure what to say, so she took the lead. "Carl Joseph . . . Daisy . . . I'm Lindsay, Josh's sister."

"Yes." Daisy had a bright orange beach bag over one arm. She looped the other through Carl Joseph's. "Josh said you were his best friend."

The ache in Lindsay's heart doubled. "He was my best friend, too." She pointed to the plastic container. "You brought some eggs?"

"Josh loaned them to us before"—he looked at Daisy, his chin quivering—"before he died."

"We wanted to be good neighbors, and good neighbors return what they borrow." Daisy took the eggs from Carl Joseph and handed them over. "You're Josh's family, so you can have them."

"Okay." Lindsay wanted to keep from crying, but she

was losing the struggle. She set the eggs on the kitchen counter. "Thank you."

Daisy rocked back and forth on her feet a few times, and she looked at Carl Joseph, then at Lindsay. "You know the story about the little girl?"

"The little girl?"

"On the fireplace." Carl Joseph pointed past them to Josh's living room. "That little girl."

"When we came over here"—Daisy thought for a second—"because good neighbors visit each other"—she nodded at Carl Joseph—"every time, Josh would tell us a story about the two older girls."

"Because he's a hero." Carl Joseph was emphatic about the point.

"And I only know three heroes altogether." Daisy looked at Lindsay's mother. "Your son is one of them."

Lindsay shot a look at her mother and saw her confusion softened by a new tenderness in her expression. Her mom blinked twice. "He was a hero?"

"Because of the two girls and the dangerous story." Admiration filled Daisy's tone.

"Josh only told us the story when we asked." Carl Joseph stepped cautiously past Lindsay and her mother and over to the fireplace. He picked up the photo of the teenage girls. "That was our best Saturday morning story, right, Daisy?"

"Yeah, because of the happy ending."

Lindsay was starting to understand. These two must've come over on occasional Saturday mornings, and when they did, they would ask Josh to tell the story about the two girls—a story Lindsay only found out about a few minutes ago.

"What . . . story did he tell you?" Her mom followed Carl Joseph and stood beside him. Daisy and Lindsay came, too, and filled in the places on his other side.

"It happened on New Year's Eve three years ago." Carl Joseph pushed his glasses higher up on his nose again.

"In Denver." Daisy gave a definitive nod. "Josh was towing cars and two girls had a question. They were two best friends."

"Yeah, they were nice girls and they were trying to find the United States, I think, right, Daisy?" Carl Joseph cocked his head. "I think it was the United States."

"No." Daisy smiled and patted Carl Joseph on the shoulder. "Not the United States. They were trying to find State Street." She looked at Lindsay. "Definitely State Street."

"So it's against the law to drive drunk but that's what the other guy was doing." He thought for a few beats. "And he had his head down, which is not the best way to drive."

"Passed out." Daisy shook her head.

"Yeah, passed out. And Josh pulled the girls out of the way so they were safe."

"And Josh got hit on the shoulder, but he wasn't too hurt and the girls were safe." Daisy's smile was wistful as she remembered these last details. "So there's a happy ending." She raised her eyebrows at Lindsay's mother. "That's one reason why Josh was a hero. Because God used him to make a happy ending."

Lindsay spotted a box of tissues on a nearby table. She gave one to her mom, who was holding the photo now, tears streaming down her face. "Why didn't he tell us?" she whispered. The words were meant for Lindsay, not Josh's neighbors.

But Daisy answered, anyway. "He only told us because we asked."

Lindsay pressed her tissue first to one eye and then the other. These two kind strangers had asked Josh about the picture of the teenage girls, but no one in his family had taken the time to learn about his heroism or the deeper details surrounding the accident. She held the tissue to her nose and closed her eyes. Inside her chest she could literally feel her heart breaking for her kindhearted brother. At the same time, she didn't want Josh's neighbors to feel they'd done something to upset her and her mother. She opened her eyes and managed a teary smile. "Thank you for sharing that story with us."

"I like the happy ending." Daisy seemed a little nervous in light of the sadness in the room. "Right, CJ? It's a happy ending."

"Very happy."

A happy ending? Lindsay stifled a series of sobs that threatened to drop her to the floor. Her brother had saved the lives of two teenage girls, yes, but he had suffered a life-changing injury that eventually killed him.

"See the little girl?" Carl Joseph carefully took hold of one of the other framed photos on Josh's mantel. "Our good neighbor never told us that story."

Daisy wrinkled her nose. "Not a happy ending, that's what Josh said."

"So . . . do you know that story? About the little girl?" Carl Joseph raised curious eyes to Lindsay's mother, and then to Lindsay.

"Josh was right." Lindsay took the photo gently from Carl Joseph. "That story doesn't have a very happy ending."

"I bought her a present." Daisy looked slightly uncertain about her gift. She took the beach bag off her shoulder, rummaged through it, and pulled out a new Minnie Mouse headband. She looked to Carl Joseph for help. "You tell it, CJ."

He looked at the mouse ears and then at Lindsay and her mother and once more he pushed his glasses up on the bridge of his nose. "Me and Daisy went to Disneyland."

"Our favorite place." Daisy smiled.

"And we wore our ears. I had Mickey Mouse and Daisy had Minnie."

Daisy set her beach bag down and held the ears up in front of her face. "With these ears, me and CJ had the happiest day of all."

"A real-life happy ending."

"So, I was at the store and I saw this new pair of Minnie ears." Daisy's shyness wore off as she got caught up in her story. "And I thought if I buy these ears for the little girl in Josh's picture then maybe a happy ending would happen for her, too."

Lindsay kept the tissue pressed to her face. This couple had clearly loved Josh. Everything about him mattered deeply to them. "So . . . you bought the Minnie ears for the little girl in the picture?" Lindsay lightly touched Daisy's arm. "You know who the little girl is, right?"

"No." Carl Joseph's answer was quick. "Because Josh said that story could wait because it doesn't have a happy ending."

But Daisy looked at the picture a little longer and her

eyes filled with a gradual understanding. "Well . . . she looks a lot like our good neighbor."

"Yes." Lindsay sniffed, struggling to speak. "That little girl is Josh's daughter. Her name is Savannah."

"Savannah?" Carl Joseph seemed stunned by the revelation. "He never said she was Savannah."

"That's a pretty name for a pretty girl." Daisy's eyes glistened with tears as she turned her face to Lindsay. "Why didn't she live here with Josh?"

"Yeah, why only a picture?" Carl Joseph put his arm around Daisy. "Because that's why no happy ending if she didn't live here."

Lindsay saw her mother look away from the photo and turn toward the patio door. Her shoulders shook from the quiet sobs washing over her. Lindsay dabbed beneath her eyes again and she cleared her throat. "That's the sad part. Savannah lives somewhere else."

"Oh." Daisy let the Minnie ears fall to her side. But after a moment, she held them out to Lindsay. "Well . . . when you see her I still think she'd like these. Because if she has the Minnie ears she'll have a happy ending, like me and CJ."

Lindsay took the headband and held it to her chest. "Thank you, Daisy. I think she'll like these very much."

"It's not Disneyland." Carl Joseph shrugged. "But it's close."

"Also . . ." Daisy looked at her friend. "We'll pray for Savannah. That she'll come out of the picture and into your arms."

Lindsay stared in awe at the young woman. Out of the picture and into their arms? What a beautiful way to pray for Savannah. She thanked Carl Joseph and Daisy once more and before they left she told them they could stop by any time in the next two weeks while she and her mother were cleaning out Josh's apartment.

"And let us know if you need anything." Lindsay's mother was still crying, but she was more composed than before. "Thank you . . . for being Josh's friends."

Carl Joseph's eyes filled with fresh tears. He crossed his arms firmly in front of his chest and stared at his feet for a few seconds. "Josh—Josh was a hero and a very good neighbor."

Daisy nodded. "We miss him a lot. We tell God all the time, right, CJ?"

"Right." He gave both Lindsay and her mother a quick hug, and Daisy did the same. The two of them left arm in arm, their heads hung, tears on their cheeks.

Lindsay watched them go and she fell into her mother's arms. They stayed that way a long time, holding on to each other so they wouldn't drown in the sea of sorrow churning around them. And they thanked God for the gift of Carl Joseph and Daisy—a couple of handicapped adults who knew more about Josh than his own family did.

All because they'd taken the time to listen.

FIFTEEN

Annie was still reeling from the visit, but she needed answers. She pulled back from her daughter and searched her eyes. "The story about the girls? Is it true?"

"It is." Lindsay walked to Josh's computer desk and picked up a stack of papers. "I found these just before you got here. A newspaper article about the accident, and a couple of letters from the girls' parents." Lindsay's voice was still thick with sorrow. "The story calls him a hero."

"And we never knew?" Annie wrestled with a mix of emotions. She was proud of Josh but her pride was tempered by pangs of anger and hurt. She motioned toward the door. "He told strangers what happened, and he didn't tell us?"

Lindsay's answer was quiet. "They asked." She handed the documents over. "Every Saturday, apparently."

Annie hated the way she felt, like she'd missed some great and marvelous opportunity to connect with her son over something good in his life. And in his last years there had been little good. She looked at the headline spread across a page that included Josh's picture and a photo of the two girls. *Tow Truck Driver Hailed as Local Hero.*

"He knew you didn't like his job." Lindsay didn't sound accusing, just honest. "He probably didn't think it would matter how he was hit that day or why. He was doing his job and it cost him his health. That made the job seem like a mistake, however the accident happened."

Annie sank into the nearest chair, the clipping and the letters still in her hands, and she stared at her son's face in print. *Dear God . . . I need one more chance, just one more chance. Please. . . .* If only she had the last three years to do over again. She would have asked more questions about the accident or come by his apartment and noticed the photograph on his mantel. *Tell me about the girls,* she would have asked him. And—as he'd done for his neighbors—he would tell her how he'd pulled the girls out of harm's way and taken the hit instead.

But none of those closest to him heard about his act of courage.

Annie felt like bits of herself were breaking off and scattering around the room and she couldn't do anything to bring them back together. She'd missed the chance to celebrate Josh within the family and among their friends, to share his act of courage and give him the credit he deserved. *God . . . why am I finding out now, when there's nothing I can do about it?*

Ten more minutes, that's all she wanted. Ten minutes to hug him and look into his eyes and tell him that she knew the truth about the accident, about what he'd done. Ten minutes to tell him she was proud of him and not disappointed, no matter how she'd acted in the past. Just ten minutes.

Lindsay seemed to understand that her mother needed

time to compose herself. She touched her mom's shoulder. "I'm going to finish going through his file cabinet."

Annie nodded, but she didn't look up. And as Lindsay set about the job of sorting through Josh's things, a thought occurred to her. What else didn't she know about her son? He'd been a hero, and she hadn't known that. So what else? Suddenly, she knew how she was going to spend these next two weeks. Not in a fog of sorrow, boxing up what remained of Josh's life. But in a quest to learn all she'd missed along the way.

My Lord . . . how could I have missed the fact that Josh saved the lives of those girls? What sort of mother am I? She squeezed her eyes shut and willed herself to pull the pieces together, to collect herself so she could set about her quest. *Help me find out everything about him, Father. He was my only son. . . . I love him so much, but—but if I didn't really know him, please let me know about him now.* She covered her face with a fresh tissue and let the tears come. *And could You do one more thing? Could You tell him I'm proud of him, God, please.*

"Mom, look at this." Lindsay walked over and handed her a full-page note in Josh's handwriting. "It's dated ten years ago, the summer after Josh graduated from high school."

And with that, her tears slowed and she embraced the task at hand. She took the page and saw it was a photocopy of a letter Josh had written to Becky Wheaton. Annie looked at Lindsay. "Did you read it?"

"I did." She sat back against the edge of the computer desk. "It's heartbreaking."

Annie stood and walked with the letter to Josh's patio

door. Leaning against the cool metal frame, she started at the beginning.

Dear Becky,

It's been two weeks since you broke up with me, and I still don't blame you. I need to get my act together, you're right about that. Last night you called and told me you loved me and that you're praying for me to figure things out. Well, I stayed up all night thinking about what you said, and I've decided to make you a promise.

I, Josh Warren, promise you, my first and forever love, that I will stop smoking cigarettes. I watched my uncle die of lung cancer, and I won't be like that—dead before I'm forty, wasting my life on some terrible addiction. I also promise to stop drinking and get serious about my life. Whatever else happens, I want my college degree. I want to be successful so that one day I can marry you and support you and have a family with you.

Believe me, Becky, you deserve someone successful, and that someone is going to be me. I promise you here and now.

This summer will be hard, because I know you need some space. Maybe I do, too. Space so I can have the time I need to figure out these changes. But the changes will come, you'll see. And one day you and I will have the life we've both dreamed about.

I'll never love anyone like I love you, Becky. Pray for me, that I can be the man you need me to be.

Love forever,

Josh

Annie read the letter over again, racked by the sincerity of Josh's great intentions, the tragedy of all he'd failed to accomplish. He had wanted to stop smoking, but that didn't happen until four years later. The drinking with his buddies continued through that summer and the next. He tried college, but only because he wanted to impress Becky and Annie and Nate. His grades were weak his first year and dismal his second, and by then Becky was seeing someone else. Josh moved to Denver and took a job at the garage, and the years began to pile up.

"I need to meet with her, show her this letter." Annie said the words more to herself than to Lindsay.

"You should." Her daughter was sitting at the desk again, going through Josh's files. She looked up and blew at a loose strand of hair. "I wonder what would've happened if Becky had been more patient."

"Or if Josh had taken life more seriously." Annie folded the letter and put it in a stack with the newspaper clipping and the letters from the girls' parents. Nate would want to see everything she found today.

As the day wore on, Annie kept her resolve, that these two weeks would be about learning whatever she could about her son, everything she hadn't known, good or bad. She especially wanted to find whatever she could about the woman Josh had been with in Vegas. Maria Cameron. And any documents or proof that would explain why Josh felt so strongly that the child was his daughter.

She and Lindsay found photos of Becky and Josh, and stacks of deposition documents related to the court case. The testimony ripped at Annie's soul for the way the insurance company's lawyers tormented Josh on the witness stand. After ninety minutes of reading through the transcripts, Annie was ready to call Thomas Flynn and ask him to file a second lawsuit—this one against the attorneys for harassment of her son.

She moved on to a broken-down box on the top shelf of Josh's bedroom closet. There were old yearbooks and awards from his participation in football and baseball, and at the top she found a thank-you card from Keith, Josh's best guy friend from high school.

Annie read the note written inside:

Hey, man . . . thanks for getting me those miles. You gave me something I would've missed otherwise—a chance to tell my dad I loved him before he died. You're the best, Josh . . . no one like you anywhere.

Keith

Again, Annie felt she was learning about a young man she'd never known. She remembered Keith's father dying a couple years back, and she knew Keith and his dad weren't close. The man rode Keith relentlessly about his sports, yelling at him in front of the other parents if he struck out. That sort of thing. When Keith was a teenager, he spent a lot of time at the Warren house, confiding in them that he was sure his father didn't love him.

Though she and Nate made a few attempts to help Keith and his father reconcile, the efforts never seemed to amount to anything.

What she didn't know, until now, was that Josh helped his friend with airline miles. Josh didn't fly, so how in the world did he come up with enough miles to get Keith back home from Ohio before his father died? However it had happened, somehow Josh had found a way to help his friend, and because of his efforts, Keith had gotten a priceless chance to reconcile with his father.

You were a hero two times over, my precious son. And I never got the chance to know that about you. Never got to tell you how proud that makes me. She held the card to her heart and for a priceless moment she had the distinct feeling she was holding Josh instead, holding him close against her the way she had when he was a little boy, when his future was still one long trail of endless possibilities.

The search continued until Annie was too emotionally exhausted to look through another envelope or file or dusty cardboard box. They would pick up the job again later, and maybe then they would find some sign that Josh was right about the girl being his daughter. But Annie doubted anything would come of the matter. If she was his child, Josh would have found out definitively by now.

In light of all Josh had hoped for his future, the child probably gave him what Becky Wheaton gave him: a reason to believe that someday the pain and torment from his accident would end. He would find a new career and financial freedom and the life he'd always wanted. That's all the little girl in the photograph really was. A reason for Josh to believe that tomorrow would be better than today.

SIXTEEN

Savannah wasn't sure what happened, or how come her life seemed so different now, but she believed the change had something to do with her daddy. Her mama didn't grab her arm like before, and twice she even let Savannah sleep in the big bed with her instead of under the desk.

"The good times are just beginning, Savannah," her mama told her this morning on their way to a place called the clinic. "A few more weeks and we'll have a big house and a maid and the best food and clothes and cars."

Savannah listened with wide eyes, and sometimes she wondered if her mama was crazy or just kidding about all that. But one thing she wasn't kidding about was the clinic. They walked from the subway to the small building, where her mama filled out a piece of paper. The place smelled like the bathrooms in Central Park, and Savannah's tummy felt topsy-turvy. Why were they here, anyway? Was this where her daddy was going to find her?

She had her little plastic cross from Grandpa Ted in her pocket and she felt it through her jeans, just to be sure it was there. Her mama finished writing on the piece of paper, and together they sat in a little room full of people who looked sad or hurt or sick. An old man sitting next to them had a cut across his arm and blood was coming through his Band-Aid. Savannah tried not to look. She leaned up to her mama's ear. "Why are we here again?"

"For the test." Her mama seemed a little nervous. Not as happy as she was when they had their hot dogs in the park or when they went to the zoo yesterday.

"What sort of test?" Savannah crossed her ankles and swung her feet. She was thirsty, but she didn't want to drink too much water. Her mama said she didn't have time for the bathroom until after the test.

"A blood test." Her mama picked up a magazine from a table next to her and she started flipping the pages.

A blood test? Savannah's stomach felt sick, because what sort of test was that? She glanced next to her at the man's reddish Band-Aid. Was he here for a blood test, too? Because she didn't want to look like that when she left. She remembered the cross in her pocket and Jesus, who was always with her. *Jesus, it's me, Savannah. I'm sort of scared about the blood test, so can You stay with me, please?*

She was waiting for an answer in her heart when a big lady in a tight white dress stepped into the little room. "Savannah Cameron?"

"Here." Her mother stood and smoothed the wrinkles in her short skirt. She reached for Savannah's hand and pulled her to her feet. "This is Savannah."

The woman looked at her notes. "Follow me."

Savannah tried not to think about the man and his bloody arm. She stayed close to her mama and the big lady took them to a room the size of a closet. "Sit here," she said. The woman and Mama talked about how " 'rangements" had been made and some other words Savannah didn't understand. Then the woman rolled up the sleeve of Savannah's sweatshirt and rubbed a wet little ball of white fur over her arm. "This won't hurt much." She opened a small white bag and took out a sharp needle and a plastic tube the size of a pencil. "Hold still."

"Very still." Her mama raised one eyebrow the way she did when Savannah had better listen, or else.

The big lady stuck the needle into Savannah's arm and held it there. "You don't have to watch, sweetie."

But Savannah did watch, because little by little her blood came from her arm into the tube. The lady was right, the needle didn't hurt too bad once it was in her. When the tube was filled, the woman pulled out the needle and put a Band-Aid on her arm—a smaller one than on the man in the room full of people. "There you go."

"The blood test is finished?" Savannah felt her stomach settle down a little.

"All done." The lady ripped a few smiley stickers from a roll on the wall. "These are for you."

"You did good, sweetheart." Her mama smiled at her.

Savannah wasn't sure what to do with the stickers. "Thank you, ma'am." She peeled off one and then the other and stuck them to the backs of her hands. She could see them there and remember that she'd done a good job on her blood test. The big lady was telling her mama that something would be sent to her in a few days.

When they were back outside in the sunshine, her mama gave her a happy squeeze. "Savannah, I have a feeling about that blood test. I think this is the beginning of a very happy time for us."

Savannah felt a little shy of her mama, this new way her mama acted around her. She nodded her head and smiled. Then she looked back down at her happy face stickers.

"Here, baby"—her mama reached for her—"take my hand."

Savannah did as she was told, and together they started walking. "Are we going to the park?"

"Yes. It'll be a beautiful day in the park, don't you think?"

"Are we gonna beg money?"

"We are." Her mama seemed less happy for a few seconds. But then she smiled big again. "Not for long, though. Your daddy is going to take care of us real good. Then we'll never beg for money again."

Savannah's heart felt suddenly light and free, like she was one of the birds over Central Park, the ones that landed on the top of the fountain and flew away whenever they wanted to. Her daddy was going to take care of them! Ever since the changes in her mama she had hoped in secret that it had to do with her daddy. She breathed in a very big breath and held her head high. The good things were finally going to happen! She was going to meet her daddy and he was going to take care of them. After so much waiting and talking to Jesus and hoping, all her dreams were finally going to come true.

Her mama stayed happy that day, even while they begged money. She waited until they were on the subway on the way home, then she decided this was the right time to ask a few questions. "The good things that are going to happen are because of my daddy, right?"

A little laugh came from her mama. "Yes, sweetie. All because of your daddy."

Savannah felt a little shiver of excitement. "So when will I meet him? Today or tomorrow? Or later this week?"

Her mama's smile fell back to a straight line. "Well . . . you're not exactly going to meet him." She had a worried look in her eyes, but then she smiled again. "He's going to send us a gift instead. A very, very nice gift."

Savannah didn't want a gift. She already had the plastic cross from Grandpa Ted and the framed picture of her daddy, which was all she needed. What she wanted was her daddy, not a present from him. She felt tears in her eyes and she wiped at them real fast so her mama wouldn't think she was ungrateful. "Will—will I meet him later, then?"

"Much later." Her mama patted her on the head. "Don't worry, Savannah. Your daddy's gift will be enough for now."

She didn't ask any more questions on the ride home. For now? She settled back against the hard, cracked seat and stared out the window at the walls rushing past. All day she'd been happy because sometime very soon she might meet her daddy. She was still going to meet him, but "much later" was a long time away. A whole week or a month, maybe. She was puzzled about her daddy because his eyes and his smile were very kind, and he wanted to send her a gift—which was also very kind. But didn't he know that all she wanted was him? A daddy to hold her and swing her around and take care of her so her mama could have the break she always talked about. Her very own Prince Charming daddy.

What could be a better gift than that?

SEVENTEEN

After one week of sorting through the pieces of Josh's life, Annie had learned much about her son, and she had a strong feeling her quest wasn't yet complete. She talked to Thomas Flynn and learned that Josh had contacted him about his friend Keith's need for airfare.

"I had a million extra miles," Thomas told her. "It was no problem donating some to Josh's friend so he could get home to see his sick father."

But the trip never would have happened if Josh hadn't made the phone call, if he hadn't cared enough to put his own pride on the line for the sake of his friend's great need.

On Annie's second day of searching through Josh's apartment, Ethel, the old woman who lived in the apartment above his, made her way downstairs and sat with Annie and Lindsay for an hour.

"I have no family," the woman explained. "Josh was like the grandson I never had. It's hard for me to get out, so one week a few years ago he asked if he could pick up a few groceries for me." She had tears in her eyes as she talked. "After that it became a routine. Every Saturday he picked up just what I needed to get through the next seven days, and sometimes he brought me an extra little surprise—a box of fresh cookies from the bakery or a small bouquet of flowers for my kitchen table."

Annie hung on every word, sometimes jealous that Josh had lavished his attention on this stranger when he might have brought the flowers to her instead. But she quickly corrected her attitude and became overwhelmed with pride over her son's decision to help a neighbor. "And you would pay him when he dropped off the food, is that how it worked?"

"Never." She touched her fingertips beneath her eyes, wiping at her tears. "Josh never let me pay for anything."

The woman's story filled Annie's heart with wonder. Her son was on an extremely tight budget, so tight that regularly he had to call her and Nate for an advance toward his settlement. Yet with what little he had, he made a point of buying the old woman's groceries every week.

Annie thought about the people who ran in their circles, the socialites and political types. Not long ago, the superintendent of Nate's school district donated five thousand dollars of his own money to the local PTA. In doing so, he threw a party for the entire PTA, complete with a free barbecue dinner for the community and a speech midway through the night. The man himself contacted the media, and Lindsay had been assigned to the story, "Local Educator Gives Gift to PTA."

No one seemed to think anything of the man's efforts to be noticed, but at the time Annie mentioned to Nate that the man's gift seemed awfully self-serving. "The Bible says when a person gives something, the right hand shouldn't know what the left hand's doing."

Nate laughed. "Every hand in the PTA knew about this one."

But not so with Josh's gift to his elderly neighbor. It was as though Josh inherently knew that the only way to feel good about a gift was to give it in such a way that no one else knew. It was a lesson Josh had no doubt heard again and again in Sunday school through the years, but until now Annie would have sworn her son had forgotten every valuable bit of Scripture from his childhood days.

Now she knew differently.

Everything she found she shared with Nate. Last night, when they were talking about the miles for Keith's flight back home, Nate's eyes welled with tears and, for a long while, he didn't say anything. When he could talk, he took hold of her hand. "Like I told you, not everyone is an all-star in sports or in life. But that doesn't mean Josh was a failure." His chin quivered and he scrunched his face, fighting the breakdown. "I always believed in Josh, that he was a good boy, a good son." He shook his head, getting a grasp on his emotions. "I appreciate these details, but they don't surprise me, Annie. Not like they surprise you."

She wanted to argue with him, but she couldn't. He was right, and rather than deny the light her discoveries were shedding on the memory of their son, she embraced it. Even the more painful pieces of information, like the letter she'd found from Maria Cameron stating that Josh couldn't have visitation or any other rights to Savannah until he figured out a way to send her four thousand dollars a month.

Your hundred dollars will never cut it, the woman wrote. *I'll keep Savannah from you until you figure out your finances. Savannah needs money, not some sentimental father figure. You won't hear another word from us until you get the money. Otherwise I'll tell her you're a loser like every other guy.*

The letter was bathed in venom. Annie felt sick to her stomach just touching the paper, as if the woman's filth might still be on the edges of the page. After reading it, she set it aside for the attorney. Her belief that the woman was nothing more than a gold digger looking for any man to bail her out doubled after finding the letter. The girl wasn't Josh's child. At the same time, she grieved the fact that her son had ever been tricked into sleeping with a woman like Maria Cameron. Josh knew better. The lessons about purity had come right along with the lessons about helping others.

For two hours after reading Maria's letter, she allowed herself to wonder where she and Nate had gone wrong that their son would go to Las Vegas, of all places, and spend the night with such a woman. But then gradually her heart softened, and she caught herself creating scenarios that might've explained Josh's poor decision that weekend.

He'd lost Becky Wheaton by then. She was tired of waiting for Josh to quit smoking and drinking, for him to get serious about life, and so she'd taken up with a young man in law school. Josh couldn't compete with that, and after moving to Denver and taking the job at the garage, he must have been very lonely. The weekend in Vegas had probably been an impulsive decision, some way to forget about the emptiness in his heart created by Becky's absence.

Who knew what Maria had told Josh? She might've had some sad story about being lonely, like him. If she needed a friend or an ear or a place to stay, Josh would have helped her. She thought about the couple with Down syndrome, and Ethel from the apartment upstairs. Yes, certainly Josh would've helped her. He wasn't wise enough in the ways of the world to recognize a trap like the one the woman had clearly set.

The entire situation was too sad to dwell on, so Annie had moved on to other boxes of belongings, other memories that made up her son's past.

Now it was Tuesday, and she was at the apartment by herself. Nate and Lindsay were coming by later that day with more empty bags for Josh's bedding. They were moving most of his furniture into an empty room at the back of their house in Black Forest. The room would be a guest suite now, a place where Josh's memory could live on.

Annie slid two more boxes into the entryway of Josh's apartment and then stood to catch her breath. As she did, she looked at her son's computer and she realized this was one area they hadn't looked at yet. She sat in his chair and reached down to hit the power button. A minute later, the screen came to life and Annie wondered where to begin. She opened Microsoft Word and checked his list of documents.

One of them read simply, "Savannah."

Annie's heart missed a beat, and she felt the blood leave her face. Was he that certain about the little girl that he'd created a document about her? How sad that he believed someone like the Cameron woman enough to care this much. She double clicked the document and it appeared on the screen. The font was small, and the text was single-spaced.

Dear Savannah, the last entry read. *It's been three days since I've written to you, so I thought I better catch up. . . .*

Annie's stomach dropped to her feet. Her son had kept an ongoing journal for the girl? As if she really were his daughter, and someday she'd actually read everything he'd written to her? Annie checked the bottom descriptor, the line that contained the information about the document. What she read took her breath away. Fifty-three pages? Her son must have been keeping the journal ever since he found out about the girl.

Everything in this document was what he might've said if he'd lived long enough to be a father. The photo on the mantel, the document tucked away in his Microsoft Word program, all of it allowed him to think and act and feel the way he might have if he'd been blessed with children. And since he never had that chance, Annie was sure every word would speak straight to her soul, to the place that would always belong to Josh.

She checked the paper supply in Josh's printer, and after a few clicks the machine came to life and the pages of his journal began falling gently onto the paper tray. But even as the document was printing, Annie finished reading the last entry:

Dear Savannah,

It's been three days since I've written to you, so I thought I better catch up. I know I've told you this a lot lately, but I'm really feeling closer to God these days. He's getting me through this trial, this stage in my life, and somewhere I know He's getting you through something, too.

I found a Bible verse I want to share with you, sweetheart. It's
from Psalm 119:50, and it says, "My comfort in my suffering is this:
Your promise preserves my life." You know about my accident, and
how I've been in a lot of pain. But lately I've been reading from the
Bible more and I find that this promise is true. Beyond true, even.
God's Word is reviving me, Savannah, and one day soon when I get my
settlement, I'll come find you. Together we can learn about Jesus and
the promises in His Word.

Annie felt tears on her cheeks, and she reached for a
tissue. Lately, she kept the box within reach. The journal to a child who probably wasn't his daughter was
one thing. But when had her son gotten closer to God?
And how come she and Nate hadn't heard about this?
She scanned the next few pages and saw that many times
over the weeks that led up to his death, Josh talked
about Jesus.

She found an entry from two months earlier, and her
eyes fell on a paragraph halfway down the page.

I was watching country videos one night and Wynonna Judd came
on, singing a song about heaven. "I Can Only Imagine," it was called.
Savannah, I can only tell you that in those next few minutes I real-
ized I'd been running from God for too long. It was like I finally got
it about having a relationship with Him, and how He wanted me to
rely completely on His strength. I've been going to church every week
since then, and I can feel God changing me. I love Him more than life,
Savannah. One day you will, too.

Annie sat back and a scene came to life in her mind. It
was the week before Josh died, and Lindsay had stopped

by to talk. But Annie was busy on a phone call, and then in a rush to get ready for another dinner, another event to help Nate get reelected to the school board. Lindsay had said something about Josh finding a song about heaven, and how he was going to church again and he was changed. The memory of Annie's response hit her like a sucker punch. She'd dismissed everything Lindsay was trying to tell her, refusing to hear the news as anything other than one more empty promise by Josh.

But here was proof that Lindsay had been right, that Josh really had found a closer relationship with God in the weeks before his death. That explained something Carl Joseph had said on his second visit this past week. He said Josh had gone to church with him and Daisy and his family. Again Annie had dismissed the idea, thinking Carl Joseph was confusing intent with action. She looked at the journal entry again. Apparently not.

Her heart warmed with the reality of what Josh had found in his renewed faith, but at the same time the guilt of her disbelief all but smothered her. What would it have taken for her to listen a little more carefully, to call Josh and congratulate him or ask for details about the change in his heart? Since Josh's death, Annie had been burdened by all her son had missed out on. But now the loss was hers alone.

She thought again about having ten more minutes with him. On top of everything else, she could talk to him about his faith and what led to his changed attitude. What a joy to have shared such a moment with him, in light of all the pain he'd been through. But Annie had missed her chance, and the reality was sadder than anything so far. *Josh, my son . . . I'm sorry.* She hung her head. *Dear God, I missed so much. What sort of mother misses moments like that?*

The only answer she had was the one that Josh had written in the last journal entry: *My comfort in my suffering is this: Your promise preserves my life.* God's Word. Yes, that's where she would find healing and comfort in the weeks and months and years ahead, in the lifetime ahead when missing Josh would be a part of every day. She would spend more time in God's Word, picking up the journey Josh had begun in the weeks before his death and finding comfort in the truth of Scripture.

Her sorrow subsided enough so she could breathe again. Josh's journal was finished printing, so she scanned the rest of the list of documents. Every one of them needed to be looked at in case somewhere in the middle of one of them there might be another detail about her son's life. For now, she wanted to check the Internet.

She opened the Safari browser at the bottom of his screen and looked at the list of bookmarks across the top of the page. Facebook was first, and Annie clicked it open. Instantly she was on Josh's personal Web site, a page with more information than she could take in at a single glance. Almost at the same time a box appeared in the lower right part of the screen. In it was a series of messages from someone named Miss Independent. The last one read, *J, I'm serious. What's wrong with you? I haven't heard from you in a week! It's like you cut me out of your life or something. Please! Write to me now!*

Annie had the strangest feeling as she scrolled down through the messages. This was a friend she knew nothing of, someone who clearly was in daily contact with her son.

Was she another Maria Cameron, or even maybe someone worse? Annie felt dizzy, but as she read through the messages she discovered a beautiful and innocent friendship. The woman's name was Cara Truman, and she was a single mother who lived in Arizona.

According to the messages, Cara had given her life to the Lord because of what she'd seen God doing in Josh's life. Here and there Annie saw a hint of romance in the messages, but nothing overt, no plans in the making. Again she felt the weight of losing Josh. This was one more detail she hadn't known about his life, one more aspect of her son she hadn't been aware of. He wasn't only a great neighbor, a giving young man, a hero, and a rededicated follower of Christ. He was a true friend as well.

In all the messages Annie saw, there was no phone number listed. Annie positioned her fingers over the keyboard. *Hello*, she typed. *This is Josh's mother, Annie. Please call me as soon as possible.* Then she typed her cell phone number and hit the send button.

An hour later she was sorting through more of Josh's computer files when her phone rang. The number on the caller ID was one she didn't recognize. "Hello, this is Annie."

"Hi. This is Cara Truman. You left me a message." There was fear in her voice, and a breathy hesitation.

"Cara, I'm afraid I have bad news about Josh." Annie expected the conversation to be quick and to the point, the way it had been when she called other old friends of Josh's or acquaintances listed in his cell phone. But Cara Truman was different. She took the news hard, as though losing Josh was one of the greatest tragedies in her life.

"He—he was the best friend I ever had," she said in a

voice broken with grief. "No one ever cared about me like he did."

The young woman spilled her heart about finding Josh during an online poker game, and then connecting with him when the game was over. "He wasn't like other guys. He wasn't looking for anything from me."

"That sounds like Josh." She closed her eyes, picturing her son and all she'd learned about him. "I'm—I'm very proud of him."

By the end of the conversation, Annie had promised to stay in touch with Cara. They both agreed that was what Josh would have wanted. Before she hung up, Cara had one question. "What about his daughter?"

Annie felt her heart lurch forward. "His daughter?" What had Josh told Cara about the girl?

"Savannah. He talked about her constantly." Cara's voice filled with fresh tears. "That's all he wanted, to get his settlement and find his little girl so he could buy a house and make a home for her—however much time he could get with her." She sniffed. "Is someone going to contact her?"

For the first time since Annie had become aware of the little girl, she felt ashamed of her attitude. However wrong it had been for Josh to go to Vegas and connect with Maria Cameron, his actions did not negate the fact that somewhere a little girl existed who possibly might be Josh's daughter. Her head spun with the admission of this new possibility. "We, uh, we aren't sure the girl is his." But even as she said the words they felt lame and rife with excuse.

"Oh." Cara's tone became kindly adamant. "Well . . . Josh was sure. I can promise you that. It seems someone should look into it, because Josh lived for that girl. Some days all that got him through was the hope that he could be her daddy."

The heartbreak surrounding her son's death seemed to know no limits. Annie sighed in a way that gave a window to the pain inside her, pain that had reached flood level. "We'll keep that in mind," she finally said. "Thank you, Cara, for being his friend."

"It's the other way around." A few stifled sobs sounded over the phone line. "Thank you for having such an amazing son."

The call ended and Annie stood and walked to the fireplace mantel. How often must her son have stood in this very spot, looking at the picture of the two teenage girls and knowing without a doubt that no matter how much pain he was in, he'd saved two lives. And how much time did he also spend looking at the family photo and yearning for the time when his parents would be proud of him? And then turning his eyes to the picture of the child. Savannah. She didn't want to see it before, but there was something in her face that reminded her of Josh. Or maybe Annie was just too overwhelmed with guilt to deny for one more day the possibility that the girl was Josh's. She picked up the picture and studied it.

Savannah Cameron.

If she was Josh's daughter, then she would be Annie's granddaughter. It was more than she could take in, and with heavy hands and a heavier heart she returned the photo to the mantel. Cara was right about one thing. They needed to finish going through Josh's things in case somewhere there was information that might lead to the whereabouts of the girl's mother.

Annie returned to her son's bedroom. So much loss made her unsure if she could survive another day of this quest, this discovery process. She comforted herself by remembering the one shining bit of information that today's search had brought to light, the fact that Josh had reconnected with the faith he'd had as a child. The joy of that was enough to help Annie draw one more breath, take one more look into a box of her son's belongings. He had missed out on his settlement and the success he hoped to have. He'd missed out on a deeper friendship with his friend Cara and on being the father he wanted to be.

But he hadn't missed out on heaven.

EIGHTEEN

Thomas hung up the phone and sent a message to his secretary to hold his calls. He needed a few minutes to process what had just happened. The notice came to him through e-mail, but just to be sure he'd called the clinic himself. He probably shouldn't have been surprised by the news, but the finality of it knocked the wind from him. The test had come back positive.

Josh was Savannah's father. There was no debating the fact now.

He covered his face with his hands and pictured Josh, the earnest way he'd looked sitting in the chair opposite his in this very office, talking about Savannah as if he'd already seen the test results. She was his daughter, he never had any doubts. It was why he'd talked about her from the witness stand, why he had gone to his grave desiring mainly one thing—the chance to be Savannah's father.

Thomas drew a long breath and leaned back in his chair. If only this news had come when Josh was still alive, when he still filled the spot across from him. His pain would've taken a backseat to the thrill of knowing Thomas had found the girl, and that she was officially his.

Instead, so much about the news was unfair. Josh had been denied the chance to know her, and now Maria Cameron was going to walk away with the settlement money. The money Josh had given his life for. He stood, but he could barely straighten his shoulders under the burden of the news. He needed to tell Annie and Nate now, before another hour passed.

He called Annie's cell phone and wasn't surprised to learn that she and Lindsay were at Josh's apartment. It was Tuesday, the third week after Josh's death, and Annie had spent nearly every waking minute looking through her son's things. Annie sounded like a different person in light of all she was learning about Josh. Like the revelation was from God alone, and day by day it was changing her, making her softhearted and kinder. Less ambitious about things that didn't really matter now that Josh was gone.

"I found out more today," she told him. "I met a friend of his I found on his computer and we talked for an hour. She says Josh taught her about Jesus. Isn't that something?"

Thomas leaned his elbows on the desk. "That is."

"And she told me that she was a single mom and Josh had given her the courage to be a better mother, to put her kids first, and—"

"I'm sorry." Her words reminded Thomas that he wanted to make it to his son's piano recital that night. Josh had made the same impression upon him. "I don't mean to cut you off, Annie. But we need to talk. Is it okay if I head over?"

Annie paused, and her tone filled with a fresh sense of alarm. "Is this good news, Thomas?"

"Let's talk about it in person."

"Okay. I'll look for you."

Thomas gathered his briefcase and his car keys and told his secretary he was leaving for the day. He would have liked Nate to be there, too, but Annie could pass on the information. The important thing was that they get the news as soon as possible.

Even if their lives would never be the same afterward.

❧

Something in his voice told Annie there'd been a dramatic and maybe terrible development in Josh's lawsuit against the insurance company. The moment they were off the phone, she called Nate and asked him to leave work, to get to Josh's apartment as soon as possible. Whatever the news, she didn't want to process it without him.

Lindsay came to her side midway through her quick conversation with Nate, and when Annie hung up, her daughter's questions came immediately. "What's wrong?"

"That was Thomas Flynn. He's on his way over." Her heart felt numb. "Some sort of news."

"Something bad?"

"He didn't say." But her tone told Lindsay what Thomas hadn't come right out and said. The news couldn't be good.

"Maybe they've reached a settlement, or an offer, at least." Lindsay took the chair closest to her mother and tucked her legs beneath her. "It's supposed to come sometime soon, right?"

"Thomas would've said so, he would've said a decision was reached. Even if he didn't want to talk about it on the phone."

"And he didn't say that?"

"No." They talked another few minutes about the possibilities. "A week ago he said a speed bump had come up regarding Josh's estate, a question of some kind."

Neither of them could make sense of that, so they waited, talking instead about Cara Truman and Keith and Ethel, and what a good guy Josh had been. Nate arrived at the apartment first. He came in, his eyes wide, face paler than usual.

Again the small talk continued, nervous and empty, anything to fill the time. In a few minutes there was a knock at the door. Lindsay opened it, and Thomas's face assured Annie that whatever was coming wasn't good. They repositioned themselves so Annie and Nate were on Josh's sofa, and Lindsay was in the matching armchair. Thomas pulled up the computer chair and for a long moment he only looked at them. In his hands was a folder, but he didn't open it.

Thomas turned to Nate. "Annie tells me you've learned a lot about Josh these last ten days."

"Yes." Nate's voice was patient, even though everyone in the room wanted to ask the obvious. What had happened that the attorney would drop what he was doing and head straight for Josh's apartment? Nate clasped his fingers and leaned over his knees. "God has been . . . very good to us, letting us see a picture of our son that we might've missed otherwise."

Thomas nodded slowly and let his eyes fall to his hands for a few seconds. When he looked up, his eyes glistened with a deeper sorrow Annie hadn't seen in the man until now. "I'm afraid I have more information about Josh."

The three of them were silent, unblinking, waiting. The

only sound was the whir of Josh's refrigerator and the subtle tick of the second hand on the clock that hung in the kitchen. That, and Annie's pounding heart. Surely everyone in the room could hear that.

Thomas released a long sigh. "In the last deposition, the one Josh gave the day before he died, he told the court that he had a daughter. That would make her his only heir."

Annie felt the room begin to spin. She slid closer to Nate and leaned on his arm, so she wouldn't slide off the sofa and pass out on Josh's beige-carpeted floor. Still, none of them said anything.

"Because of Josh's testimony, I was obligated to do my best to find the girl's mother, Maria Cameron of New York City." He pursed his lips. "I found her the Friday after Josh's death, and left her a message later that day. By law I was required to tell her that the girl could be the heir to a settlement." His disdain sounded in his tone. "Needless to say, she contacted me first thing the following week."

"Why . . . didn't you tell us all this?" Nate didn't sound angry, just baffled.

"I wanted to believe the search would lead to nothing." Thomas breathed in through his nose. "I didn't want to worry you over nothing."

"But . . ." Nate didn't need to ask, really. Everyone in the room could see where the conversation was headed.

"I ordered that the girl be subjected to a paternity test. We had Josh's results already. Standard in a case like this where he suspected he was the father of a child and where paternity hadn't been established."

His words ran together, and Annie felt her world slipping off its axis.

"The woman was very compliant, of course, and very sure that Josh was her daughter's father." He lifted the file in his hand and let it fall again. "The results came in right before I called you." He made eye contact with each of them one at a time. "Without question, the girl is Josh's daughter."

Annie grabbed on to Nate with one arm and the edge of the sofa with the other. No—no, it wasn't possible. All this time Josh had been right? He'd had a daughter and he'd been denied the chance of seeing her or holding her or knowing her? She sucked in her next few breaths and then stood and paced to the patio door and back. "You're sure?"

"The test is conclusive." Thomas handed the folder to her. "The details are all there."

She dropped the folder on the sofa and crossed her arms. The results must have had a million implications, but the first one, the one that stabbed straight through her heart, was this one: Josh had a daughter, but he'd missed out on being a father.

Thomas was going on, saying something about the settlement, and the girl being Josh's only heir, and how the entire amount minus any debt Josh had incurred would now go to Josh's daughter, and—

"Wait." The room stopped spinning. Annie drilled her eyes into those of the attorney. "Are you saying that we won't have control over Josh's settlement?"

"That's right."

"The entire amount will go to this—this child?" Nate's voice was incredulous.

"Yes. But her mother will be in control of it until she turns eighteen."

"But my parents are the executors of my brother's estate. Can't they determine whether the girl should really be an heir in this situation?" Lindsay was on her feet, her voice slightly raised. "I've written stories about things like this." She turned to Annie and then to Nate. "We can fight it."

"You can certainly try." Thomas sat a little straighter. He nodded, still in the game, not quite ready to throw in the cards. "Your case would be better if Josh hadn't said on the witness stand that he had a daughter, if he hadn't acknowledged her."

Annie remembered something. She hurried to Josh's bedroom and returned with the letter from Maria Cameron, the one where she threatened never to let Josh see the girl unless he paid her thousands of dollars per month. "Listen to this." She read a few choice paragraphs from the meanest sections of the letter. "The woman blackmailed Josh. She refused to even let him meet the girl. There's no way his accident money can go to her and a daughter he never met."

"Actually," Thomas said, sounding more tired than hopeful, "the law is pretty clear in this situation. In the case of estate law, any money belonging to the deceased automatically goes to the heir of the estate unless the deceased stated in writing before a witness that he or she did not want any or all of the estate to be given to that heir."

"In other words, if Josh had put in writing that he didn't want his money going to this girl, or rather her mother, then there wouldn't be an issue." Nate was still sitting on the sofa, but he'd slid to the edge, his back straight, clearly doing his best to understand the situation they were suddenly in.

"Exactly." Thomas looked like he wasn't sure how to

say this next part. "The thing is, I had this talk with Josh a number of times. I advised him not to mention the girl on the witness stand, since there had never been a paternity test and since he had no idea where she was or any other details about her."

Annie knew where Thomas was headed with this. She closed her eyes and she could hear him still, hear the pleading in her son's voice as he tried to convince her and Nate that the child was his daughter.

"Josh wouldn't hear of it. He told me that Savannah was his daughter and he would never deny the fact, not in court or anywhere else."

Her eyes opened and she looked at the photo over the fireplace. For the first time in all these years she saw the resemblance as clearly as if she were looking into the face of her son at that age. They had the same eyes. Annie must've seen it all along, seen it and denied it all at the same time so that her brain wouldn't allow her heart to acknowledge the obvious. That this little girl was Josh's daughter, their granddaughter.

"I'll look into case law on the matter first thing tomorrow." Thomas pursed his lips.

"I can check on the story I wrote, the one about a case like this," Lindsay said. "The woman already tricked Josh once." She looked at Annie and Nate. "I don't think any of us can stand back and let her trick Josh again. Not when that settlement meant so much to him."

The conversation continued another five minutes, then Thomas left with promises to call sometime around lunch tomorrow. If they were going to contest the idea that the child was Josh's rightful heir, they needed to form a battle plan as soon as possible.

After Thomas was gone, Nate pulled Annie into his arms. "I have a few more hours left at the office." He nuzzled his face against hers. "Don't worry about this. We'll get everyone at church praying and God will help us. The right thing will happen, I have no doubt whatsoever."

Annie nodded, too weary to speak. The news had knocked the wind from her, and after the initial burst of indignation, she was unable to feel anything but one very clear emotion: doubt.

Lindsay needed to go, too, and she asked Annie to join her. "Come to my house, Mom. We'll pick up a few salads on the way and you can spend a little time with Ben and Bella." Lindsay leaned in and kissed her forehead. "They miss you."

"I'm not hungry." Annie looked past her daughter to the boxes that still hadn't been sorted through. "I'll come over later. In an hour or so."

Reluctantly, Lindsay left, but only after Annie promised she wouldn't stay more than an hour longer. Annie understood her daughter's concern, but being here among Josh's things, his words and music, his greatest treasures, had become almost enjoyable, a routine that made Josh a part of her life again.

When she was alone, Annie returned once more to the picture on the mantel. Savannah was Josh's daughter, and neither she nor Nate had ever wanted to admit that fact. But what if they had? What if they'd taken the time to hire an investigator and search out Maria Cameron? They might have forced a paternity test based on Maria's own admission that the girl belonged to Josh. And then with the results in hand, Maria would've had no choice but to allow Josh a role in the girl's life.

Which meant Josh might have had his daughter after all. If only she and Nate had once, just once, believed him.

Her tears came in convulsive spasms, taking over her heart and soul, her lungs, and her ability to think clearly. What had they done? So what if the woman had slept around? Did it really matter that she'd been married at the time of her Vegas tryst with Josh? Even if she'd been with a hundred men that month, there was a chance Josh was the father. A single chance, and that chance was worth exploring, wasn't it? Didn't Josh deserve at least that? He didn't have any resources to wage that sort of search, that type of custody battle. The only way would have been if he'd received help.

Help that Annie and Nate had unequivocally denied him.

Dear God, what have we done? She took hold of the photo and slowly, painfully, she dropped to her knees. The little girl in the picture had never known her daddy, and now it was too late.

Josh had never gotten to cradle his newborn daughter, never spoken to her in the quiet coos and gentle whispers that existed between a father and his child. He had been robbed of the chance to hold her hand while she toddled across the room, and he'd missed the drive to school on her first day of kindergarten.

She had never known her father's hugs, his strong arms. Never had she run to him down the hall of her home when strange noises made her frightened in the middle of the night. She'd never walked hand in hand with him to the park or giggled out loud while he pushed her high on a swing until her feet brushed against the sky.

Josh had known she was his little girl, and there'd been nothing he could do about it. So he'd kept the journal and fought the lawsuit, knowing that the moment he had the settlement he would do what he'd longed to do since he first heard about the girl. He would fight Maria Cameron for custody. Annie remembered one time when the subject came up, the earnest look in Josh's eyes, the passion with which he talked about the child.

"Even if I get only one week a year, I want her to know me. I want her to know she has a dad who loves her."

Annie swallowed another sob. What had she done when Josh said that? Change the subject? Ask Josh if he wanted a second helping of spaghetti? Nothing about the child seemed even a little real. People didn't go off to Vegas, have a one-night stand with a married woman, and wind up the father of her child. Annie couldn't bring herself to acknowledge the possibility.

And now it was too late.

She held the photo close to her heart. "I'm sorry, Josh. I didn't know."

The conversation from earlier played in her thoughts again—the news from Thomas and her reaction, the way she was instantly sure she wanted to fight the girl's mother. Nate's comments, too, about how nothing had meant more to Josh than receiving this settlement.

That's where she stopped. She struggled to her feet, her eyes never leaving those of the girl's. No wonder she'd been feeling overwhelmed with doubt, both then and now. She'd denied the truth for seven years, denied that even a possibility existed that this child was Josh's daughter. She caught herself, forced herself to rethink the way she viewed the little girl in the photograph. She wasn't *that girl*, or *that child*. She was Savannah, Josh's daughter. *From now on I'll think of her by her name,* Annie told herself. *I owe Josh at least that much.*

If Annie was sure the settlement would go to Savannah, then there would be no war to wage, no battle to fight. Josh loved her, even if he never met her, and he would have wanted her taken care of. But that wouldn't happen. Thomas said so himself. The money would go to Maria Cameron as Savannah's guardian. By the time Savannah turned eighteen, the money would be gone, the insurance money wasted in the hands of a woman who had done everything in her power to ruin Josh's life.

That was something worth fighting against.

But even so, Annie asked God for wisdom and understanding greater than herself. *Please, Lord, lead the way in this legal nightmare. I've spent the last seven years denying even the slightest chance that Savannah was Josh's daughter, and I was wrong. I don't want to be wrong again. Please, God, lead us.*

"Josh, I promise I'll never forget that you're Savannah's father. Not ever again." She whispered the words through a fog of agony and she silently prayed at the same time that somehow God would let Josh hear them.

Especially after so many years of denying Savannah's relationship to Josh.

She and Nate and Lindsay could form a team and fight for Josh's settlement, and even now she was convinced that was the right thing to do, the only way to keep his money from falling into the hands of a woman who did nothing but hurt him. But they couldn't tell themselves that nothing mattered more to Josh than the settlement. That was hardly true.

Josh cared about the settlement, certainly, and the decision that the drunk driver's insurance company should pay for the losses he'd incurred. He cared about getting the money and buying a house and building a future for himself. But his top concern wasn't the settlement. That spot belonged to one person and one alone. Cara Truman had confirmed the fact again in their conversation earlier today. The answer was obvious to everyone who knew and loved Josh. What mattered most wasn't the lawsuit but his daughter, Savannah Cameron.

And now, one way or another, Savannah would have to matter to the rest of them, too.

NINETEEN

Cody Gunner couldn't shake the feeling that he needed to contact Josh Warren's parents. It was Wednesday, more than three weeks after Josh's death, and every day since then the thought had all but consumed him. He hadn't slept well once since hearing the news, because he knew a truth that maybe Josh's parents should know, too. On the other hand, the situation really wasn't his business. He waffled between whether to say something or not, and the inner conflict left him a little more worn out each day.

Now he sat on the front porch of the ranch home he shared with his wife, Elle, and once more he voiced his feelings. "I keep telling myself it's none of my business." He reached for Elle's hand and stared out across their property. "I mean, what if his family doesn't even know about the little girl?"

"What did Josh say, exactly?"

"It was a talk we had on the way home from church, the last time he went with us. You were in back with Carl Joseph and Daisy, and Josh looked like he had the weight of the world on his shoulders."

"That's right. I thought something was wrong with him."

"I saw it, too, so I asked him. I told him he looked like he had a lot on his mind." Cody remembered the conversation perfectly. He could hear Josh's voice, see the lines on his forehead all over again.

"My lawyer keeps asking me about Savannah," he had said.

"Your little girl?" Cody knew her name because Josh had talked about her before.

"Yeah. He thinks the subject might come up in court soon. If the other lawyers ask about her, he wants me to say that as far as I know I don't have any children." Josh's eyes narrowed with his concern over the issue. "You know, because there's never been a paternity test or anything."

Cody remembered how his heart went out to Josh. He and Elle had been married for just over two years and she was expecting their first baby—a boy, if the ultrasound was right. Already the protective feeling he had for their first-born surpassed any emotion he'd ever known. He could only imagine what it would feel like to be Josh, to be sure that the child was his and then advised by his own attorney to deny his relationship to her in a court of law. Cody had pushed the issue a little further, curious about the intentions of Josh's lawyer. "Why wouldn't he want you to tell it like you believe it to be, that as far as you know you're Savannah's father?"

"Because of the settlement." Josh had squinted against the glare of the sun in his eyes. "If I tell the court I have a daughter, and if something happens to me, then Savannah will get all the money."

"All of it?" The thought had concerned Cody, especially since there was no real proof of Savannah being Josh's daughter.

"My debts would be repaid first, so my parents and my sister would be taken care of for everything they ever loaned me. And they'd do a paternity test before Savannah would get a dime, that sort of thing." He shrugged one shoulder. "But yeah, after all that she would get the rest."

"Is that what you want?"

"If I die before I get the settlement? Yeah, it's what I want." He had never sounded so sure about anything since Cody had met him. "That little girl hasn't had her daddy all these years. If something happens to me, I at least want her taken care of financially. So she can grow up knowing I cared that much about her. You know?"

Cody understood better now that he was about to be a father. Coming back from the memory, he looked deep into Elle's eyes. "At the time, I let the conversation end without giving it another thought. I mean, Josh was in a lot of pain, but I didn't think he was about to die."

"Of course not." Elle's expression told him she understood his dilemma. She put her hand on her stomach. "The baby's kicking a lot tonight."

"Is he?" It was the third week in October and temperatures were cooling down at night. He put his arm around Elle's shoulders.

"I think he's gonna ride horses like his daddy."

"Bulls, you mean?"

"Horses." Elle raised her eyebrows at him. "We have a deal."

"I know." Cody smiled. He moved closer and kissed her

slowly, enough that it left them both breathless. "No bulls for this baby. I promise."

They kissed again, and Elle drew back first. "What are you going to do?"

"About the conversation with Josh?"

Elle nodded. "His parents need to know their son's wishes."

"You're right. I'll call them tomorrow." He thought about Carl Joseph. "My brother's having a hard time with this."

"Daisy, too."

"Yesterday he called and asked me about heaven." Cody drifted as the conversation came to life again.

"Heaven's where Ali is, right, Brother?" There'd been uncertainty in Carl Joseph's voice.

"Right. Ali's been there almost five years."

"That's a long time."

"It is." Cody rarely hurt over the loss of Ali anymore, but in that moment the pain was as fresh as the day his first wife had succumbed to cystic fibrosis. He swallowed his sorrow. "A very long time."

"You think maybe my good neighbor is getting to know Ali in heaven?"

Cody had smiled at the picture. "That would be nice, wouldn't it?"

"Yeah, because Josh was a really good neighbor, Brother. And if Ali needed a good neighbor in heaven, I wish God would put their houses right next to each other."

"Me, too."

"But I really wish Josh still lived across the parking lot in Apartment J-8, because we can't exactly stop by on Saturdays and visit him in heaven."

"Not yet."

"One day?" Carl Joseph let a little hope creep back into his voice.

"Yes. One day when we're all in heaven together I'm sure Josh will be your neighbor again."

"I hope so, Brother." Carl Joseph sighed. "He was a very good neighbor, and he gave us eggs for late breakfast and he didn't even put them all in one basket. He used a plastic container instead."

Cody's heart had been touched by his brother's description. "Josh was a good guy."

"Yeah, so the people in heaven are lucky to have him."

Cody pulled Elle close against his side. "That brother of mine has a good heart. He was the one at Ali's funeral who told me he hoped God would give Ali a horse in heaven. Because she was a good horse rider. Now he's hoping that Josh can be a good neighbor in heaven the way he was here."

"I love that guy." Elle pressed her cheek against his. "Daisy has called me three times in the past week, crying. She tells me she's worried Carl Joseph will die, because maybe dying is contagious." Elle sighed. "Other than when our father died, Josh is one of the only people Daisy has ever lost. It's been hard on her."

Cody could only imagine how hard the past few weeks had been on Josh's family. And if his family did, indeed, include Savannah, then somewhere a little girl had lost her daddy. Whether she knew it or not. There was nothing he could do about the pain Josh's loss was causing the people around him, but he could do something about the conversation he'd had with Josh on the way home from church. He'd make the call first thing in the morning tomorrow.

Maybe after that he'd be able to get a good night's sleep.

❧

Annie and Nate were at home that night going over the paperwork from the lawyer's office. Thomas had gone over the documents contesting Savannah's position as Josh's heir, and now it was up to them to sign the papers. When they signed and returned the papers to Thomas tomorrow morning, the battle would officially begin.

A hearing would take place, and evidence would be presented. Annie found another letter from Maria, this one stating in more specific terms that it would cost Josh dearly if he wanted even an afternoon with his daughter. That correspondence would be presented, as would a number of witnesses who could state Josh's determination to find Savannah and accept her as a daughter, all to no avail because of Maria's decision to keep that from ever happening.

Unless and until Josh could come up with the money.

Beyond that, they would hire a private investigator who would show the judge the sort of person Maria was, how she'd tricked Josh into sleeping with her even though she was married. When it was all said and done, the investigator would know exactly how many men Maria had been with, lending credence to the fact that Savannah's father could have been any of the men her mother had bedded, the point being that Maria Cameron hadn't been interested in establishing Josh's paternity until there was money at stake. And since at the same time she refused Josh access to his daughter, Thomas thought they had a chance of winning the case.

If the situation had been different, if Maria had been in contact with Josh and if she'd been a more fit mother, Annie and Nate wouldn't mind letting the money go to Savannah. But the woman's greed and character had already been established. Now Annie and Nate sat across from each other at their kitchen table and talked about the battle ahead.

"What did Thomas say about setting up a college fund?" Annie's head was swimming with the legalities of taking on the system. In the meantime, the attorneys for the insurance company were nearer every day to a settlement. Thomas would have to make his case about Savannah not being a legitimate heir quickly. Otherwise, the money would go to Maria Cameron without a fight. Once she took hold of it, the chances of winning it back from her were almost non-existent.

Nate locked his fingers behind his head and leaned back in his chair. "It's possible. We can tell the judge we'd like to put an amount, a hundred thousand dollars, say, in a trust fund for Savannah's college years. Two hundred thousand, even. Her mother couldn't touch it because the money wouldn't be for Savannah's care and support. It would be only for her college expenses."

"Then that's what we'll do. That way everyone wins." She thought about that. "Besides, the judge will be more likely to see things our way if he knows we're willing to help Savannah. It's her mother we're trying to avoid."

They'd been home for several hours, but not until Nate stood for a glass of water did he notice the blinking light on their home phone answering machine. He pressed a series of buttons and a tiny voice filled the room. "This is

Marybeth Elmer, manager of your son's apartment buiding. We've spoken before. I need to tell you that a Cody Gunner is looking to talk to you. He left his phone number." The woman went over the number twice slowly. "Maybe you can give him a call and see what he wants. His brother is one of our tenants."

Nate played the message again and wrote down the phone number of Cody Gunner. Annie had never heard of the guy, but if he was the brother of one of the tenants, maybe he knew something about Josh—another detail that would add to the new way they'd come to see and know their only son.

"It's too late to call him tonight." Nate set the piece of paper with Cody's number on the counter next to the phone.

"Remind me to call him in the morning."

"Okay." Nate sat back at the table and pulled the paperwork close. He flipped through the top five pages and took a little longer with the sixth and final page. "I think we should sign it. We're doing the right thing, Annie."

"There's no way Josh would've wanted that woman taking his settlement."

"Absolutely not."

In the distant rooms of her heart, Annie remembered her prayer, her promise that she would let God show her if at any point in the battle for Josh's settlement they were doing something that went against the Lord's plan in all this. But today there had been no voice advising them not to move ahead with their motion. Maria Cameron had used Josh one too many times already, without her walking off with his money.

After all, the accident cost him his life, his chance for a future with Becky Wheaton, his dreams of making a new career for himself, and saddest of all, his opportunity to be a father to Savannah. It belonged to Josh's family to decide where Josh would have wanted the settlement money to go—not to a stranger like Maria Cameron.

For a slight moment, Annie wondered what it would be like to meet Savannah, to look into her eyes and see a part of her son looking back at her. If they lost the battle, Annie had every intention of asking for visitation rights. If the courts deemed Savannah to be Josh's rightful heir, then the privilege would have to come with a responsibility on the part of Maria Cameron—to connect her daughter with Josh's family.

At least Annie hoped that would happen if they lost.

But what if they won? Would that mean they'd never have the opportunity to meet the child, to hug her even one time the way Josh had never been able to? Annie didn't like the way that felt, as if winning the legal battle was more important than meeting Savannah. But maybe somehow God would allow both—their rightful victory in court, and a meeting with Josh's little girl.

She wasn't sure about much of anything except that they needed to sign the papers. Nate went first, and then it was her turn. But as she signed her name on the line clearly marked by their attorney, it took everything Annie had to remind herself that this battle was against Maria Cameron.

And not against Josh's precious Savannah.

TWENTY

The twitches and rapid heartbeats were happening more often, constant fleshly reminders that she had to play it straight. Very straight. At least until the settlement came. Maria looked at the glowing red numbers on the table next to her bed. Seven-fifteen. She sat on the edge of her bed and stretched her arms over her head. Life had become crazy and she had no idea how to handle the pressure. At least not sober.

Maria had an attorney now, someone Freddy had recommended. The attorney was his idea after a call from Thomas Flynn last Thursday telling her that Josh's family was fighting for the money. Of all the nerve. Savannah was Josh's only kid, his only heir, as Josh's lawyer liked to say. The case should be open-and-shut, and three months from now she and Savannah should be sitting in the lap of luxury. That's what her attorney said. He'd found out the numbers Thomas wouldn't tell her during that first phone call: a cool two million dollars. That's what she and her baby girl stood to win if things went right. Two million. Josh had finally reached the big time. He'd gotten himself hit by a rich drunk driver, and now the payout was weeks away.

Maria picked up the business card on the table next to the alarm clock. "Harry Dreskin, Attorney-at-Law," the card read. Harry was a good guy. He worked out of a tiny office on the Upper West Side. Maria had met with him twice already and as far as she could tell Harry was beside himself to be working on a respectable case like hers. Helping his client rope in a settlement for a kid without a father? What could be more honest and good than that?

Harry didn't want money up front, which made him the perfect lawyer. But he'd hinted around that a little bedroom action could cut his fees quite a bit once the settlement came. Maria was mildly interested, but she turned him down because mothers—real mothers like the ones she saw playing with their kids in the park—didn't sleep with men as a way of bringing down the cost of legal fees, or rent, or blow, or anything else.

Maria thought about the day ahead. She and Savannah couldn't sit around Freddy's place. Not today. They had to clean it and get lost. Freddy had a business deal with a group of characters who scared even Maria. After that, more scary was the trip she had to take to Denver tomorrow. First time she'd flown anywhere since the junket to Vegas eight years ago.

The trip was part of this new fight for the money, naturally. Her attorney said it would take some time since they couldn't afford the airfare and would have to borrow a car and drive to Colorado, so Josh's attorney bought tickets for her and Savannah. He was even going to put them up in a fancy hotel—a Holiday Inn with a free breakfast. The trip wasn't the scary part. The reason she was going, that's what made her afraid. Some judge in Denver said she had to come and testify about Savannah being Josh's daughter, and how come she never let Josh visit her.

She'd come up with one lie after another since she got news of the trip. The attorney would ask her why she hadn't let Savannah see Josh, and she would smile sweetly and say, "I gave Josh the chance to see his daughter, but he wasn't interested." Maria's heart picked up speed. No, maybe that lie wouldn't work. Josh's family probably knew how hard he'd tried to see Savannah.

She bit her lip. There was the other lie. "I gave Josh the chance to spend time with his daughter, but he could never afford to make the trip." Again, she would give the attorney her sweetest smile. "I kept hoping he'd find a way to visit us, to connect with Savannah, but it never happened."

Somehow between today and Wednesday—two days from now—she would have to come up with something solid, a believable story that would prove she hadn't intentionally kept Savannah from her father. Otherwise, there could be some question as to whether Savannah should be his rightful heir.

She reached out her toe and nudged Savannah's foot. "Wake up, sleepy. It's a new day." Maria's heart was still racing, her right eye still twitching just beneath her lower lashes. Every part of her body screamed for a drink or a hit—anything to dull the anxiety closing in around her. But even so, she silently congratulated herself at the way she talked to Savannah just now. She almost sounded like a real mother.

Savannah sat up and moved her blankets to the corner of the room, far enough beneath the desk that they were out of sight. " 'Morning, Mama." She yawned and blinked a few times. "Is there breakfast today?"

The question frustrated Maria. "When have we missed breakfast? Not for two weeks now, right?" Maria started to roll her eyes but she caught herself. Harry told her that the attorneys for Josh's family would probably put everyone breathing on the witness stand. That meant some stranger could come sniffing around asking Savannah what sort of mother she had, and whether Savannah was happy living with Maria.

If she was going to be in charge of the girl's two million dollars, then Maria didn't want a single doubt about whether her daughter would tell the lawyers she was happy. Happy and well fed. Maria led the way out of the bedroom. They needed to clean the place today. Freddy's orders. Keep Savannah happy, keep enough food in the kitchen, pay the rent, clean the place. So much to worry about. Maria walked to the cupboard and pulled out a box of Cap'n Crunch. The pressure would be a lot easier to handle if she could drink just a little. A swig of whiskey now and then.

They were finished with breakfast and halfway through the cleaning job when the phone rang. Normally, Maria avoided Freddy's phone, but since the whole settlement thing had come up, she didn't miss a call. She picked it up on the second ring and reminded herself to use her best motherly voice. "Hello?"

"Maria, it's Harry."

"Hey." She relaxed. "I got Flynn's package in the mail. I'm all set for tomorrow's trip to Denver."

"Right, well, that's why I'm calling. I filed a motion with the court and the judge thinks he can resolve the case without your testimony."

Maria's eye stopped twitching. "What does that mean?"

"It means you don't have to fly to Denver." He allowed only a quick break in between sentences. "That's not saying you won't have to fly out some other time to testify, but for now you can stay home. We'll be talking to the judge and I'll call you later this week."

The thrill of victory rushed through Maria's veins like a drug. "Well, that's the best news of the day."

"I'm sure it is. I'll be in touch." When he hung up, she eyed the whiskey bottle tucked back in the corner of the kitchen counter. "Savannah?"

"Yes, Mama?" Her voice came from the bathroom upstairs. "Do you need something?"

"Are you almost finished up there?"

"No." Her voice sounded closer and there was the sound of her feet on the stairs. When she was in sight, she gave Maria a nervous look. "I still have to wash the windows and the sink."

"Okay." Maria gave a lighthearted laugh. "Just checking. I want to make sure we have plenty of time in the park later. Plus Freddy has that meeting here."

"I'll hurry." Savannah's eyes were wide with concern as she hurried back up the stairs.

Maria waited until she heard the girl working in the bathroom again, then she grabbed the whiskey bottle and jerked the top from the glass neck. Being sober was one thing, but no one would know if she took a small drink. How else could she celebrate the attorney's great news? Whatever had happened between the two lawyers, Harry Dreskin had clearly won this first battle. She didn't need to fly to Denver, which meant she didn't need to lie about letting Josh see Savannah.

This legal thing was a breeze, and one day soon she'd get a check in the mail for two million dollars. She held the bottle of golden liquid to her nose and breathed deep. The whiskey smelled wonderful. She could feel herself relaxing just from the intoxicating scent of it. She glanced up at the stairs one more time and reminded herself to hurry. She couldn't have Savannah find out she'd been drinking again. Even Harry Dreskin told her to stay clean if she wanted the money.

This was different, though. She had a reason to celebrate, and besides, no one would ever know. She put the bottle to her lips and took a small sip. The liquid felt smooth and seductive on her tongue, and it burned deliciously as it slid down her throat. She took another sip and another. Already the alcohol was spreading through her, warming her and slowing her heart rate. She needed this—she deserved it. But if she was going to soothe her cravings she needed more than a few quick gulps. Who knew when she'd have the chance to drink again?

Once more she looked for Savannah, listened for her footsteps. When she was sure the girl wasn't going to catch her, she turned the bottle bottom side up and guzzled several long swigs. Enough so that she'd really feel it. Then she quick twisted the top back on and slid the bottle back to its place on the counter. The dizzying euphoria flooded through her, over her. This was the life, filling herself with warm, welcoming whiskey and having all day ahead to enjoy the feeling.

She finished tidying the kitchen, cleaning the counters

and sweeping the floors. She wasn't quite steady on her feet, but that part would wear off before they left the apartment. Maria remembered the routine, even if it had been a while.

Savannah came down after a while and for a long moment she studied Maria. Finally, a nervous laugh came from Maria's lips, a laugh that was probably too loud. "What ya lookin' at?"

"Mama? Are you—are you okay?"

"Jus' tired, baby girl." She laughed again, quieter this time. "All this work has me tuckered out."

Savannah looked doubtful. She looked around the kitchen until her eyes seemed to fall on the place where the whiskey bottle sat. "Did you drink, Mama? Is that what you did?"

"Of course not." Maria turned her attention back to the broom in her hand. How could a seven-year-old be so smart, anyway?

"Did you drink Freddy's whiskey?"

"Listen!" Maria spun around and glared at her daughter. "Are you callin' me a liar?"

"No, Mama." Savannah took a step back.

Maria hated this, when Savannah acted afraid of her. She closed the distance between them and grabbed Savannah's arm. "Don't call me a liar, you un'erstand?"

"Sorry. Sorry, Mama." Savannah started to cry. "You told me you weren't gonna drink."

"And I didn't drink. You never saw me drink, okay?"

"Okay." Savannah jerked her arm free and rubbed the place where a line of red marks stood out. "I'm sorry."

"You better be." Maria gave her daughter a shove for

good measure. Brat. Trying to ruin a perfectly good day. She was about to say so when she remembered she was supposed to be treating Savannah differently. Better than before. She swept the other half of the kitchen floor, and she was almost done when she realized how dizzy she was. The whiskey was making the room tilt, and Maria was angry at herself for drinking so much. She could have done with half of what she'd gulped down. The floor felt wobbly beneath her, and suddenly she leaned wrong on the broom and wound up flat on the floor. Quickly, she lifted herself to her hands and knees and cursed softly.

"Mama." Savannah rushed to her side. "Are you hurt?"

"No." She used her daughter's shoulder to stand up and then she smiled her nicest smile. "Mama's sorry about earlier. I'm jus' tired, like I said." She messed her fingers through Savannah's reddish-blond hair. "Let's get ready for the day, okay?"

Savannah still looked nervous, but she nodded. They got dressed and took the subway to Central Park, same as always. Halfway to their spot, Maria grabbed a fistful of dirt and rubbed it on her face and Savannah's.

"I hate this, Mama. No more dirt, please!"

"Shhh." Maria put her hand against her daughter's mouth. The effects of the whiskey were already wearing off, her body already craving one more swig, one more rush. "We won't beg much longer, baby girl. We have to have the dirt or people won't give us anything."

She had made a sign last week that read "Please help me feed my daughter." She carried it in a grocery bag and when they found their spot on a bench across from the zoo entrance, Maria pulled it out. It seemed to work. People tossed fives and tens their way without thinking twice. Yesterday they'd brought home more than a hundred dollars, most of which she gave to Freddy for rent. She was paying her way now. It was more respectable that way, more like a mother should be. But today the money would be hers, and she could take Savannah out for pizza later or maybe to a movie. That would keep the kid happy, and keeping Savannah happy was very important now.

That's what mothers were supposed to do, keep their kids happy. But Maria had to be honest with herself, trying to be a good mother had to account for at least some of her twitches and racing heart. They begged for five hours without a break. After that, they went out for pizza, and when Savannah took a trip to the bathroom, Maria ordered herself a pitcher of beer.

When Savannah returned she noticed right away. "You said you weren't gonna drink alcohol."

"This is a party." Maria kept her tone happy, but under the table she dug her fingers into Savannah's arm, to warn her against saying anything else. "We made a hundred and twenty-two dollars today, baby girl. I'll drink what I want."

One pitcher became two and then three and the room was spinning hard. A waitress told her it was time to leave, but Maria didn't want to go. She was having a party with her daughter, and what was wrong with that? But then the waitress had two people with her, two big ol' guys, and they told her she needed to pay for her tab and be on her way.

"Listen!" She stood and pushed the nearest guy in the

shoulder. "No one tells me what to do!" She was yelling, but she didn't care. "I'm a millionaire. I do what I want!"

Savannah shrank down in her seat and covered her face.

"Ma'am, if you don't pay your tab and leave, we'll have to call the police."

"Mama!" Savannah shrieked at her. "Please just pay him."

"Shut up." Maria was sick of the girl, sick of playing the role of perfect mother. She slapped Savannah hard across the face. "I hate being your mama, can't you see that?"

The man from the restaurant grabbed her arm. "That's enough," he hissed at her. Then he turned to the other guy. "Call nine-one-one."

Nine-one-one? The police couldn't come or everything would be ruined. They wouldn't give two million dollars to a drunk who slapped her daughter. And if the guy called the police then everyone would know that's what she'd done. "No, you don't!" Maria screamed right in the man's face. Then she reeled back and took a swing at him, but she missed. Somehow the action sent her spiraling to the floor, and on the way down she hit her head on something sharp and hard. The table, maybe.

When she next opened her eyes, a roomful of policemen stood around her. They pulled her to her feet and put handcuffs on her. Maria cussed and kicked at them, but they took her anyway, threw her into a police car, and drove off with her. Not until they pulled into the precinct parking lot did she remember Savannah.

"My little girl!" she screamed. She leaned as far forward as she could. "Where's my little girl?"

"We took care of her." The policeman behind the wheel glared at her. "Sit back and shut your mouth."

Maria realized how badly she'd blown it. She would have to work harder than ever to make the lawyers and the judge believe she was a good mother now. Her head hurt as she pressed herself into the back of the cruiser. On the good side, she was getting a break from Savannah, from the girl's constant questions and scrutiny. The kid was more a spy than a daughter. But she'd have to find a way to make the girl happy, to keep herself sober and in line, or Maria knew she'd lose everything.

After they booked and printed her, they pushed her into a stinky cell and slammed the door shut. Maria felt afraid and alone, drunk, and depressed over the mistakes she'd made that night. She curled up on a wooden bench along one wall of the cell and hoped she hadn't blown it. Because for the first time in her life, she had reasons to believe things would be good again, reasons to believe she would have the house and the car and the future she'd always wanted. With or without Savannah. If she could get herself out of this mess, she had reasons to believe in tomorrow.

Two million wonderful reasons.

❧

Savannah lay in the dark in the strange bed and held tight to the only thing that mattered. The photograph of her daddy. After the trouble at the restaurant, a nice policeman had taken her to Freddy's house. Savannah wasn't sure how they knew where to go, but they looked through her mama's wallet and maybe something in there told them the directions.

At Freddy's, the lights were out and the nice policeman took her hand and walked her inside so she could get her things. He turned on the bedroom light when they reached the room Savannah shared with her mama. Savannah got down on the floor and crawled under the desk. One at a time she pulled out her pillow and her blanket and her pile of clothes.

"Is this your bed?" The policeman pointed to where Mama slept.

"No." She felt shy about not having a bed, because maybe other kids her age didn't sleep on the floor. She pointed to the spot beneath the desk. "I sleep down there."

The nice man's face said that he wasn't happy with that news. Savannah was scooping her things into one pile, but the officer said she didn't need her blanket or pillow. "Your foster parents will have all that, sweetie."

Foster parents. Wasn't that what Mama had always said might happen? If Savannah complained too much, then the police would take her to foster parents? She was suddenly very afraid about that news. "Who are the foster parents?" Her voice sounded quiet and little and scared.

"They're very nice people." He patted her on the arm. "Don't worry, Savannah. It'll be okay."

"I want Mama." She wasn't sure why she said that, because her mama didn't want her. She even said so out loud in the restaurant. But Mama was all she had until the day her daddy came to get her.

The policeman looked closer at her arm. "What's this?" He ran his finger over the marks on Savannah, the ones her mama had put there.

She tried to be brave, but she moved a little because the spots hurt. "Nothing."

"Your mother did this, didn't she?"

"She didn't mean to."

The officer shook his head and said, "I'll bet." Then he took Savannah's things from her so she didn't have anything to carry except her small bag with the plastic cross and the picture of her daddy.

They drove for a long time and crossed two bridges before they pulled up in front of a nice house, nicer than anything Savannah had ever been inside. She heard the officer tell someone on the radio that the foster family lived in Queens, so that's where they must be. Together they went inside. An old man and lady lived there. They showed her to a room upstairs with a bed that was just the right size for Savannah, gave her a new toothbrush and some toothpaste, and said it was time to brush. Then they gave her a new nightgown and told her it was bedtime.

"Do you believe in Jesus?" the old woman asked her. She had nice eyes.

"Yes." Savannah remembered Grandpa Ted. "Are we going to talk to Him?"

"We are." The old couple sat together on the edge of her bed and talked to Jesus for a long time. "We know You have plans for Savannah. We pray that You protect her and help her find those plans. Please be with her mother and let her know that with You she can find true and lasting change."

After that they said good night and sweet dreams and they left her alone. But they kept one small light on. "Just in case you're afraid," the old woman told her.

As soon as she was alone, she snuck out of bed and

pulled the picture of her daddy out of her bag. She had Jesus in her heart, but when she was really afraid she would sleep better if she had Daddy in her hands. She looked at his smile and his friendly eyes. *Daddy, where are you? Why aren't you coming for me?* She felt little stinging feelings in her eyes and she blinked back some wetness. *Dear Jesus, it's me, Savannah. Can You tell my daddy that I'm waiting for him?* She sniffed real quiet, so the nice people wouldn't come back in the room. *Tell him I'm at the foster house and Mama doesn't want me anymore. So now would be a good time to come find me.*

She talked a bit more to Jesus, and then she yawned two times and looked at the picture again. Her daddy was so handsome, so strong. He never would have let anyone put marks on Savannah's arms. She yawned once more, and her eyes started to close. The picture was rough around the edges, but Savannah didn't care. She hugged it close to her heart and pushed her face deeper into the pillow. Her mama's voice came in all around her, all the mean things she'd said at the restaurant.

Shut up! I hate being your mama!

The words lined up again and again in her mind, until finally she thought about Jesus again. Because Grandpa Ted said Jesus loved her, and that meant it was up to Jesus to bring her daddy to her. As she fell asleep, she begged Jesus to love her enough to make that happen. Because she needed to be with her daddy right away, before the foster people gave her back to Mama and something really bad happened. Her daddy better hurry and get here, because she needed her Prince Charming to rescue her.

Even if she had to find him herself.

Annie was aware that she'd lost the first round. Maria's attorney was some creep from Manhattan, and he'd insisted that Maria was a single mother whose routine couldn't be disrupted simply because some jilted family members didn't want their son's settlement money going to his own daughter. At least that's the way Thomas had depicted the scenario to them. Apparently, the judge was convinced, because he ruled that more evidence would need to be presented, enough to make a decent argument that Savannah wasn't Josh's daughter in any way other than by blood.

If they could make that argument strong enough, then the judge would consider ordering Maria out to Denver for a hearing.

Annie was reading through the documents on Josh's computer, and her determination had never been stronger. How dare the woman get an attorney and battle for Josh's money? Could she honestly sleep at night knowing she was fighting for money that should never be hers? She rubbed her eyes and looked around the apartment. They'd moved Josh's furniture out this past weekend. Nate rented a U-Haul and took his bedroom set to what would now be the guest room in their house in Black Forest. The rest—the sofa and chair, his pots and pans and dishes and linens—all had been donated to Goodwill.

When the place was empty except for Josh's computer and desk and several boxes of things they'd already gone through, she and Lindsay and Nate spent a day cleaning. It was important that they leave the place the way it had been given to Josh. He would have wanted them to do that much for the manager.

Now, with only a few days left in October, Annie was glad they were nearly finished. She still had to decide which boxes of his personal belongings they should keep, and which— like the box of hiking magazines—should be dropped off at the recycling center. When she needed a break from the paperwork, she spent time on Josh's computer, opening one document at a time and either printing or deleting it.

She opened Josh's iTunes library, selected his Favorites playlist, and hit the play button. The heartrending, haunting sounds of Josh's favorite song filled the space around her. The plink of the piano chimed in, and then the words that Josh loved.

"*I can only imagine, what it will be like . . . when I walk by Your side. . . .*"

Sorrow, like an old friend, put its arms around her, and for the hundredth time since her son's death, she felt tears in her eyes. *You don't have to imagine anymore, Josh . . . never again.* She pictured her baby, her son, walking alongside Jesus, looking long into His face. Was he hurt that his own parents hadn't really known him? Was he angry, disappointed in her the way she had once, a lifetime ago, been disappointed in him?

She knew him so much better now. Her discoveries made her want to have Lindsay write a story about his life for the *Gazette*. That way the busybodies with the public library and the teachers union and the PTA could know that Josh Warren had been a success in all the ways that mattered. No matter how his life looked to people who didn't know him.

Shallow people, like Annie had been.

She breathed in deep and let the words of the song fill her soul. A ray of light warmed the cold, dark sadness inside her. Josh wasn't angry with her or disappointed, he had no regrets. His only concern now was whether to dance for Jesus or fall to his knees in awe of a God so merciful, so loving. Josh was okay, and one day she'd have the chance to hold him in her arms and tell him what she hoped he already knew.

That she couldn't possibly be prouder of him.

The music kept playing, but she returned her attention to the files on Josh's computer. The next one was marked Hours. She opened it and saw a spreadsheet with Josh's assigned hours for the month. Next to each calendar date, Josh had added a check mark—designating, it seemed, that he had completed the shift in question.

Thomas had told her to print anything dealing with his work as a tow truck driver, so she hit the print button and waited. As she did, someone knocked at the door. Carl Joseph and Daisy had been by several times now, once with a plate of cookies and most recently with a seedling pine tree. "Because when you see it you'll remember Josh," Daisy had told her.

"And Josh was too good to forget." Carl Joseph's earnestness was refreshing.

She figured they were probably back again, maybe to check if she'd enjoyed the cookies or to bring her a pitcher of iced tea. Daisy had asked last time if she liked iced tea on hot days. Annie smiled to herself as she turned the knob and opened the door. But standing there instead was a striking dark-haired young man with high cheekbones and eyes deep enough to fall into. "Mrs. Warren?"

"Yes." She stepped aside. "How can I help you?"

"I'm Cody Gunner, Carl Joseph's brother."

"Ah. Your brother speaks very highly of you." Annie made the connection immediately. "Come in." She motioned to a couple of bar stools that remained along Josh's short kitchen counter. "I'm afraid there aren't many places to sit."

"That's fine. I won't be long." He gave her a polite smile and moved to the closest seat. He waited until she was seated opposite him before he began. "My wife and I were talking recently about a conversation I had with Josh a couple of weeks before he died." The grief in Cody's eyes told Annie that he, too, had cared about her son. "I left a message for you. I'm not sure if you got it."

Annie didn't remember the message from the apartment manager until just then. She frowned. "We got the message. I meant to call you the next morning, but . . ." She looked around.

"I know, you've been distracted." He gave her a sad smile. "I was at my brother's and I saw your car. I decided to take a chance."

"I'm glad you did." Annie was no longer surprised by

anything she might learn about Josh. Whatever piece of Josh's life story Cody was bringing with him now, Annie didn't fear it. She craved it the way women in wartime craved the next letters from their sons on the battlefield. "Can I get you some water?"

"No, thanks." Cody put his hands on his knees and looked at the mantel over Josh's fireplace. The photos were still there, where they would stay until they closed his door behind them for the last time. Cody turned his eyes to her. "What do you know about the little girl in the photo?"

"Much." Annie sighed. She turned her attention to the picture of her granddaughter. "Our attorney had a paternity test done, and it was conclusive. She's Josh's daughter, Savannah."

They were quiet for a few moments. "That's what Josh believed—that she was his." Cody seemed uncomfortable with whatever he was about to say. "This is none of my business, Mrs. Warren, but Josh's settlement . . . Has there been a determination about where the money will go?"

Annie was surprised by Cody's question. He was right, the topic was none of his business, but if this had something to do with a conversation he'd had with Josh, then . . . Her insides tightened sharply. "Actually, we're working with Josh's attorney on that. The money will automatically go to Savannah by way of her mother unless our lawyer can convince the judge otherwise." She felt the strange need to defend herself. "Obviously, we're contesting the fact that Savannah is a rightful heir to the settlement. We're trying to set up a college fund for her, anything to keep the money out of the hands of her mother. We don't think she'll use it for Savannah at all."

"Yes, well, that's what Josh and I talked about that day. We were on our way home from church."

Again Annie felt the loss of all she'd missed out on. She never believed Josh had found his way back to God, and so her son had spent his last two months attending services with people who were virtually strangers. She hid her heartache and forced herself to listen.

"We were talking about Savannah, how Josh's attorney didn't want him to mention her if the subject came up during one of his depositions. That was before anyone knew for sure whether she was his daughter."

Annie wondered if they might have avoided all this if Josh had only taken his lawyer's advice.

"Josh said he knew why his attorney wanted him to deny having any children. It was because of the settlement, so the money would go to his family if something happened to him before the case was settled."

Annie felt for her son, troubled by the conflict between his certainty that Savannah was his daughter and the urging of his lawyer to publicly say otherwise for the sake of a pile of money. She could almost sense where Cody's story was headed. "Did he—did he tell you his wishes?"

Cody hesitated. "Yes, ma'am. That's why I'm here."

"Hold on." Air, that's what she needed. She stood and slid the patio door open and breathed in until her lungs were full. Then she returned to the seat opposite Cody. She had prayed for God's wisdom, His leading. Now she needed to listen very carefully, no matter how she thought things should go. She searched Cody's eyes. "Tell me. Please."

"He wanted you and your family to be repaid. Everything you ever loaned him." Cody narrowed his eyes, empathy flooding his voice. "But after that, he wanted the money to go to Savannah."

"All of it?" Annie felt suddenly light-headed, as if the moment were something from a dream or a nightmare. She had ideas for how to use the settlement, once Josh's debts were repaid. She pictured setting up a college fund for Ben and Bella, and of course for Savannah, and then maybe they would use the money to help Nate get reelected one more time. There would be money for their church and several of their charities, and something for Carl Joseph and Daisy, so they might never have to pay for bus fare again. She and Nate would pay off their house, because Josh had worried about their retirement when he'd had to borrow so much from them, often bringing up the financial concerns that plagued some retired people. That sort of thing. She asked the question again in a tortured whisper. "The entire settlement?"

Cody nodded. "I'm sorry. I figured this would be hard for you. I was surprised, too."

Annie wondered if Josh was upset with them, if that was why he could fathom giving his entire settlement to a child he'd never met—whether she was his own daughter or not. "Did he say . . . I mean, was he angry with us? Was that why?"

"It wasn't like he actually thought it would happen. He was in a lot of pain, but he didn't think he had weeks to live." Cody's tone told her that he'd thought all of this through a number of times already. "Like I said, he wanted his debts repaid. But I think he just loved that little girl with all his heart."

Annie could almost hear the Lord telling her to pay attention. "Did he say anything else?"

"He told me Savannah hadn't had her daddy all these years. If something happened to him, at least he wanted her taken care of financially." Cody sat up a little straighter. "He said he wanted her to grow up knowing how much he cared for her—whether he was alive or not."

Just like that, Annie felt everything change, felt the fight drain from her body like water from a sink. She'd asked God to show her the right thing, and now through Cody's words He had. She kept her thoughts to herself as she and Cody talked a few more minutes about Josh's renewed faith, how he loved singing along during the worship part of the service, and how he hung on every word the pastor said. "My wife and I had the feeling Josh was just starting to live." Cody gave a sad shake of his head. "I'm sorry, Mrs. Warren, for your loss."

She saw him to the door and thanked him for his honesty. After he was gone she stood unmoving in the silence of the empty living room. The settlement belonged to Josh. Until now they could tell themselves that Josh would have wanted Savannah's college education taken care of, but not her current needs, not if they had to go through Maria first. Until now they could have made themselves believe that he wouldn't have wanted a dime going to Maria Cameron, not after what she'd put him through.

But now . . .

The conversation with Cody was all the proof Annie needed. When Nate heard what their son had said about Savannah and the money, Annie was sure her husband would see things the same way. God might as well have come through the door and told her the news Himself. The message was that clear.

She started the song over again and closed her eyes, picturing Josh walking the streets of heaven free from pain and worry over when the lawsuit would be settled and how he was going to connect with his daughter. He'd left them to sort through what remained of his life, and they would remember him differently because of that. But he'd also left behind a daughter, and his wishes that she receive his settlement money. Even if her mother spent every dollar before Savannah's eighteenth birthday.

Annie wandered to the photograph on the mantel one more time. She picked up the wooden frame and stared into the eyes of her granddaughter. If Josh wanted her to have all the money, then so be it. She would call Nate, and then call Thomas Flynn, and the fight against Maria Cameron would be officially dropped. But she would demand one thing before walking away from the matter forever. Something that was almost worth two million dollars all by itself.

A visit with Josh's little girl.

TWENTY-TWO

The call to Josh's lawyer was merely a routine favor Lindsay was doing for her mother. Her parents had been through so much in the past month that, even with her workload at the newspaper, she tried to do everything she could to help.

Lindsay dialed Thomas Flynn's number and waited while the line began to ring. Already this morning they'd all met at Josh's apartment to load the rest of his things in the back of her father's pickup truck. The last things her mother packed were the three photographs that had sat over Josh's fireplace. She wrapped them in a pillowcase and set them on the front seat of the truck.

Before they left for the last time, she and her parents stood in the doorway and her father had prayed. "Lord, You showed us so much about our son this past month." His voice was strained as he continued. "Thank You for giving us this time and place so we could learn what we didn't know about our son."

Lindsay and her mother both had tears on their cheeks as Nate continued, thanking God for the neighbors who had known Josh and for the ways in which they'd come forward to fill in the memory of all Josh had meant to this world. "A person doesn't have to have a college degree or an investment portfolio or a big house to be successful, Lord. You showed us that this past month, and in the process You gave us a season of grieving and discovering that none of us will ever forget."

When they finally closed the door and locked it, they took Josh's keys to the apartment manager and returned to their separate cars. Lindsay's parents looked emotionally exhausted. They took Josh's final belongings back to their house, and Lindsay returned to her home to make a few phone calls. This was one of them, to see if there'd been any response from Maria Cameron since she'd gotten the news that Josh's settlement money was hers.

A secretary patched Lindsay through to Mr. Flynn, and Lindsay kept her question short and to the point. But even before she could finish, Josh's lawyer cut her off. "I was just going to call your parents." His words came fast and colored with concern. "I got news from Maria Cameron's attorney. She's been arrested and put in jail for two weeks. Apparently, she got drunk and put on some public display." His tone fell. "She tried to hit a waiter, and she slapped Savannah with a whole restaurant full of people watching."

Lindsay was on her feet, pacing from the kitchen to her dining room and back again. "So where's Savannah if her mom's in jail?"

"In foster care. Her lawyer says the district attorney is sorting through a stack of warrants trying to figure out what to charge her with." Mr. Flynn barely broke for a quick breath. "This could change things. Here's what I'm thinking."

For the next fifteen minutes, Lindsay listened, and when the call ended, she picked up the phone and dialed her parents. Her mom answered almost immediately. "Lindsay? Did he have any news?"

Lindsay steadied herself against the doorway in her dining room. "In fact, he did. How soon can you meet me?"

"I was headed to the cemetery." Her mom still sounded tired, drained. "I bought flowers for Josh's grave."

None of them had spent time at the graveside. They'd been too busy sorting through Josh's life to spend much time dwelling on his death. "Meet you there in an hour."

Her mind raced with the details Thomas Flynn had shared with her. With Savannah in foster care, Lindsay was still trying to absorb the fact that her mother's prayers might be answered sooner than any of them thought.

If Mr. Flynn was right, a visit with Josh's daughter might be only an airline ticket away.

❧

Annie reached Josh's grave first. She didn't bring a chair or a blanket, because this wasn't a long visit, more just a chance to pay her respects. Josh's stone should be marked by flowers at least, so that people who passed by would know he was missed and that he mattered. If there was one thing Annie knew now, it was that single truth.

Josh's life did matter.

She studied the temporary marker. Nate had ordered a permanent stone and an inground container to hold flowers, but they wouldn't be ready to install until Thanksgiving time. For now there was only the simple piece of cement with Josh's name engraved across the top: *Joshua David Warren.*

"I miss you, son . . . so much." She closed her eyes and lifted her face to the breeze drifting down from the mountains. Sometimes on days like this the light wind felt like Josh's presence beside her, like she could reach out and touch him, his memory was so close. If she could—if she could have just one more time with him she wasn't sure she would even know what to say. Carl Joseph had said it all, really. Josh was a hero, but as wonderful as that was, Annie had missed the fact. Tragically and completely, she'd missed it.

"Mom."

For a fraction of a second, the voice belonged to Josh. Not Josh the way he'd sounded the last time she talked to him, but Josh the way he'd sounded when he was ten or eleven and he had a frog or a flower to show her. But before the thought had time to root itself, Lindsay's voice was soft beside her. "Sorry . . . I didn't want to frighten you."

Annie opened her eyes. "Sometimes I can feel him." She smiled—that painful sort of drenched-in-sadness smile. The one that would be her trademark whenever she thought about Josh for the rest of her days. "As close as wind against my skin."

"Hmmm." Lindsay folded her hands and stared down at Josh's marker. "I feel it, too. But it's not the same."

"No." She breathed in slowly through her nose, savoring the smell of evergreen on the breeze. "Thomas had news for us?"

"You're sure you don't want to sit down? We could talk about it in the car."

Annie cocked her head and took another look at her son's name on the temporary stone. "I'm okay. I need this time, the serenity of it."

Lindsay looked like she wasn't sure where to begin. "He got news about Maria Cameron. Mom . . . she's in jail. Public intoxication, and she has a list of warrants for her arrest. I guess she hit Savannah."

The details kept coming, but Annie couldn't get past that one. She felt something fierce and protective come to life within her, and in the middle of Lindsay's story she held up her hand. "She hit Savannah?"

"With everyone watching." Lindsay bit her lip. "Mr. Flynn says Savannah has bruises on her arms. She's in a foster home for now."

Annie wasn't sure whether to scream or break down in light of this latest sad development. All this time she'd had nothing but disdain for Maria Cameron, but only because of the way she'd treated Josh. Until now she hadn't thought for a minute about how she'd treated Josh's daughter.

The truth nearly dropped her to her knees. What sort of life had Savannah lived? As Lindsay shared the rest of what the lawyer had told her, a frightening picture came into focus. Savannah and her mother lived with a known drug dealer, and Savannah slept on the floor beneath a desk—which was an improvement from the three times when police had picked the pair up in Central Park where they sometimes slept beneath a bridge near the pond.

Annie wasn't sure how much more of the story she could take. If Josh had known these details, he would have found a way to reach Savannah if he had to walk across the country. Again she was hit by the truth that if she and Nate had paid more credence to Josh's insistence that Savannah was his daughter, then together they might have found out about her situation sooner, gotten the paternity test, and figured out some way to rescue her.

Annie's determination to find and help her granddaughter grew like a wildfire within her. Maria Cameron would never hurt Savannah again, not if Annie had anything to do about it. "If her mother isn't fit, then Savannah should come live with us. What did Thomas say about that?"

"Well, that's the worst part." Lindsay folded her arms. Her voice blended with the wind, every word washing over Annie whether she wanted to hear it or not. "Mr. Flynn says that Maria hasn't been arrested in more than a year, and her landlord says that she's usually a model mother."

"Which is clearly a lie."

"But the system is bound to pay attention to that. If her attorney can get the warrants dismissed, then she'll probably get Savannah back. That's what he said." She took her mother's hand. "But he also said that if you act fast, you can meet Savannah while she's still in foster care."

"What?" Annie couldn't explain the sense of joy that burst through her pain in that single moment. She was going to get to meet her granddaughter. Her dream of looking into the eyes that were so like Josh's was going to come true. God had heard her prayers, and now in a matter of days she would meet the girl Josh had loved for the past seven years.

She called Nate while she and Lindsay walked back to their cars. Once she had his okay, she called Thomas and then the airline. Lindsay and Nate wanted to go, too, so she booked three flights to LaGuardia. Thomas recommended that all of them go, because there was no telling what Maria would do once she had custody of Savannah again, once she had the money. The woman was under no obligation to stay in contact with the Warren family, despite the fact that they had willingly dropped the fight for Josh's settlement.

Thomas felt strongly that once Maria had the money, she and the girl would disappear, move to another state or another country, and that would be that. Which meant this might be their only chance to meet the girl Josh had longed to hold, the one he had planned to love and care for as soon as he had the chance to meet her. Annie tried to imagine what might have happened if Josh and Becky had gotten back together, if he'd finished college and if they'd married. Her grandchild would've had a different mother and a different life, and Josh would never have been working for the garage that night. Never would have had a reason to find himself suddenly in the path of a drunk driver.

Annie drove home from the cemetery lost in a maze of questions. What would the girl be like? If she'd been abused or neglected, would she be quiet and withdrawn? Would meeting Annie scare her or confuse her? Did she love her mother despite the life she'd lived? Was she being treated kindly in the foster home where she'd been placed? But the question most pressing on Annie's heart was the obvious one, the one she had thought about ever since the results of the paternity test came in.

Did Savannah know about Josh?

TWENTY-THREE

Some nice people were coming to see her today, that's all Savannah knew. Her foster parents bought her new clothes—a sundress, they called it, and a sweater. The sweater was white, and the dress . . . the dress was white with little purple and green flowers across it, and best of all, the sundress was brand-new!

"Who are these people?" she asked her foster mother.

"They're very nice from what I understand, and they love Jesus."

That part made Savannah less scared about the meeting. But still it didn't answer her question. "How do they know me?"

"They'll explain it to you, sweetheart." That's all her foster mother would say. The people would explain it when they showed up after lunchtime.

It was after lunch right now, so Savannah sat on her knees on the sofa next to the front window and studied every car that passed by. There would be three of them. That's what her foster parents said.

Savannah had wondered something ever since she knew the nice people were coming. What if one of them was her daddy? He was out there somewhere, and her mama said she was going to meet him later. Much later, but still . . . this was much later than then. Maybe her daddy had a family and he was bringing them along. That's what other people did, because when she and her mama were in Central Park and other people walked along with their kids sometimes there was a whole group all together.

She had always wondered what it would be like to be part of a whole group.

"You okay in there?" Her foster mother poked her head into the room. "You need anything, Savannah?"

Just my daddy, she wanted to say. But she gave the old woman a nice smile. "No, thank you." Then she thought about kneeling on the sofa and maybe that wasn't allowed, so she covered her mouth real quick and felt her eyes get big. "Want me to get off the sofa?"

The woman laughed real soft. "No, sweetie. You go right ahead and kneel on the sofa. The thing's old as time anyway."

Savannah smiled. "Thank you." She felt better now. Her foster mother was nice. At first Savannah thought about running away and finding her daddy, because that was all she really needed. Then she wouldn't be a trouble to her mama, and she wouldn't take up the time of the foster parents. But her foster mother was very nice, and she probably would've been sad if Savannah ran away. So she stayed and asked Jesus every day to bring her daddy very soon.

Her foster mother walked back into the kitchen and Savannah looked out the window again. Just then, a blue car stopped in front of the house, and after a few loud heartbeats, a man got out from the driver's side. Savannah made her eyes squinty and looked at him real hard. He sort of looked like her daddy, but not really because he had gray hair. Mostly gray.

Next came a woman from the other front seat, and a younger woman from the backseat. Savannah sucked in a little gasp, because the first woman, the one from the front seat, was very pretty. Like the queen in *Sleeping Beauty*, but with hair down to her shoulders. The three of them talked for a minute by themselves and then they started up the walk.

Savannah quick ducked down beneath the windowsill. Why were people who didn't know her coming for a visit? Were they friends of her mama's? Or maybe friends of Freddy's? Savanna poked her head up just enough to see them. No. They weren't friends of either her mama or Freddy because they dressed in nice clothes and their eyes looked different. More like the people who gave them money when they begged in the park.

"They're here!" She shouted the news because she wanted her foster mother to answer the door. That was the right way of things for regular people, and Savannah wanted these nice people to think she was regular. When her mama drank too much whiskey or stayed up too late, she was the one who answered Freddy's door. But that wasn't regular at all.

Her foster mother came into the room wiping her hands on a towel. She moved to the door and all of a sudden Savannah had a warm feeling inside her. So many times when she and her mama begged money, she wondered what it would be like to spend time with the people who *gave* the fives and tens, instead of always being on the taking side.

And now, even though she still didn't understand, she was about to find out.

❧

Annie had never been so quiet in all her life.

The whole way here—on the trip to the Denver airport, during the flight through O'Hare to LaGuardia, while they waited at the rental car counter, and during the drive here to Queens—she had no interest in making small talk. All she could think was that this should have been Josh's trip. Now that they'd found Savannah, now that they knew for sure she was Josh's daughter, the chance to meet her and get to know her even for a short time belonged to Josh.

So she spent the time wondering what he would have been thinking, and anticipating the moment when she would first see Savannah the way Josh would have looked forward to it. This was the single goal through all of his pain and suffering, the one moment that mattered more to him than any other.

Annie linked hands with Nate, and a few steps behind them came Lindsay. That moment was finally here, and Annie wondered if she'd remember to breathe. It was the first Wednesday in November, but the afternoon was still warm, the leaves every shade of orange and yellow and red. Twenty years from now Annie knew without a doubt she would remember everything about this minute. The way Nate's hand felt in hers, the clutter on the front porch of the foster family, the colors in the leaves, and the feel of fall in the air. Her heart beat so hard she wondered if it would burst through her chest. Nate went to knock on the front door, but before he could reach it, an older woman opened it and smiled at them. "You must be the Warrens."

"Yes." Nate fell back beside Annie. "Thank you for making this possible."

"Anytime I can be part of something good for these kids, it makes my day." She held out her hand. "I'm Marti." The three of them introduced themselves, and Marti explained that Savannah didn't know who they were or how they were connected. "I figured I'd let you take care of that part."

The questions came again in a wild rush. What if she didn't understand? What if she had no idea who Josh was or that he was her father? How could they erase seven years of having no relationship in a single afternoon? Nate must have seen her anxiety, because he squeezed her hand and gave her a look that said not to worry. Everything would be okay.

Marti welcomed them in and moved aside. There, standing at the far end of the room, was Savannah, the girl from the picture. She was older now, her eyes more guarded than they'd been when she was four. But they were Josh's eyes. Annie was sure that Nate and Lindsay could see that as easily as she could. Marti stepped into another room, saying something about leaving them alone so they could get to know each other.

Annie couldn't focus on anything but the little girl, Josh's daughter. "Hi, honey." Annie took a few steps closer to the girl and then stooped down so she was at eye level with her. "I'm Annie."

"Hi." Savannah gave a little wave of her hand, but she kept her chin tucked down, too shy to make a move in their direction. "I'm Savannah."

How often had Josh longed to hear those simple words? Annie pressed her finger to her upper lip, refusing the tears lining up along the back side of her soul. "Nice to meet you, Savannah."

Nate and Lindsay took turns introducing themselves, and then Annie motioned for the three of them to take seats around the room. Savannah stayed standing in the far corner. Nate coughed a few times, and Annie could tell he was fighting tears. "Would you like to sit for a minute?"

"No, thank you." Savannah did a half twirl one way and then the other, and though she still had shy eyes for them, a smile tugged at her lips. "I got a new sundress and a new sweater."

Annie wanted to take her to FAO Schwarz and let her buy whatever she wanted. She dismissed the thought. If this was their only chance to meet Savannah, her attention couldn't be on all the girl didn't have. Nate nodded at her, silently asking her to take the lead in the conversation that needed to happen before they could spend the afternoon with her.

Annie slid forward a few inches and looked at her granddaughter, at the eyes that were so familiar. "Honey, you don't know who we are, right?"

Savannah shrugged one dainty shoulder. "You're nice people, that's what my foster mother said. And you love Jesus."

"Right." Annie appreciated the woman's comments.

They needed all the help they could get to make this little girl understand who they were and why they were here. She exhaled, silently begging God for the right words. "What do you know about your daddy, Savannah?"

As soon as the question was out of her mouth, Annie saw the child respond. Her eyes began to dance and she clasped her hands the way young children do on Christmas morning when they wake to find the rocking horse or doll or train set they'd always wanted. That's how Savannah looked, and she moved her gaze from Annie to Nate to Lindsay, and back to Annie again. "Can you wait a minute?"

"Sure, honey." Annie glanced at the others while Savannah ran off down the hall toward the back of the house.

"At least she knows who he is." Nate dabbed his knuckle beneath one eye and then the other. "Did you see her light up? I think she knows, don't you?"

"Definitely," Lindsay whispered. "I can't believe how much she looks like Josh."

"She looks like you, too." Annie had realized it as the girl reacted to the mention of her father. Her excitement changed something in her face, and suddenly Annie felt like she was looking at a mix of Josh and Lindsay at that age.

They heard Savannah's feet coming down the hall, running as fast as she could by the sounds of it. *Breathe*, Annie ordered herself. *Breathe so you don't pass out on the living room floor. Please, God, help me breathe.*

Savannah rounded the corner and stopped short. In her hands was a framed photo—a five-by-seven. She held it out in front of her and with a look that was pure adoration, she studied the picture. Then she turned it so they could see the photo.

Annie gasped softly and put her fingers over her lips. The picture was Josh a few years ago, before the accident. Savannah's eyes shone as she looked from the picture back to Annie. "This is my daddy." She smiled with a pride that knew no limits. "He's a Prince Charming."

Across the room, Lindsay looked away, probably so Savannah wouldn't see her tears. Annie felt Nate put his arm across her shoulders. She hadn't counted on this; none of them had. The idea that Savannah might not only know who her dad was, but that she'd have a picture of him, that she'd so completely adore him.

Annie could barely force any words from her mouth, let alone her heart. The image of Josh's daughter holding his picture and calling him a Prince Charming would stay with her forever. She locked eyes with her granddaughter. "How do you know about him, Savannah? Who told you?"

A ribbon of fear wove its way through Savannah's smile. "My mama." She squirmed as if maybe that part wasn't quite true. "I think she knew him a long time ago, because she had this picture. She put it in the trash one day when she was cleaning out our room, way back when I was a little girl. She said once it was my daddy." Savannah swallowed hard and her eyes found Josh's in the picture again. "She told me he was a real Prince Charming. Since she didn't want the picture, I took it." She held it close to her chest. "Mama doesn't know, but . . . I've kept it ever since then."

A few seconds passed while Annie processed what her

granddaughter was saying. Basically, Maria had tried to end Josh's presence in Savannah's life, but she'd found the picture and asked about it. All Annie could figure about the Prince Charming bit was the obvious—Maria had meant the comment sarcastically. But Savannah had been too young to understand sarcasm, so she'd taken her mother's comment to heart. She'd also taken the photo and kept it in hiding every day since then.

Annie wanted to take the little girl in her arms and tell her the truth about Josh—that he really was a Prince Charming. That he had lived for the chance to meet her, but that he'd lost that chance forever. And the worst part of all—that her daddy from the photograph was dead.

Nate leaned closer to Savannah. "Your mother doesn't know you have the photograph?"

A worried look darkened Savannah's countenance. "You're not going to tell her, are you?"

"No, dear." Nate's answer was quick. "Definitely not."

"Mama told me I would meet my daddy later. Much later." She looked out the window to the street beyond. "I thought maybe you were going to bring him to me."

"Well, that's why we asked you about him." Annie slid over and patted the spot on the sofa between her and Nate. "Want to sit here with us?"

Savannah hesitated, but then she tucked the framed picture beneath her arm and slowly crossed the room. She sat on the slightest edge, half standing, and she studied the picture. "He looks like a Prince Charming, don't you think?"

Annie could hardly believe they were sitting here with

Josh's daughter. "I can tell you this, honey. Your daddy was definitely a Prince Charming. We just learned that about him."

Savannah's eyes lit up again and she turned fully toward Annie. "You know him? My daddy?"

Annie wondered how many times a person's heart could break. How could they be the first real connection to her daddy the child had ever known, and in the same breath tell her that he was no longer alive? *Tell me what to say, God. . . . Help us get through this time with Savannah.*

I am with you, daughter. . . . I will give you the words.

The peace of God's promises gave Annie the strength she needed.

Even if it was only enough to survive a few minutes at a time.

TWENTY-FOUR

The time had come to tell Savannah the truth about who they were. Annie wanted to take hold of her granddaughter's hand, but it was too soon, so she stayed in her spot. On the other side of their granddaughter, Nate did the same. Lindsay was still crying softly across the room, taking in the scene.

Savannah was waiting for an answer.

"Yes, honey, we know him." She could feel herself being led along by the Holy Spirit, feel God leading her in what to say and when to say it. "Your daddy is our son—mine and Nate's."

"And he's my brother." Lindsay touched her fingers to the place above her heart. "We all love him very, very much."

Savannah was on her feet. Her smile took up her whole face and she ran to Lindsay, putting her small hands on Lindsay's knees. "You're his sister?"

"Yes. He's always been my best friend."

"Really?" She raised her eyebrows high up into her forehead. "Mine, too!" She darted back to Nate. "And you're his daddy?"

"Yes, honey." Nate touched the girl's shoulder. "You know what that makes me?"

She looked like she might have an idea, but she wasn't sure enough to voice it. Instead, she shook her head.

"It makes me your grandpa, Savannah."

"Like Grandpa Ted!" Savannah gasped and put both her hands over her mouth. When she dropped them she rushed into Nate's arms and flung her hands around his neck. "Grandpa Ted's in heaven, but you're right here. I didn't even know I had another grandpa, so now you can be my grandpa Nate, okay?"

Nate's chin was quivering. He had one hand on Savannah's back, and with the other he squeezed the bridge of his nose. He nodded, and Annie knew it was because he couldn't say anything. After another big hug, Savannah turned to her. "Then . . . are you my grandma?"

Annie wanted to freeze the moment. She held out her arms toward Josh's daughter. "Yes, honey. I'm your grandma."

Savannah didn't rush into a big hug the way she had with Nate. Instead, she seemed mesmerized by Annie, by the idea of having a grandmother. "I never had a grandma before."

"You do now." Annie couldn't fight the tears another minute. They came despite her smile. "I'll always be your grandma, because your daddy is my son."

Savannah nodded slowly. "You're"—she reached up and gingerly touched her little girl fingers to Annie's dark hair—"you're very beautiful, Grandma Annie."

A small sob escaped from Annie and she tenderly took the girl into her arms. "You're beautiful, too, Savannah.

I see your daddy in your eyes." They hugged for a long time, and Annie wanted the moment to end right there, without the admission of anything so sad as Josh's death. The ending was all wrong. She sniffed and ran her hand along Savannah's small back. "Would it be okay if we took you to the park?"

"Central Park?" Savannah looked suddenly afraid. "You mean, to beg for money?"

Annie was horrified. "No, honey. The park at the end of the street. So we can play on the swings and talk about your daddy."

Again the girl's smile was as wide and innocent as a sunrise. "I'd like that very much."

They told Marti they were leaving, and the four of them climbed into the blue rental car. A few minutes later they pulled into the lot of Maple Leaf Park, and once they were outside they headed for the swings. Annie whispered quietly to Nate and Lindsay. Sometime in the next hour she wanted a few minutes alone with Savannah, so she could tell her the truth about Josh in a way that wouldn't seem overwhelming. It was what they'd agreed to before the trip, and Nate and Lindsay both whispered their agreement.

Annie wanted to delay the news as long as possible. Savannah held her hand as they walked to the playground and when they were ten yards from the swings, she broke free and ran to the closest one. "Can I ride one, please?"

"Of course." Despite so much that was sad about the visit, Annie couldn't help but be filled with happiness at the sight of Josh's daughter begging for a ride on a swing. Like their time together was as normal as that of any other grandparents spending an afternoon with their granddaughter. "Go ahead." Annie laughed. "Climb on and I'll push you."

Savannah grabbed hold of the metal chains and sat down awkwardly, as though she wasn't sure the swing would hold her up. "Not too high, okay? I've never been on swings before."

The news shifted Annie's emotions one more time, and hit her hard. Her granddaughter had never been on swings? "I thought you said you and your mother spent a lot of time in Central Park."

"We beg money there." Savannah looked embarrassed at the fact. "Mama always said that people wouldn't give money if we looked like we were at the park for fun. So no swings for us."

Annie was glad she wasn't meeting Maria Cameron on this trip. She wasn't sure she would be responsible for her actions if she had a chance to address the woman in person. She let go of her anger and frustration, so that Savannah wouldn't think for a second it was directed at her. "Here." Annie put her hands around Savannah's smaller ones. "Hold tight to the chains and I'll push you really slowly. Just tell me if you feel like you're going too high."

She moved around behind her granddaughter and gave her the most delicate pushes. "Don't let go."

"I won't." Savannah was clearly petrified, but as the ride continued she relaxed and began to giggle. "I like this, Grandma Annie. It's like I'm flying."

"Tell me if you want to go higher."

"Okay." Savannah's giggle became a full-fledged laugh. "Higher, please."

Annie did as she was asked. This was how all of life might have been for Savannah, only Josh should have been the one pushing her, and Annie should have been on the park bench next to Nate and Lindsay. She was a delightful child, and if Josh had known her these past seven years, no doubt the five of them would have shared countless happy times like this one.

They moved from the swings to the monkey bars, and then to the double slides. Annie even climbed up and rode down next to her granddaughter until she felt brave enough to tackle the slide on her own. After her fifth time down, Savannah set her feet in the sand and caught her breath, her narrow sides heaving with the exertion, her cheeks red and full of life.

She angled her pretty face at Annie. "Did my daddy like going to the park when he was a little boy?"

"Yes." Annie sat on the end of the second slide. She pictured the free spirit Josh had been at Savannah's age. "He would run from the swings to the slide and back again until he could barely take another step."

Savannah giggled. "I can't wait to meet him." She put her hand on Annie's knee. "Do you think he could push me on the swings when he comes here?"

For a crazy instant Annie thought about keeping the charade going. What was the difference whether Savannah knew about Josh's death? Could any harm come from her holding on to the image in the photograph, believing her Prince Charming daddy was going to come for her one of these days? The answer was as obvious as daylight. Annie reached for Savannah's hand. *God, please. . . . I can't do this without You.*

"And hey"—Savannah grinned at her—"if you know my daddy, could you tell him to hurry? I don't want to meet him much later, but right now. Today, if that's okay with him."

"Savannah"—Annie felt God giving her the ability to speak the words that had to be said—"honey, your daddy isn't coming for you."

The news seemed to hit her slowly, like a gradual rain, the kind where it took several drops of wetness before the reality of the storm sank in. Her thin shoulders slumped forward a little and her eyes held a mix of shock and betrayal. "Why not?" Her mouth hung open, and the beginning of tears sprang to her eyes. "I've been waiting for him a very long time."

"I know." Annie wondered how much her heart could take. "You see, honey, a month ago your daddy went to sleep and he never woke up. He went to heaven instead."

"To heaven?" Savannah stood and stared at Annie. "My daddy is in heaven? Like Grandpa Ted?"

"Yes, baby." Annie reached for Savannah's hand.

But the child took a step back and shook her head. "No." She scrunched up her face and began to cry. "No, he can't be in heaven. That's too far away." She shook her head harder, faster. "He's my Prince Charming, and he was going to come for me and . . . and . . ." She turned around and ran across the sand to the swings. She flung herself onto the farthest one, grabbed the chains hard, and hung her head halfway to her lap.

Annie caught a look of pity from Nate and Lindsay. The two of them stood and started walking along a path in the other direction. They could hear the details later. These next few minutes were for Annie and Savannah alone. Annie stood, and as she trudged through the sand toward her granddaughter she wore her son's loss like a heavy coat.

He should have been here right now, to take Savannah in his arms and soothe away her hurt and sadness. Annie stopped a few feet from the girl, and again she knew she'd remember the sight of Savannah—sitting on the swing weeping, her heart breaking—for as long as she lived. Although she was only seven years old, the child understood the significance of Josh being in heaven.

Annie took the swing beside her and waited several minutes until Savannah's angry sobs eventually subsided. Finally, she sniffed and turned her red eyes to Annie. "Grandpa Ted told me sometimes things don't go the way we want this side of heaven."

"That's true." Annie wasn't sure who Grandpa Ted was, but she had a feeling he had been Maria's father. "This side of heaven can be pretty sad sometimes."

"So here's what I want to know." She sniffed again. "How do I get to *that* side of heaven? So I can be with my daddy?"

Annie couldn't talk through her tears. *That side of heaven.* If she could take Savannah there now she would. "Ah, Savannah, baby. If only there were a way to make that happen."

"Grandpa Ted said there was." She had fresh tears on her cheeks, but her anger was gone now. In its place was a sad desperation, a last-ditch hope that she might some-how find a way around the terrible news. She wiped her nose. "He told me if I loved Jesus, then one day I'd go to heaven, too. So then I'd be on that side with my daddy."

"Your grandpa Ted was right." Annie brushed her wrists across her cheeks. "One day you'll be on that side of heaven with your daddy and your grandpa Ted and—and all of us who love Jesus. Just not until you're much, much older."

"But"—her voice broke and she looked smaller than she had an hour ago—"my daddy wasn't old. So how come he's on that side of heaven and I'm here on this side?"

Annie swallowed a sob before it could consume her. "I don't know. I've wondered that same thing."

When Savannah saw that Annie didn't have any more of an answer than that, she squeezed her eyes shut and lowered her head again. "I was going to live with him, and he was going to give me hugs, and . . . and . . ." Her tears came harder, and it was difficult to understand her. "He was going to take me to his house and bring me to school and push me on the swings and race me down the slide. And everything was going to be happily ever after." She lifted the saddest eyes and looked deep into Annie's face. "What about that?"

"I'm sorry, Savannah." Annie reached out her hand once more, and this time Savannah stood, and after a few seconds of inner struggle she came to Annie and flung her arms tight around her neck.

"I wanted to meet him so bad, Grandma Annie." Savannah nuzzled her face in close against Annie's neck. "Now I have to wait for heaven."

"Yes." Annie let her tears come. "We both have to."

They hugged for a long time, until finally Savannah pulled back. She searched Annie's face. "That's why you came, isn't it? To tell me my daddy was in heaven?"

"Yes, honey." Annie didn't want to mention the rest. "And because we wanted to meet you and tell you about your daddy. He loved you very much." Annie had made a copy of Josh's journal. It was in an envelope in the car. "Before we go I have something for you. Lots and lots of letters your daddy wrote to you from the time you were a baby until the day before he died."

"Why—why didn't he come see me before he went to heaven? Before it was too late?"

The afternoon sun was slipping behind the trees that lined the playground, and the temperature was falling. Annie wasn't sure how much to say. "He wanted to, baby. Every day he wanted to."

The pieces seemed to come together slowly but surely in Savannah's mind. She thought for a long time, and then she bit her lip. "It was 'cause of my mama, right? She didn't let him come, because she threw his picture in the garbage."

"That's right, Savannah." She didn't want to turn the girl against her mother, especially when the woman was most likely all she would ever have in the years ahead. But the truth needed to be spoken. "Your mother didn't want Josh to be a part of your life."

"Josh?"

"That was your daddy's name. Joshua David Warren."

Savannah repeated his name slowly. "I like Prince Charming Daddy better."

Annie smiled. Her tears were drying in the late afternoon breeze. "I like that, too."

"My mama shouldn't have kept him away from me."

"No." Annie ran her hand along the back of Savannah's head. "But she can't keep him away in heaven. So you'll always have that to look forward to."

They talked a few more minutes about heaven and how Josh had loved Jesus very much. Then they met up with Nate and Lindsay, and Savannah hugged each of them. "Grandma Annie told me about my daddy. I'm sorry he went to heaven so soon."

"Us, too." Nate held her hand as they walked to the car. "We miss him every day."

When they got back to the foster home, Savannah found Josh's picture on the sofa where she'd left it. "Is it okay if I still keep this picture? So I can think about my daddy and what it's like on that side of heaven?"

"Yes, sweetie." Lindsay hadn't said much, but now she knelt near Savannah and touched the girl's strawberry-blond hair. "My brother wanted to be your daddy so much. I want you to know that."

"He is my daddy. It doesn't matter if it takes a long time to meet him." Savannah was accepting the situation a little better now. "Plus, I have my picture, so he'll always be close by, even if he's in heaven."

"Right." Lindsay kissed Savannah's cheek. "We have to go now. But I want you to remember us, okay?"

Savannah moved on to Nate and hugged him, too. But as she pulled away she looked confused by the good-byes. She turned to Annie. "Are you leaving, too?"

"I have to, honey. We live in Colorado, on the other side of the country."

Her eyes lit up, but not like they'd done earlier in the afternoon. "How 'bout I go with you? My mama doesn't want me." She glanced at Nate. "She told me in the restaurant. She doesn't want to be a mama anymore."

The admission ripped at Annie and made her want to pack up the girl's things and take her home. Let the courts figure out a way to make the arrangement legal. If Maria didn't want her daughter, then Annie and Nate would be happy to step in. But Maria definitely wanted her daughter. As soon as she was sober, she would certainly come back to her senses. There could be no settlement money if she gave up Savannah. Thomas figured Maria and her attorney would pull out all the stops so that Maria could regain custody and get her hands on the money.

Annie gave her granddaughter one more long hug. What she was about to say next was only what she had to say, so that Savannah wouldn't fear the life that lay ahead of her. "Listen to me, honey." She searched Savannah's eyes, the eyes that were so like Josh's. "Your mother didn't mean what she said. She's sick right now, but when she gets better she'll make things right with you."

"Know something?" Savannah's voice was too soft to hear across the room.

"What?" Annie touched her finger to the tip of her granddaughter's nose.

"My mama doesn't love Jesus. She told me she doesn't believe like Grandpa Ted."

Another blow, not that Annie was surprised. "Well, honey, maybe one day you'll help her believe." They needed to go. One afternoon was all Child Protective Services would allow given that Savannah was in emergency foster care. And now their plane was set to leave in just three hours. Annie cradled her hand around the back of Savannah's head. "I'm going to ask Jesus every day that we have the chance to see you again. Okay?"

Savannah nodded. She looked shy again, her expression a mix of hurt and disappointment and a sorrow that seemed all too familiar. "I'll ask Him, too." She took a step back and gave each of them a little wave—Annie last. Then she hugged the picture of Josh to her chest. "Thank you for telling me about my daddy."

Annie had brought the envelope from the car and now she handed it to Savannah. "Can you read, sweetie?"

"Not yet." Again there was shame in her voice. "Mama said I could learn later. Right now we have to beg for money."

Anger threatened to taint the moment. Annie gritted her teeth and made a mental note to talk to Thomas about Savannah's living conditions. If the courts returned the child to her mother then the entire system was flawed. She put the thought out of her head for now. "Inside that envelope are the letters I told you about." Her face softened and she squeezed Savannah's hand once more. "The letters from your daddy. Keep them with your picture of him, so that one day you can read for yourself how much he loved you."

"How much he still loves me." Savannah held the photo tighter to herself. "People can love all the way from heaven."

"Of course." Annie kissed the top of Savannah's head.

"Inside the envelope is our phone number. In case you ever need anything."

Savannah nodded, but the confusion in her eyes told them she didn't really understand. She couldn't possibly have understood how far away Colorado was, or why her daddy's family was leaving so soon after finding her. When Annie couldn't take another moment of the good-bye, she turned, left the house, and walked to the car. Nate and Lindsay followed, and the last image they saw as they pulled away for the airport was Savannah's sweet pixie face in the front window of the foster parents' house. Marti was beside her and Savannah wasn't somber or pouting or indifferent.

She had one hand raised to the glass and she was sobbing.

TWENTY-FIVE

Back in the Springs the days passed slowly, each one drenched in the sadness of Josh's absence. Every few afternoons, Annie called Thomas for an update, and one week after their return home from the quick visit to see Savannah, Thomas passed on word that a local judge had ruled Maria fit to regain custody of the child. No surprise, Annie knew. But when she read in Scripture that week about God's faithfulness, she remembered the song at her son's funeral service and the little girl on the other side of the country praying for a happy ending, and she had to wonder.

God had a plan, no doubt, but in this case she was better off not trying to make sense of it.

Annie debated the situation with Thomas, because she needed to talk to someone about the insanity of it. "The woman told Savannah she didn't want to be a mother anymore."

"I know."

"She hit her on the face in front of a crowd of people."

"The judge was aware of that."

"So how, Thomas . . . how can they overlook her warrants and the fact that she begs for money and return Savannah to that environment?"

Thomas could only release a sigh that sounded drenched in futility. "I wish I could explain it, Annie. I'm sorry."

The outcome for Savannah was exactly as they feared it might be, and as the day of the settlement neared, Annie was sure that Maria would do just what they expected—flee the city and any ties to the court or to the Warren family, most likely in case she might have to share the money if she kept in touch.

Now, with each day that passed, she not only missed Josh, but his little Savannah, too. She would always be glad for the few hours they'd had with the child, but it made the grief she and Nate and Lindsay shared even stronger than before. Annie kept her word and prayed every day that Jesus would allow them the chance to meet again, to know each other. But Jesus hadn't let Savannah see her daddy, and now it didn't look like the rest of them would ever get to see Savannah again, either.

The settlement came in late November. After three years of updates, depositions, hearings, and meetings, Thomas called with the news they'd been waiting for. The decision had been made. The judge had analyzed the accident, the damage caused by the insurance company's client, and the fact that Josh's need for pain medication had ultimately led to his death. Instead of the two million dollars Thomas asked for, the judge ruled that the insurance company pay out $2.3 million.

The case was a landslide victory for Josh's estate, and one of Lindsay's colleagues at the *Gazette* covered the story.

A few days after the article appeared, Annie spent an

afternoon in what had become a new kind of routine. She brought two Starbucks soy lattes to Carl Joseph's apartment and talked for an hour with him and Daisy.

"We saw the story about Josh." Carl Joseph pointed to the bulletin board on his kitchen wall. "Daisy cut it out for me."

"Yeah, but"—Daisy wrinkled her nose—"it wasn't long enough. It didn't say that Josh was a hero, and Cody says that's bad journalism."

"Because bad journalism isn't good." Carl Joseph shook his head. "You should've written the story, Annie."

She wished she could have. But what she knew now about Josh would have never fit in a single newspaper feature. She could have written a book about her son's life, and once in a while she almost convinced herself she should do just that, even if their family and Josh's friends were the only ones who ever read it. She could always use the book as a reason to find Savannah again, years from now.

After her visit with Carl Joseph and Daisy, Annie went to the local Whole Foods and picked up the same items she'd been buying every week since the end of October: a half gallon of milk, a loaf of bread, two small containers of strawberry yogurt, a bag of frozen salmon fillets, a bag of rice, and an assortment of fruit and vegetables. The food fit neatly into two grocery bags, and Annie carried them easily up the steps to Ethel's apartment.

"Hello, dear." The woman smiled as she opened the door. She took the groceries, clucking her tongue about how Annie didn't need to do this and how she'd be happy to pay for the food if only Annie would let her. "Have I ever told you," Ethel said as Annie set the groceries down on the small kitchen table, "every time I open the door and see you standing on the porch with my groceries, for just a short minute I can see Josh again. The two of you have the same eyes."

Ethel said the same thing each time Annie came, and always Annie left with a promise to be back the next week. Not on Saturday, but on Monday—the day she'd set aside to keep in touch with the people she'd met because of Josh. Today she had more than her usual stops to make. She drove across town to a small café at the foot of Black Forest. The meeting was set to take place at one of the tables near the window. It was the first week in December, and snow was forecast for that night.

Annie parked and thought about all she wanted to say, all she never would have had the chance to say if the person she was meeting hadn't pursued this private, early dinner, hadn't been willing to drive in from Denver. Annie spotted the young woman as soon as she entered the restaurant.

Becky Wheaton raised her hand so Annie would see her. As she reached the booth, Becky stood and gave her a quick hug. "Thanks for coming. I—I felt bad asking."

Annie took her seat opposite Becky and once she was situated she reached across the table and briefly took hold of Becky's hands. "That's why I wanted to come here today. I think we have a few things to talk about."

"I thought you'd think it was awkward, sitting down with me after all these years."

A sad smile tugged at Annie's lips. "That's one of the things Josh taught me. The only awkward thing between people who care about each other is missing out on the chance to sit down and talk things out."

"Yeah." Becky was wearing her blond hair shorter these days. She was already sipping a cup of coffee. "I see what you mean."

They ordered dinner, and then Becky got to the point. "Ever since Josh's death, I've been buried under, I don't know, a sense of guilt. Like maybe if I'd stayed with Josh none of this ever would've happened."

They were the same thoughts Annie had experienced at first, but not in a long time. "You did what you had to do, Becky. No one faults you for that. Josh certainly didn't blame you." Annie had come today with one goal in mind—to give Becky the freedom to move on with her life. But first they had to talk through the things Becky was feeling.

"I asked him to stop smoking and stay in college." She set her coffee cup down and leaned on her forearms. "But every night I fall asleep thinking I never should've expected that of him." Her eyes glistened. "I loved him so much. I still haven't ever felt that way about anyone else."

Annie had wondered whether she should share with Becky just how much Josh had still cared for her. As long as Becky was being painfully honest, Annie figured she might as well tell the whole story, too. She settled back into the booth. "Josh didn't blame you, Becky. He respected all you wanted from him. He stopped smoking a few years after he moved to Denver. I wasn't sure you knew that."

Her eyes showed her surprise. "I had no idea."

"He heard your engagement fell through, and he was hoping to get his settlement and open a business. He needed back surgery and he was trying to lose the last forty pounds he'd gained. But once he had all that figured out, he was planning to call you." She studied the young woman across from her. If things had been different, she might have been her daughter-in-law.

"I—I didn't know any of that."

"Josh loved you. He had a lot to work through, and he wanted to find his daughter. But he always saw you as part of his future plans. At least he prayed you might be."

Becky dropped her gaze to her hands. "That only makes it worse."

Annie understood what she meant. All along the process of discovering who Josh had really been, she'd experienced that same feeling: that the depth of Josh's loss grew the more good she found out about him. But that's not the way God wanted either of them to feel about Josh, and now it was Annie's responsibility to help relieve Becky of the burden she was carrying.

"You need to understand something." Again Annie put her hand over that of the young woman across from her. "You'll keep Josh in your heart, the same way I'll keep him. But you need to let your guilt and regrets go." Annie hoped she sounded sincere. "Josh made his own decisions, and it took him a little longer to understand the sort of life you wanted."

"I didn't want any sort of life, though." She looked up and there were tears on her cheeks. "I wanted Josh. That's all."

"I want him, too. Just for ten more minutes so I can tell him how proud I am of all he was, all I didn't know about him." Annie gave a slow shake of her head. "But that isn't going to happen for either of us." She thought about Savannah. "Not this side of heaven, anyway."

"I feel like I missed out on a kind of love I'll never know again."

"But you will." Annie wanted the young woman to believe that. Otherwise she would be paralyzed by her past. "You'll love again, but first you need to let go of Josh and everything you're feeling about him."

"How?" Her question seemed trapped in a heart that had never rebounded from a love she'd found when she was only fifteen years old. "How do I move on?"

"You tell yourself that you can only keep those times you and Josh *did* have. Beyond that, you can't grasp at days that never existed. For all you know, you and Josh might've been too different to make another go at things."

Becky seemed to ponder that for a few seconds. "Maybe. Still, I don't know if I can go a day without wondering."

"Wondering is part of life. As long as it doesn't keep you from living."

Their dinners came and they talked about Becky's job as a therapist, and a young man at the practice who'd asked her out to dinner twice in the past month. Josh didn't come up again until the end of the conversation, after the meal was over. "I still see him, this dark-haired gorgeous guy sitting in the stands at the first football game our sophomore year." Becky's eyes grew distant, the memory clearly alive again. "Everyone was talking about him, but after the game he came and found me. He said it'd been a long time." She laughed.

"Let me guess—the two of you had never met until then." Annie would always remember her son's sense of humor.

"Not once." She lifted her hands and let them fall back to her lap. "He was making the whole thing up, pretending that we'd met at a game the previous year, when he attended the school across town. By the time I figured out he was only teasing me, it was too late. I'd already fallen for him."

"And he for you." Annie remembered. "He came home after one of the football games that fall and told me he'd met the girl he was going to marry. She had blond hair the color of sunshine and her name was Becky."

A wistfulness clouded Becky's eyes. "I guess we'll never know."

"Which is why you can't spend today wondering about yesterday, my dear. Josh is gone." The words would always hurt to voice them. "He's gone and you have to let him go. It's what he would've wanted for you."

She still didn't look sure.

"You believe in God, right?"

"Of course. I talk to Jesus all the time." Becky's cheeks grew slightly red in anticipation of what was coming. "I ask Him to tell Josh how sorry I am, and that I never stopped loving him."

"Okay, then . . . I want to give you something." She pulled a small greeting card from her purse and handed it over. "Read it."

Becky opened the envelope and read the inside of the card. Besides restating everything Annie had already said, the card contained the Bible verse that had meant so much to Josh in his final days. Psalm 119:50.

" 'My comfort in my suffering is this: Your promise preserves my life,' " Becky read the verse out loud. "Really? That verse meant a lot to Josh?"

"Right up until his death." Annie crossed her arms, warding off the sadness that threatened to consume her. "I think Josh would want you to take that verse to heart. Stay grounded in God's Word, Becky. Let the Lord's truth revive you so that you can date that young man from your work, and so you can let Josh take his rightful place in your life. As a part of your past, a very fond part."

For the first time since Annie had spotted Becky sitting at the booth, the young woman's eyes looked less troubled, as if a cloud had lifted from her heart. The process of letting Josh go wouldn't happen in an instant or overnight. But this was a beginning, and Annie felt sure she'd done the right thing by meeting with her. They said their good-byes and agreed to stay in touch. Annie had a feeling that someday in the not too distant future, she and Nate would be invited to Becky Wheaton's wedding.

Night had fallen as she drove home to Nate. They had plans to watch *Monday Night Football* that evening and go over the last phase of Nate's reelection plans. The election had taken a backseat in their lives since Josh's death, and neither of them felt driven to return to the frenzy for votes that had defined their lives prior to losing their son. They were involved in their church's Bible study again and were planning to take meals to the homebound starting in January.

The settlement funds had been transferred to Savannah in care of her mother, and at any time she expected to hear from Thomas that Maria had changed her phone number or moved without any forwarding address. Thomas explained how at the last minute he'd worked out the settlement so that Maria couldn't have access to all of it right away. But the details no longer mattered. The money was gone, and very soon Savannah would be gone, too.

In the meantime, she comforted herself with something Cody Gunner had told her that afternoon in Josh's apartment. In light of Josh's faith, Cody and his wife had figured Josh was just starting to live. Annie understood now how true that was.

He really had just started to live. Just not the way she and Nate and Lindsay and the others had expected.

The beautiful thing was this: She hadn't only discovered what her son meant to other people, the sort of true success he'd been while he was alive, but she'd discovered something about herself, as well. In taking over the love and friendships Josh had begun, Annie had become a better person in the process. More of the person God had intended her to be.

If only she could have forced Maria Cameron into a shared custody arrangement with Savannah. Then she could be absolutely sure that not only would she spend the rest of her days proud that Josh was her son, but that he would spend eternity proud that she was his mother. She pulled into the driveway, parked her car in the garage, and found Nate waiting for her inside.

"How was dinner?" He pulled her into his embrace and rocked her slowly.

"Good. I told her she needs to move on. Let Josh go because that's what Josh would've wanted for her."

Nate nodded. "The game's already started."

"I figured." She set her purse down. "Any score?"

"Not yet." Nate moved to sit down, but then he stopped himself. "I almost forgot. There was a message for you on the machine when I got home. Thomas Flynn. He wants you to call him first thing in the morning."

Annie nodded absently as she took her place beside her husband. Thomas was good about giving her updates on the case, even now, after it was long since settled and the funds dispersed. She stretched out her legs and focused her attention on the football game. When it came to the lawsuit or the painful time after Josh's accident, Annie believed God wanted her to take the same advice she'd given Becky. Let it go and move on.

No matter what bit of information Thomas had for her this time.

TWENTY-SIX

Maria didn't want to admit to herself that she was worried. Harry Dreskin would take care of the mess she was in. Ever since she met him, Harry always took care of her messes, right? She gripped the bars of her jail cell and shouted at an officer as he walked by. "Where's my attorney? He should've been here an hour ago."

The officer scowled at her. "When he shows up, we'll tell you."

"That's not good enough." She cursed at the man and stormed to the opposite side of the boxy cell. She'd been sitting here for nearly three days, and she hadn't talked to Harry Dreskin since she was arrested. How was she supposed to get out of here if he didn't make more of an effort?

Two men were fighting in a cell across the hall, yelling at each other, getting on Maria's nerves. "Shut up!" she screamed. "Officer, get back here and tell them to shut up!"

They turned on her instead, shouting vile things at her. Maria didn't care. She tuned them out and sat on the wooden bunk bed in the corner of the cell. Ever since her arrest she'd done everything in her power to get her attorney back to the jail, back into a conversation about what might happen next.

What worried Maria was Harry's attitude. Normally, her lawyer was as cocky and full of himself as any man she'd ever met. Harry prided himself on finding ways around the system. Creative representation, he called it. Caught writing a bad check? Harry could make it look like a mistake. Public intoxication? A case of depression gone bad. The slap across Savannah's face? An exaggeration on the part of the restaurant employees. Harry hated judges, all judges. If he thought he had even the slimmest chance of winning a case, he made promises and predictions and he bragged about his abilities until the victory was his.

But this time Harry had promised her nothing.

An hour after her arrest, he'd met her at the jail. They sat in a windowless conference room for thirty minutes. Harry had spent half the time poring over the booking sheet, stopping only to ask a snappy question or two. "You kiddin' me, Maria? You stole two grand from a pawnshop in Harlem?"

"I needed start-up money." Maria was indignant. "I told the guy I'd pay him back in a week. So what?"

"You tried to buy a bag of coke from a cop?"

"He wasn't exactly wearing a uniform, okay?"

He read a little more and his eyes opened wider. "With your kid standing there watching?"

Savannah was a sore subject right now. "Keep her out of it." Maria had wanted to kick the guy in the leg. "Come on, Harry. Give me a pep talk. That's what I need, because you're the best, right? Isn't that why I hired you?"

Harry didn't respond. He read the details on the booking sheet again, pointing at a line here and there and shaking his head. "This is bad stuff. Real bad."

"Quit it, Harry. You're scaring me." She gave him a light shove in his shoulder. "This is just like the other times. No big deal, right?"

"First"—Harry's tone changed—"don't shove me." He straightened his coat sleeve. "Second, hittin' up a pawnshop and dealing to a cop's a very big deal. Especially with your rap sheet. You could lose your kid for good this time, Maria. I mean it." He raised a wary eyebrow at her. "What kinda down payment you got?"

Maria had been stumped by the question. "I just paid you thirty grand. What do you mean down payment?"

"That was my cut a' the settlement." He thumped his chest. "I earned that. This"—he flicked the booking sheet—"is a new case. I don't work for free, got it?"

"Okay." Maria thought about the money. "I can afford you. So get on it, already."

"I need up-front money. When I come back I want two g's to get started on this mess."

Their thirty minutes was up, and Harry told her he'd be back in the next day or two. Only she hadn't heard a word from him since then and it was going on the end of the third day. She dropped her head in her hands and tried once more to shut out the shouting from across the hall. What had she gotten herself into? This was supposed to be the beginning of the big time, the best days of her life.

She went over the series of events again and tried to figure out where things had gone wrong. The answer was easy.

Josh Warren.

The guy had been bad news from the beginning, talking about his plans for success and then failing to see a single one of them come to pass. He'd gone and knocked her up, and once her old man ditched her she was nothing but a single lady with a kid on her hip. Savannah was a nice girl, but she'd cramped Maria's style long enough. What sort of big time was she going to find trying to make a living for the two of them?

She'd believed Josh Warren, thought he'd be good for eighteen years of monthly payments, but he'd let her down. And since she couldn't count on him for child support when Savannah was a baby, what was she thinking to count on him for the settlement money? Maria rubbed her thumbs into her temples. Her head pounded, her body screaming for a drink. Sure, the settlement seemed like the answer to all her cares. Like she'd hit the lottery without buying a single ticket. But when the money finally came there were more strings on it than a frayed sofa.

Thomas Flynn saw to that.

Right off the money went into an account with Savannah's name—not hers—on it. Maria told Harry to fix the problem, but he told her his hands were tied. The money belonged to Savannah, not Maria. Then she found out about some guy called an administrator who had the job of giving Maria a couple thousand dollars a month. Pennies, really.

"The stipend is intended so that Savannah is taken care of. The rest of the money can only be withdrawn by Savannah, and only on or after her eighteenth birthday," Harry told her.

"How 'bout if I'm the administrator?"

"Flynn said you can't be because you have a criminal record. I checked it out, and he's right. Nothing I can do about it."

Thomas Flynn had a lot of nerve, rubbing that in her face. Everyone had a past. With two million dollars she had every intention of being a respectable mother. But on two grand a month? What did the system expect, that she'd get a job waiting tables to supplement the money?

Harry suggested she draw up an expense sheet, prove to the judge that she needed more money to keep Savannah comfortable. Five g's or maybe seven a month. But Maria never got around to writing up the details. She ran into one of Freddy's guys first. Big Pete was his name, and he gave her an idea for making money all on her own, without Savannah's help or the administrator's permission. A career only she could take credit for. "It's a business venture," he told her. "But you'll need start-up cash."

The venture turned out to be dealing drugs to high rollers, guys who took the subway each morning to Manhattan's financial district. "We got no one running drugs for that crowd." Big Pete winked at her. "With your looks, shouldn't take no time to get clientele."

It was Big Pete's idea that Maria hit the pawnshop. "I know the guy who runs it." Pete shrugged. "Go in on a Friday night. Make like you got a gun in your pocket and when he gives you the cash, tell him you're good for it. You'll pay him back in a few days."

Big Pete set up the buy. Maria would take the money and meet secretly with one of the biggest drug dealers in the city. She'd buy a half-gallon bag of coke and break it into smaller bags. "You'll triple your investment in a week," Big Pete said. "Oh, and I'll get twenty percent of everything you make—since you're using my contacts."

Maria wasn't sure what went wrong. She got the money without a hitch, wore the ski mask, kept her identity a secret, the whole nine yards. The day of the big buy, she went to the right corner, looked for the guy with the right description, and used the right code words. Only instead of some big-time drug dealer the guy she tried to buy from was an undercover cop.

A frustrated sigh slid through her teeth. Figures. And now even Harry was worried. Maria stood and walked from one side of the cell to the other. Harry was wrong. She'd get through this and find the big time on the other side. Big Pete had given her an idea. If the high rollers from the financial district took the subway every morning, then she could do the same thing. She could take some of the monthly stipend money and fix herself up real nice. A better haircut, better clothes. And then some morning soon she would hit on the right guy and all her problems would be solved.

All except two.

When was she going to get out of jail, and what was she going to do with Savannah?

⁂

Two weeks had passed since Thomas learned of Maria Cameron's arrest, and as he hung up the phone with the social worker, he could hardly believe how quickly the system was working. Especially less than a week before

Christmas. The way things were happening, it was like God was moving heaven and earth to help Savannah find her way home for the holidays.

Thomas stared out the window at the rainy Denver sky and reminded himself of all that had transpired in the past fourteen days. After Maria's arrest, the investigating officer found evidence on more than just the crimes in question. Maria was now being charged with enough to send her to prison for at least twenty years. She'd confessed to using a gun in the robbery and, on top of that, the investigating officers were able to connect her with a bad-check writing ring. All that combined with her attempt to buy from an undercover officer, and no one thought Maria would see the light of day before Savannah turned eighteen.

Thomas even called Harry Dreskin, Maria's less than reputable attorney, and the man had been straight about his client. "She's got no money. I'm repping her as a favor." He sounded weary of the case. "I'm gonna try to cop a plea for five years, but I'll be happy with ten."

Harry said he'd shared the information with Child Protective Services for two reasons. "First, the kid deserves a family if she can get one. Second, Maria doesn't want to be a mother. Not in prison or out. She's tired of pretending."

Under other circumstances, Thomas would have been heartbroken for the little girl—living with a new set of short-term foster parents and without a mom or dad to love and care for her. But Savannah wasn't any other child. She was heir to a multimillion-dollar estate, and her very existence came with a stipend for care that would put to shame the typical monthly amount given to foster parents.

It was a detail Thomas wanted CPS to keep secret from any potential long-term foster or adoptive parents.

But mostly Thomas wanted CPS to keep quiet about the money because he had a different plan for Savannah, a plan he hoped God was orchestrating. Before he could say anything to Annie or Nate Warren, he wanted to make sure Maria's case couldn't slip through the cracks, that Maria wouldn't wind up Savannah's guardian again in a few weeks or a month.

Now that problem had been solved for good.

The phone call he just ended was from the social worker, with the best news Thomas Flynn had heard in a very long time. "Savannah Cameron is officially a ward of the court," the woman said. "I thought you'd like to know."

"So"—he pushed back from his desk, adrenaline flooding his veins—"her mother's rights have been severed?"

"Forever."

Thomas closed his eyes. *Thank You, God. . . . You're doing this; I can sense Your presence opening the right doors.* He drew a steadying breath. "So you're saying Savannah Cameron is legally available for adoption?"

"Yes." The woman's voice held an undeniable smile. "Let me guess. You have someone in mind?"

Thomas grinned at the memory of the recent conversation. He picked up the phone and dialed Annie Warren—first her home number, and then her cell. Both times he left her the same message. "I have an update on the situation with Savannah. Call me as soon as you can."

It was lunchtime, and Thomas ordered chicken salad to be delivered to his office. Otherwise he might miss Annie's call, and this was one connection that couldn't wait. His eyes found the plaque on his desk and he was struck by the faithfulness of the promise. For indeed, all things had worked to the good for the people who loved God—Annie, Nate, Lindsay, and Savannah. Even for Josh, who was safe in heaven.

Thomas was halfway through a slice of sourdough bread when his secretary alerted him, "I have Annie Warren on the phone."

"Thank you." His throat was suddenly thick, and as he reached for the receiver, he thanked the Lord again for all that lay ahead, all the good that would happen now because of these recent developments. Most of all, he thanked God for hearing the prayers of sweet Savannah, a fatherless little girl Thomas would meet one day soon.

And for loving her enough to give her a second chance.

TWENTY-SEVEN

Annie and Nate were by themselves this time. They'd arrived in New York late yesterday, and after lying awake most of the night, they were sitting in the waiting room at the Manhattan office of Child Protective Services trying to believe this wasn't all some wonderful dream. Especially three days before Christmas.

"I can't believe she's going to be ours." Nate could hardly sit still. "I prayed for this, but still . . . Josh would be so happy, Annie."

"I keep picturing him, all those years wishing Savannah could be a part of his life and ours, a part of her cousins' lives." She couldn't stop smiling. "Everything he wanted is going to happen."

She didn't state the sad obvious—that Josh was the only one who would miss out. All that mattered now was Savannah. Annie leaned against her husband and remembered Thomas's phone call. His question was a simple one. "Would you and Nate be interested in adopting Savannah?"

Annie would always remember what she did next. Nate was sitting across from her at their dining room table, and

Annie let out a happy cry as she placed the call on speakerphone. "Say it again. Please, Thomas."

And Josh's wonderful attorney had laughed. "I said, would you and Nate be interested in adopting Savannah?"

The question was a rhetorical one, of course. Annie had talked about pursuing a custody battle for Savannah from the moment Josh's wishes became clear, after the conversation with Cody Gunner. But always the answer was the same—if the local Child Protective Services didn't deem Maria an unfit mother, then no one could force her to let Annie have custody even one day a year.

Ironically, when it came to establishing paternity, the courts didn't care if Josh had been denied access to his daughter. Savannah was his heir and with the exception of only the rarest cases, nothing would change the court's mind. But when Annie talked about seeking visitation rights or custody, those same facts worked against them. Thomas had explained that since the girl had no prior relationship with Annie and Nate, no one could force her to have one now.

Up until the call from Thomas, it looked like their family wouldn't see Savannah again, at least not until she was an adult. Even then there would be the matter of finding her. Annie folded her hands in her lap and tried to keep from giggling out loud. Those days were behind them now. Thomas had worked quickly, filing the right paperwork and requesting a rushed adoption.

Even Thomas was surprised when the judge overseeing the adoption agreed, under the circumstances, to sign paperwork on Monday afternoon. There would be a home study conducted and other paperwork to complete in the months ahead, but the documents she and Nate would sign later today would give them temporary custody until then.

Annie remembered Josh's funeral service and the words of the song played at the beginning and the end. *Great is Thy faithfulness . . . Oh, God my Father . . . there is no shadow of turning with Thee. . . .*

The words were true, after all. His mercies really were new every morning. Today was tangible proof. And no matter what happened from here, Annie would never doubt them again. God's good plans for Josh, His faithfulness to her youngest child, had taken him straight to heaven, to a better life than this one. And now Annie and Nate would care for his daughter all the days of their lives.

Annie tapped one toe on the dingy carpet that covered the waiting room floor. She wished the social worker would hurry. It was hard to think of Savannah in a room behind the closed door. After all she'd been through in the past few months, she needed the love of her grandparents more than ever. She thought about the other details Thomas had shared with them. He expected that sometime before the end of the year, Annie and Nate would be named coadministrators of Savannah's settlement. In light of all they now knew, they told Thomas they would only take the monthly stipend if Savannah needed it for clothing or a car when she was a teenager. Otherwise, the money would wait for her—the way Josh intended.

Annie stared at the brand-new pair of Minnie Mouse ears sticking out of her purse. She hadn't brought them the first time they'd come here to see Savannah because she couldn't have faced Daisy with the sad ending. Daisy, who had prayed every day that Savannah would come out of the picture and into Annie's arms.

But now . . .

Annie heard the sound of a door handle, and she and Nate looked up at the same time. The social worker opened the door and smiled at them. "Mrs. and Mr. Warren?"

"Yes?" Nate was on his feet.

Annie stood at his side. "Is Savannah ready?"

"She is." The woman motioned to someone in the other room, and after a few seconds Savannah appeared in the doorway holding a small worn plastic Little Mermaid suitcase. The zipper was broken on one side.

She set the bag down and put her fingers to her mouth, her chin tucked against her chest. In her eyes was the same shy uncertainty she'd had the last time they met—nearly two months ago. This time Savannah wore jeans that were an inch too short and her rumpled white sweater hung on her skinny frame. Someone had placed a blue bow in her hair, and the effect made her look closer to six years old than almost eight. "Savannah"—the social worker put her hand on the child's shoulder—"you remember your grandparents?"

"Hi, honey." Annie gave her a little wave. "It's Grandma Annie and Grandpa Nate. Remember us?" Only then did Annie realize that the look in Savannah's eyes wasn't shyness or uncertainty. It was a hurt, borne from feelings of abandonment and betrayal. With her eyes, Savannah seemed to ask, "How can I trust you again? You left and look what happened."

Nate must have recognized the look, too, because he

got down on one knee and held out his arms. "We're very sorry, Savannah. About what's happened to you."

She searched his face, and then she lifted her eyes—the eyes so familiar to Annie. Gradually, like the break of day, a sparkle came to life in her eyes, and when she couldn't hold back another moment, she ran to them, ran for all she was worth, and flung herself into their arms. They circled her, holding her close and giving her the security she'd never had for a single day in all her life.

Sobs came over their granddaughter, the same heart-rending sobs that had marked her when they'd said good-bye back in early November. Annie pressed her face in close to Savannah's. "Oh, honey. We're never going to leave you again." Annie felt tears in her eyes, but she couldn't cry—not with the joy consuming her. Still, for all the good ahead of them, Savannah needed to cry, needed to grieve all she'd lost before she could embrace all she was about to have.

Annie and Nate stayed that way, knees on the floor, their arms around Savannah, and they let her cry. The whole time, Annie couldn't stop thinking about Josh and how she had held out unrealistic expectations for her only son. Every mistake she ever made with Josh she promised herself and God she would never make with Savannah. Whatever the girl wanted to do when she grew up, Annie and Nate would love her and encourage her. They would tell her they were proud of her as often as they had the chance. The way Annie had failed to do with Josh.

The social worker left the room. The legalities had been cleared and they could take Savannah whenever the three of them felt ready to leave. After a few minutes, Savannah dragged her fist across her face. "Can I have a tissue, please?"

Nate hurried to the receptionist's desk and snagged several from a flowered box. "Here, sweetie."

"Thank you." She dried her face, blew her nose, and then stood and dropped the crumpled tissue in the trash can. When she came back to them, she put one hand on Annie's shoulder, the other on Nate's. "I'm glad you came back. Know why?"

Annie ran her thumb ever so gently beneath Savannah's eye, catching one last wayward tear. "Why, honey?"

"Because remember how my daddy is on *that* side of heaven?"

"Yes." Nate was completely enamored of their granddaughter. He soothed his hand over the back of her head.

"Well"—she looked at Nate and then at Annie—"since I can't go there yet, I need you both to tell me stories of my daddy. So I can know everything about him." She sniffed. "Okay?"

The tears Annie didn't plan to cry came unbidden. What would her answer have been several months ago? If Josh's daughter had asked for stories about him, Annie would have treated the question the same way she treated the inquiries from people like Babette. She would have had to work to find something good, and stretch the truth to keep from dwelling on all the bad.

But now—now she could spend the rest of her life telling Savannah about how her daddy had rescued two girls from certain death, and how he'd told the hurting people in his life about Jesus, and how he could find friendship with a person even if they were handicapped or too old to drive to the market. How he would go the distance so a buddy might have a final conversation with a father he'd never connected with. How he'd helped a friend find Jesus. All that and so much more.

Annie brushed the tears from her cheeks with her fingertips and smiled at Savannah. "Actually, honey"—she coughed to clear her voice—"I've learned a lot about your daddy since he died." She fought her emotions so she could finish her thought. "He was a hero, did you know that?"

"Really?" Her eyes danced. "So he was a Prince Charming *and* a hero?" She grinned. "I bet that's a really good story, Grandma Annie. The kind with a happy ending."

"Yes." Annie breathed in sharp through her nose to keep her control. And in that split second she knew, with everything in her, that one day she would write Josh's story, even if no one but her family ever read it. She sniffed again. "Yes, a very happy ending." Savannah tilted her head and patted Annie's hair with the softest little-girl touch. "I'm glad you can tell me about him. Because those stories about my daddy are all I'll have. Those and my picture of him and the letters." She smiled. "I still have the letters. They're in my Mermaid suitcase."

Annie pulled the Minnie Mouse ears from her purse. "Here." She handed them to Savannah. "These are from some friends of your daddy's. You'll meet them soon." Annie felt her throat tighten again. "They're a special gift."

"They're pretty." She turned them one way and then the other.

"Want to wear them?"

"Okay." She handed them back to Annie. "I never had a pair of Minnie ears before."

Annie steadied her hands and slid the headband into place. "There. You look beautiful, Savannah."

"Thanks." She felt lightly against the ears. "I think I'll like Daddy's friends."

Annie smiled. "You will." She gently patted her arm. "Ready to go home, Savannah?"

"Really?"

Nate rose to his feet, grabbed her pink suitcase, and reached out his hand. "Really."

"Forever? Until heaven, I mean?" She tucked her fingers into his. She still looked wary.

"Yes, honey." Annie took hold of her other hand. "You're our little girl now."

Savannah smiled and nodded. "I'm ready." The three of them headed for the door, and even before they reached the sidewalk, Savannah was talking about Josh again. "Maybe you could tell me the hero story on the subway. We are taking the subway, right?"

Annie cherished the full feeling in her heart. What more could God have given them in light of all they'd lost? The chance to know that Josh was with his Savior, and the opportunity to raise his daughter with the love and acceptance she deserved. And most of all the great privilege of teaching Savannah everything she could ever want to know about her daddy, her Prince Charming.

This side of heaven.

❧

Already Savannah loved her grandma Annie and grandpa Nate more than anyone except Jesus and her daddy. They had wonderful stories about him, and on Christmas morning Aunt Lindsay and her husband and her two kids came over and everyone sat around the tree and Grandma Annie read to them out loud.

The letters her daddy had written to her, every single one of them.

She knew so much more about her daddy, because Grandpa Nate found lots and lots of pictures and so now she didn't just have her favorite one with the wooden frame, she had a whole stack of books with pictures. Her daddy was handsome and happy and he loved Jesus. He also loved her, because he said so in the letters a hundred million times.

Savannah still couldn't wait to meet him, one day on that side of heaven. She had seen a few videos of him, and she was pretty sure she'd know him right away because she would recognize his laugh. And of course he would look like a Prince Charming, which he was.

But in the meantime she felt like Snow White, living out a fairy tale. Because all those years when she prayed to find her daddy, she was never really sure if she ever would, and so she didn't know how her own story was going to end. But now she knew, because she had so much love, more than she could believe. She had new friends, Carl Joseph and Daisy and Mr. and Mrs. Gunner, and a pair of Minnie Mouse ears prettier than any she could have dreamed about.

But most of all she had Grandma Annie and Grandpa Nate and Aunt Lindsay and Uncle Larry and Ben and Bella, who were like built-in best friends. All that, and one day heaven, and a Prince Charming daddy who was a real-live hero.

And what could be a happier ending than that?

Dear Friends,

I'm not sure about you, but having just finished *This Side of Heaven*, I have tears streaming down my face. I long for the chance to hold Savannah in my arms and love away all her sorrow and loneliness, and I would pay dearly for a front-row seat to see that far-off reunion between her and her daddy, her Prince Charming who loved her so much.

My characters always feel real to me. That's why my husband can catch me at a moment like this and temporarily feel a great sense of alarm. Why in the world would his normally happy wife be sitting at her computer crying her eyes out? It's why he teases me that one day I'll make a very interesting old lady—when I can no longer tell the difference between my kids and my characters, and I pester him with questions about how come Carl Joseph hasn't been by to borrow eggs in a while.

Yes, the characters feel real to me.

But in this book, the characters, the story line, the haunting sorrow, and the bittersweet triumphs were very close to home. You see, *This Side of Heaven* was inspired by the story of my brother, Dave. Like Josh, Dave chose to forgo college to become a tow truck driver. And like my main character, Dave pulled two teenage girls out of harm's way and took the blow from a drunk driver one cold, wet New

Year's Eve seven years ago. The story line about Maria Cameron is entirely fictional.

After that, the lines blur between Dave's real story and the one that came pouring from my heart and into the pages of this book. In the real story there was no major settlement, no multimillion-dollar windfall. The lawsuit and depositions in Dave's case all amounted to nothing more than so much extra heartache. And rather than my mom, it was I who wondered about Dave's life—whether he had sold himself short and settled for mediocrity when he could have really been something.

Dave had struggled in his faith for many years, despite prayers and efforts on the part of me and my family and so many extended family members. We all have people in our lives like that, don't we? People who seem determined to take the hard road in life. But for Dave, the change happened as it happened with Josh—through a Wynonna Judd country music video late one night in the solitude of his lonely apartment.

She was singing "I Can Only Imagine," and at the end of the video, she raised her hands to our mighty God— God who in that moment became deeply real to Dave. He searched for the song and found the MP3 by a group many of you are familiar with, MercyMe. Afterward, he played that song all day and into the next, and that's when he called me.

By then, when it came to Dave, I'd grown a little jaded. He had rejected every offer to attend church or join our weekly Bible study, so when I saw his name on the caller ID that Wednesday afternoon I figured he'd be calling for one reason—to borrow more money. I almost walked away, almost missed out on one of the greatest moments in my life. But by God's grace and mercy, I was compelled to pick up the phone.

"Hello?"

"Hey, Karen." I could hear the song playing in the background. "You won't believe it." He talked loud so he could be heard over the music. "I found this song, and it's like I finally get it about God."

I had to sit down just so I could process what was happening. My brother was not speaking to me in his usual stifled grunts and distant tones, but he was pouring out his heart about a change that was dramatic and undeniable. He told me about the video and about finding the song, and finally he laughed with unbridled joy. "Can I go to church with you this weekend? I mean, really. I can hardly wait."

Dave had been hooked on OxyContin for three years by the time he found that deeper faith. He would be at one of our family get-togethers, and I'd head into the kitchen to refill the water pitchers, and he'd be standing in the kitchen, unshed tears in his eyes, gritting his teeth and clutching the countertop. Sweat would have broken out across his forehead and he'd give me an apologetic look. "I'm sorry . . . the pain is so bad, Karen. I can barely stand it."

But once he developed a craving for God and His Word, once he found the joy of singing worship songs to the Creator of the universe, Dave no longer talked about his pain. Oh, it was still there, I'm certain of that. But it no longer defined him the way his faith and hope for the future defined him.

Every weekend for six weeks in a row, Dave attended

church with us at our favorite Saturday night service and again with my parents at their service Sunday morning. I remember the service that sixth week like it was yesterday. We were running late—three of the boys still in their soccer uniforms and one holding a napkin to a suddenly bloody nose. Amid the chaos and the rush of getting the younger four boys signed into Sunday school, we hurried into the darkened sanctuary after the first song was already in progress. People were on their feet, but my brother was six foot six, and I could easily see him near the front, in the third or fourth row.

He was doing what any of us do when we're at church waiting for someone to join us. Every few seconds he was glancing over his shoulder, searching the back of the church, looking for me. Donald and I and our two older kids took a row in the back, and I excused myself. I had to at least tell Dave we were there, and since everyone was standing, I didn't think anyone would notice.

No one except Dave.

He saw me coming, and as I came nearer he stepped out into the aisle and pulled me into his arms. "I love you," he whispered near my ear. "Thank you for never giving up on me."

Our hug lasted a few more seconds, and then we shared a smile and I returned to my family at the back of the church.

It was the last time I ever saw my brother.

I was at a book signing the next Saturday, a beautiful sunny morning in October, and Dave had planned to attend my nephew's football game. Only he never showed up. I was ten minutes into meeting with a hundred or so readers when I suddenly noticed that my husband was there. He had a strange look on his face, and my first thought was something must've happened to one of the kids. They were busy with soccer and theater and any number of things could have gone wrong.

I asked my next reader friend if she could wait a few seconds, and then I stepped close to Donald. "Is everything okay?"

"No, honey. It isn't." He took my hand and led me a few feet away, never breaking eye contact. "Your brother's dead. He died in his sleep last night."

What happened next was a beautiful picture of the family of God. That bookstore became a church, the readers gradually sharing the awareness of what had just happened. In no time they circled me and prayed for me, giving me the grace to spend a few minutes in the store's break room to call my parents. In the end, I decided to stay and finish the signing because, after all, that's what I write about—the heartache of real life, the hope of the Cross. The promise that in the end all things really do work to the good for those who love the Lord.

My reader friends that day were kind and compassionate, hugging me and telling me how sorry they were. One lady had tears in her eyes after I told her that my brother had a daughter, but that he never had the chance to know her. "I lost a grandbaby last week," she told me. "Maybe tonight your brother is holding her in heaven."

But even with that, and with the firm knowledge that Dave was with the Lord and no longer in pain, I had regrets. In the weeks after his death, I learned much about the goodness of my brother, his care for others and his compassion for the weak. I wondered why we didn't take the whole family up front and sit with Dave that last time in church. And how come I'd grown distant and jaded by my attempts to invite him to Bible study, when God never grows distant and jaded with me? The one consolation that remained, the one that remains with me now, comes in the form of my brother's final words.

"Thanks for never giving up on me."

And so, my friends, that brings me to the reason I wrote this book. I wanted to share the story of a character like Dave who maybe wasn't an all-star or a first-place winner or a financial success. Someone who didn't earn a degree or gain a title or write a bestselling novel. Someone who wasn't popular and successful the way the world defines those things. Because all of us have people in our lives like Dave, people like Josh. My challenge to you—the one that comes at great personal cost—is to look for the good in these less-noticed people.

Our pastor, Matt, said something last week that stays with me still. "Jesus was about the least, the last, and the lost."

Yes, and we ought to be about those people, too. I would encourage all of us to renew our love for the least and last and lost in our lives, and most of all—no matter how jaded we might have grown—to never, ever give up.

For only if we keep on loving, keep on believing in these precious people, will we allow God room to work a miracle the way He did with Josh.

The way He did with Dave.

᠊ᡣᠵ᠊

Always, as I finish a book, I spend many hours praying for you, my reader friends. Sometimes God needs to take us back in time to the place where one of our relationships became strained, to the place of new love and second chances, before we let go of our own ways and grab on to Him for life. At some point, all of us will hear the voice of God calling us back or drawing us closer in some way: through a conversation with a friend or a sermon on the radio or the loss of a loved one.

Maybe even through Life-Changing Fiction™.

If during the course of reading this book you, like Annie Warren, found yourself crying out for God to give you strength, for Him to find you again, for the chance to become the person deep inside your heart that once upon a yesterday you used to be . . . then I pray that you will connect with a Bible-believing church in your area. There, you should be able to find a Bible, if you don't already have one. That life-saving relationship with Christ is always rooted in His truth, the Scriptures.

If you are unable to purchase a Bible or if you can't find one at your local church, and if this is the first time you are walking into that relationship with Jesus, then write to me at my Web site, www.KarenKingsbury.com. Write the words "New Life" in the subject line, send me your address, and I will send you a Bible. Because between the covers of that precious book are all the secrets to a new life.

For the rest of you, I'd love to hear your thoughts on *This Side of Heaven*. My guess is that there are a great many of you out there who can relate to having a person in your life like Josh Warren. Tell me how Josh's story and

Annie's new understanding about her son spoke to you, and how it maybe even changed you.

Contact me at my Web site, and while you're there, take a moment to look at the ways you can get involved with the community of other Karen Kingsbury readers. You can leave a prayer request or pray for someone else, tell me about an active military hero or a fallen one, and send me a picture so that all the world can pray for your soldier. You can also join my club and chat with other readers about your favorite characters and books.

If this is your first time with me, thank you for taking the time to read. My Web site lists my other titles in order, as well as by topic, in case you're looking for a specific type of Life-Changing Fiction™.

Again, thank you for your prayers for me and my family. We are doing well and trying to keep up with our kids, all of whom are growing up way too fast. In addition, we are making that special determination to be proud of them—regardless of their trophies or lack thereof.

We feel your prayers on a daily basis, and please know that we pray often for you, too.

Until next time,

In His light and love,

Karen Kingsbury

www.KarenKingsbury.com

DISCUSSION QUESTIONS

Please share these questions with your book clubs, church groups, friends, and family. Discussion makes the experience of reading so much richer!

1. Talk about Annie's relationship with her son prior to his death. What was her opinion of him, and why?

2. Nate plays a lesser role in this story. What was his relationship with Josh, and how did it differ from Annie's relationship with him?

3. Talk about a time when you or someone you know has been tempted to value the people in your life based on performance or perfection. What was the outcome of that attitude?

4. How do you define success in the lives of the people you love? How important is it to tell the people you love that you're proud of them?

5. Have you ever experienced a loss that made you doubt God or feel angry toward God? Explain.

6. Annie was struck by the song at Josh's funeral, "Great Is Thy Faithfulness." Have you ever doubted God's faithfulness? Talk about that time.

7. Lamentations talks about God's mercies being new every morning. How was that true for Annie? How has it been true in your life?

8. Explain the emotions Annie went through as she made the series of discoveries about Josh after his death. When have you or someone you know been wrong about the way you viewed someone you love? How was the discovery made of that person's real character?

9. Maria Cameron made many poor choices in her life. What were some of those choices? Talk about how those choices can affect people in real life.

10. What common theme seemed to dominate Maria's life? How can greed get in the way of loving the people God has placed around us?

11. Thomas Flynn was a good and godly attorney. Why do you think so many attorneys have a bad reputation? Talk about a situation that may have tainted your view of lawyers.

12. Why is it important that we have people of integrity in the field of law? Tell about a situation where a lawyer of great virtue made a difference.

13. The sign on Thomas Flynn's desk reads, *"In all things God works for the good of those who love him, who have been called according to his purpose,"* a Scripture found in Romans 8:28. How have you seen that verse apply in your life and the lives of those you love?

14. Tell about a time when you doubted the promise in Romans 8:28. How did that situation resolve, and if it hasn't, how might you find a way to apply that Scripture to your life?

15. Josh prayed daily for the chance to meet his daughter, Savannah. At the same time, Savannah prayed that she would meet her daddy. Neither of those prayers seemed to be answered this side of heaven. Talk about a time when your prayers weren't answered the way you wanted. How can we see God in moments like that?

16. Becky Wheaton had regrets about her relationship with Josh. Explain Annie's advice to Becky. Tell about a time when you or someone you know had regrets about a relationship. What are some ways to handle that type of situation?

17. Annie was willing to fight to the end to protect Josh's settlement. Why was this? Do you think Annie was a greedy person? Why or why not?

18. Cody Gunner wasn't sure about going to Annie with the story of his last conversation with Josh. Tell about a

time when someone came to you with life-changing news. What did Cody's admission mean to Annie?

19. Annie's prayers that she would have time with Savannah were answered very dramatically. Talk about that. Whom are you praying for right now? What can you focus on so that you'll be encouraged to continue to pray? Tell about a time when a prayer in your life was answered after someone spent time praying for you.

20. Many different types of love are illustrated in this book. Talk about a few of them, and explain what types of love are illustrated in your life.

If you enjoyed *This Side of Heaven*,
you'll love
Just Beyond the Clouds,
the unforgettable story of two brothers
and the woman whose love can set them both free.

Still aching over the death of his wife, Cody Gunner can't bear the thought of letting go of his brother, Carl Joseph, who has Down syndrome. Cody wants his brother home, where he will be safe and cared for, not out on his own in a world that Cody knows can be heartless and cruel. So when Carl Joseph's teacher, Elle, begins championing his independence, she finds herself at odds with Cody. But even as these two battle out their differences, they can't deny the connection they share, and Cody faces a crisis of heart.

What if Elle is the one woman who can teach Cody that love is still possible? If Cody can let go of his anger and pain, he might see that sometimes the brightest hope of all lies JUST BEYOND THE CLOUDS.

Available now wherever books are sold.

And be sure to check out
Like Dandelion Dust,
Karen's bestselling novel about a couple's love for
their son and the lengths to which they will
go to keep their family together.

Jack and Molly Campbell are right where they want to be, enjoying an idyllic life with their adopted four-year-old son, Joey. But everything changes when the Campbells receive a phone call from Joey's social worker: Joey's biological father has been released from prison. He's ready to start his life over, but not without getting custody of his son.

A judge's quick decision deals a devastating blow to the Campbell family: Joey must return to his biological parents. The day after the ruling, in a haze of grief and disbelief, the Campbells watch their adopted son pick a dandelion and blow the feathery seeds into the wind.

In the days that follow, Jack Campbell conceives a desperate and dangerous thought. What if they can devise a way out? What if they take Joey and just disappear . . . LIKE DANDELION DUST?

Available now wherever books are sold.

You'll also love
A Thousand Tomorrows!

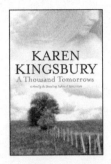

Cody Gunner is a nationally renowned bull rider—cocky, brash, and a legend among his peers. Abandoned as a child by the people he needed most, Cody swears he will never allow himself to love again.

Recognized horsewoman Ali Daniels denies love as well. Carrying a terrible secret, she lives life to the fullest, taking risks and refusing relationships. When Cody and Ali meet, their first instincts are to hide behind their emotional walls, seemingly doomed to repeat the patterns they have established for most of their lives. But their attraction is too strong, and despite their fears, they bare their souls to each other.

Only after three years—a thousand tomorrows later—do they realize at what cost their relationship comes. In the end, they must decide if love is worth the ultimate prize.

Available now wherever books are sold.

Other Life-Changing Fiction™ by Karen Kingsbury

September 11th Series
One Tuesday Morning
Beyond Tuesday Morning
Every Now and Then

Lost Love Series
Even Now
Ever After

Stand-Alone Titles
Oceans Apart
Between Sundays
When Joy Came to Stay
On Every Side
Divine
Like Dandelion Dust
Where Yesterday Lives

Redemption Series
Redemption
Remember
Return
Rejoice
Reunion

Firstborn Series
Fame
Forgiven
Found
Family
Forever

Sunrise Series
Sunrise
Summer
Someday
Sunset

Red Glove Series
Gideon's Gift
Maggie's Miracle
Sarah's Song
Hannah's Hope

Forever Faithful Series
Waiting for Morning
Moment of Weakness
Halfway to Forever

Women of Faith Fiction Series
A Time to Dance
A Time to Embrace

Cody Gunner Series
A Thousand Tomorrows
Just Beyond the Clouds
This Side of Heaven

Children's Titles
Let Me Hold You Longer
Let's Go on a Mommy Date
We Believe in Christmas

Miracle Collections
A Treasury of Christmas Miracles
A Treasury of Miracles for Women
A Treasury of Miracles for Teens
A Treasury of Miracles for Friends
A Treasury of Adoption Miracles

Gift Books
Stay Close, Little Girl
Be Safe, Little Boy
Forever Young: Ten Gifts of Faith for the Graduate